Experiment Central

Understanding Scientific Principles
Through Projects

Experiment Central

Understanding Scientific Principles
Through Projects
Second Edition

VOLUME 1: A-CH

M. Rae Nelson
Kristine Krapp, editor

U·X·L
A part of Gale, Cengage Learning

GALE
CENGAGE Learning

Detroit • New York • San Francisco • New Haven, Conn • Waterville, Maine • London

GALE
CENGAGE Learning

Experiment Central
Understanding Scientific
Principles Through Projects
Second Edition
M. Rae Nelson

Project Editor: Kristine Krapp

Managing Editor: Debra Kirby

Rights Acquisition and Management:
   Margaret Abendroth, Robyn Young

Composition: Evi Abou-El-Seoud, Mary
   Beth Trimper

Manufacturing: Wendy Blurton

Product Manager: Julia Furtaw

Product Design: Jennifer Wahi

© 2010 Gale, Cengage Learning

For product information and technology assistance, contact us at
Gale Customer Support, 1-800-877-4253.
For permission to use material from this text or product,
submit all requests online at **www.cengage.com/permissions.**
Further permissions questions can be e-mailed to
permissionrequest@cengage.com

Cover photographs: Images courtesy of Dreamstime, Photos.com, and iStockPhoto.

Library of Congress Cataloging-in-Publication Data

Experiment central : understanding scientific principles through projects. -- 2nd ed. / M. Rae Nelson, Kristine Krapp, editors.   p. cm. --
   Includes bibliographical references and index.
   ISBN 978-1-4144-7613-1 (set) -- ISBN 978-1-4144-7614-8 (vol. 1) --
ISBN 978-1-4144-7615-5 (vol. 2) -- ISBN 978-1-4144-7616-2 (vol. 3) --
ISBN 978-1-4144-7617-9 (vol. 4) -- ISBN 978-1-4144-7618-6 (vol. 5) --
ISBN 978-1-4144-7619-3 (vol. 6)
   1. Science--Experiments--Juvenile literature. I. Nelson, M. Rae. II. Krapp, Kristine M.

Q164.E96 2010
507.8--dc22   2009050304

Gale
27500 Drake Rd.
Farmington Hills, MI, 48331-3535

978-1-4144-7613-1 (set)	1-4144-7613-2 (set)
978-1-4144-7614-8 (vol. 1)	1-4144-7614-0 (vol. 1)
978-1-4144-7615-5 (vol. 2)	1-4144-7615-9 (vol. 2)
978-1-4144-7616-2 (vol. 3)	1-4144-7616-7 (vol. 3)
978-1-4144-7617-9 (vol. 4)	1-4144-7617-5 (vol. 4)
978-1-4144-7618-6 (vol. 5)	1-4144-7618-3 (vol. 5)
978-1-4144-7619-3 (vol. 6)	1-4144-7619-1 (vol. 6)

This title is also available as an e-book.
ISBN-13: 978-1-4144-7620-9 (set)
ISBN-10: 1-4144-7620-5 (set)
Contact your Gale sales representative for ordering information.

Printed by China Translation & Printing Services Limited,
Guangdong Province, China. 1st printing. 05/2010
1 2 3 4 5 6 7 14 13 12 11 10

Table of Contents

Experiment Central, 2nd edition

Experiment Central, 2nd edition

Experiment Central, 2nd edition

Experiment Central, 2nd edition

Reader's Guide

Experiment Central: Understanding Scientific Principles Through Projects provides in one resource a wide variety of science experiments covering nine key science curriculum fields—astronomy, biology, botany, chemistry, ecology, food science, geology, meteorology, and physics—spanning the earth sciences, life sciences, and physical sciences.

Experiment Central, 2nd edition combines, expands, and updates the original four-volume and two-volume UXL sets. This new edition includes 20 new chapters, 60 new experiments, and more than 35 enhanced experiments. Each chapter explores a scientific subject and offers experiments or projects that utilize or reinforce the topic studied. Chapters are alphabetically arranged according to scientific concept, including: Air and Water Pollution, Color, Eclipses, Forensic Science, Genetics, Magnetism, Mountains, Periodic Table, Renewable Energy, Storms and Water Cycle. Two to three experiments or projects are included in each chapter.

Entry format

Chapters are presented in a standard, easy-to-follow format. All chapters open with an explanatory overview section designed to introduce students to the scientific concept and provide the background behind a concept s discovery or important figures who helped advance the study of the field.

Each experiment is divided into eight standard sections to help students follow the experimental process clearly from beginning to end. Sections are:

- Purpose/Hypothesis
- Level of Difficulty

- Materials Needed
- Approximate Budget
- Timetable
- Step-by-Step Instructions
- Summary of Results
- Change the Variables

Chapters also include a "Design Your Own Experiment" section that allows students to apply what they have learned about a particular concept and to create their own experiments. This section is divided into:

- How to Select a Topic Relating to this Concept
- Steps in the Scientific Method
- Recording Data and Summarizing the Results
- Related Projects

Special Features

A "Words to Know" sidebar provides definitions of terms used in each chapter. A cumulative glossary collected from all the "Words to Know" sections is included in the beginning of each volume.

The "Experiments by Scientific Field" section categorizes experiments by scientific curriculum area. This section cumulates all experiments across the six-volume series.

The Parent's and Teacher's Guide recommends that a responsible adult always oversee a student's experiment and provides several safety guidelines for all students to follow.

Standard sidebars accompany experiments and projects.

- "What Are the Variables?" explains the factors that may have an impact on the outcome of a particular experiment.
- "How to Experiment Safely" clearly explains any risks involved with the experiment and how to avoid them.
- "Troubleshooter's Guide" presents problems that a student might encounter with an experiment, possible causes of the problem, and ways to remedy the problem.

Over 450 photos enhance the text; approximately 450 custom illustrations show the steps in the experiments.

Four indexes cumulate information from all the experiments in this six-volume set, including:

- Budget Index categorizes the experiments by approximate cost.
- Level of Difficulty Index lists experiments according to "easy," "moderate," or "difficult," or a combination thereof.
- Timetable Index categorizes each experiment by the amount of time needed to complete it, including setup and follow-through time.
- General Subject Index provides access to all major terms, people, places, and topics covered in the set.

Acknowledgments

The author wishes to acknowledge and thank Laurie Curtis, teacher/researcher; Cindy O'Neill, science educator; and Joyce Nelson, chemist, for their contributions to this edition as consultants.

Comments and Suggestions

We welcome your comments on *Experiment Central*. Please write: Editors, *Experiment Central*, U*X*L, 27500 Drake Rd. Farmington Hills, MI 48331-3535; call toll-free: 1-800-347-4253; or visit us at www.gale.cengage.com.

Parent's and Teacher's Guide

The experiments and projects in *Experiment Central* have been carefully constructed with issues of safety in mind, but your guidance and supervision are still required. Following the safety guidelines that accompany each experiment and project (found in the "How to Experiment Safely" sidebar box), as well as putting to work the safe practices listed below, will help your child or student avoid accidents. Oversee your child or student during experiments, and make sure he or she follows these safety guidelines:

- Always wear safety goggle is there is any possiblity of sharp objects, small particles, splashes of liquid, or gas fumes getting in someone's eyes.

- Always wear protective gloves when handling materials that could irritate the skin.

- Never leave an open flame, such as a lit candle, unattended. Never wear loose clothing around an open flame.

- Follow instructions carefully when using electrical equipment, including batteries, to avoid getting shocked.

- Be cautious when handling sharp objects or glass equipment that might break. Point scissors away from you and use them carefully.

- Always ask for help in cleaning up spills, broken glass, or other hazardous materials.

- Always use protective gloves when handling hot objects. Set them down only on a protected surface that will not be damaged by heat.

- Always wash your hands thoroughly after handling material that might contain harmful microorganisms, such as soil and pond water.

- Do not substitute materials in an experiment without asking a knowledgeable adult about possible reactions.

- Do not use or mix unidentified liquids or powders. The result might be an explosion or poisonous fumes.

- Never taste or eat any substances being used in an experiment.

- Always wear old clothing or a protective apron to avoid staining your clothes.

Experiments by Scientific Field

Chapter name in brackets, followed by experiment name. The numeral before the colon indicates volume; numbers after the colon indicate page number.

BOTANY

CHEMISTRY

ECOLOGY

FOOD SCIENCE

GEOLOGY

Words to Know

Abdomen: The third segment of an insect body.

Abscission: Barrier of special cells created at the base of leaves in autumn.

Absolute dating: The age of an object correlated to a specific fixed time, as established by some precise dating method.

Acceleration: The rate at which the velocity and/or direction of an object is changing with respect to time.

Acid: Substance that when dissolved in water is capable of reacting with a base to form salts and release hydrogen ions.

Acid rain: A form of precipitation that is significantly more acidic than neutral water, often produced as the result of industrial processes and pollution.

Acoustics: The science concerned with the production, properties, and propagation of sound waves.

Acronym: A word or phrase formed from the first letter of other words.

Active solar energy system: A solar energy system that uses pumps or fans to circulate heat captured from the Sun.

Additive: A chemical compound that is added to foods to give them some desirable quality, such as preventing them from spoiling.

Adhesion: Attraction between two different substances.

Adhesive: A substance that bonds or adheres two substances together.

Aeration: Mixing a gas, like oxygen, with a liquid, like water.

Aerobic: A process that requires oxygen.

Aerodynamics: The study of the motion of gases (particularly air) and the motion and control of objects in the air.

Agar: A nutrient rich, gelatinous substance that is used to grow bacteria.

Air: Gaseous mixture that covers Earth, composed mainly of nitrogen (about 78%) and oxygen (about 21%) with lesser amounts of argon, carbon dioxide, and other gases.

Air density: The ratio of the mass of a substance to the volume it occupies.

Air mass: A large body of air that has similar characteristics.

Air pressure: The force exerted by the weight of the atmosphere above a point on or above Earth's surface.

Alga/Algae: Single-celled or multicellular plants or plant-like organisms that contain chlorophyll, thus making their own food by photosynthesis. Algae grow mainly in water.

Alignment: Adjustment in a certain direction or orientation.

Alkali metals: The first group of elements in the periodic table, these metals have a single electron in the outermost shell.

Alkaline: Having a pH of more than 7.

Alleles: One version of the same gene.

Alloy: A mixture of two or more metals with properties different from those metals of which it is made.

Amine: An organic compound derived from ammonia.

Amino acid: One of a group of organic compounds that make up proteins.

Amnesia: Partial or total memory loss.

Amperage: A measurement of current. The common unit of measure is the ampere or amp.

Amphibians: Animals that live on land and breathe air but return to the water to reproduce.

Amplitude: The maximum displacement (difference between an original position and a later position) of the material that is vibrating. Amplitude can be thought of visually as the highest and lowest point of a wave.

Anaerobic: A process that does not require oxygen.

Anal fin: Fin on the belly of a fish, used for balance.

Anatomy: The study of the structure of living things.

Anemometer: A device that measures wind speed.

Angiosperm: A flowering plant that has its seeds produced within an ovary.

Animalcules: Life forms that Anton van Leeuwenhoek named when he first saw them under his microscope; they later became known as protozoa and bacteria.

Anther: The male reproductive organs of the plant, located on the tip of a flower's stamen.

Anthocyanin: Red pigment found in leaves, petals, stems, and other parts of a plant.

Antibiotic: A substance produced by or derived from certain fungi and other organisms, that can destroy or inhibit the growth of other microorganisms.

Antibiotic resistance: The ability of microorganisms to change so that they are not killed by antibiotics.

Antibody: A protein produced by certain cells of the body as an immune (disease-fighting) response to a specific foreign antigen.

Antigen: A substance that causes the production of an antibody when injected directly into the body.

Antioxidants: Used as a food additive, these substances can prevent food spoilage by reducing the food's exposure to air.

Aquifer: Underground layer of sand, gravel, or spongy rock that collects water.

Arch: A curved structure that spans an opening and supports a weight above the opening.

Artesian well: A well in which water is forced out under pressure.

Asexual reproduction: A reproductive process that does not involve the union of two individuals in the exchange of genetic material.

Astronomers: Scientists who study the positions, motions, and composition of stars and other objects in the sky.

Astronomy: The study of the physical properties of objects and matter outside Earth's atmosphere.

Atmosphere: Layers of air that surround Earth.

Atmospheric pressure: The pressure exerted by the atmosphere at Earth's surface due to the weight of the air.

Atom: The smallest unit of an element, made up of protons and neutrons in a central nucleus surrounded by moving electrons.

Atomic mass: Also known as atomic weight, the average mass of the atoms in an element; the number that appears under the element symbol in the periodic table.

Atomic number: The number of protons (or electrons) in an atom; the number that appears over the element symbol in the periodic table.

Atomic symbol: The one- or two-letter abbreviation for a chemical element.

Autotroph: An organism that can build all the food and produce all the energy it needs with its own resources.

Auxins: A group of plant hormones responsible for patterns of plant growth.

Axis: An imaginary straight line around which an object, like a planet, spins or turns. Earth's axis is a line that goes through the North and South Poles.

Bacteria: Single-celled microorganisms that live in soil, water, plants, and animals that play a key role in the decay of organic matter and the cycling of nutrients. Some are agents of disease.

Bacteriology: The scientific study of bacteria, their characteristics, and their activities as related to medicine, industry, and agriculture.

Barometer: An instrument for measuring atmospheric pressure, used especially in weather forecasting.

Base: Substance that when dissolved in water is capable of reacting with an acid to form salts and release hydrogen ions; has a pH of more than 7.

Base pairs: In DNA, the pairing of two nucleotides with each other: adenine (A) with thymine (T), and guanine (G) with cytosine (C).

Beam: A straight, horizontal structure that spans an opening and supports a weight above the opening.

Bedrock: Solid layer of rock lying beneath the soil and other loose material.

Beriberi: A disease caused by a deficiency of thiamine and characterized by nerve and gastrointestinal disorders.

Biochemical oxygen demand (BOD5): The amount of oxygen micro-organisms use over a five-day period in 68°F (20°C) water to decay organic matter.

Biodegradable: Capable of being decomposed by biological agents.

Biological variables: Living factors such as bacteria, fungi, and animals that can affect the processes that occur in nature and in an experiment.

Bioluminescence: The chemical phenomenon in which an organism can produce its own light.

Biomass: Organic materials that are used to produce usable energy.

Biomes: Large geographical areas with specific climates and soils, as well as distinct plant and animal communities that are interdependent.

Biomimetics: The development of materials that are found in nature.

Biopesticide: Pesticide produced from substances found in nature.

Bivalve: Bivalves are characterized by shells that are divided into two parts or valves that completely enclose the mollusk like the clam or scallop.

Blanching: A cooking technique in which the food, usually vegetables and fruits, are briefly cooked in boiling water and then plunged into cold water.

Blood pattern analysis: The study of the shape, location, and pattern of blood in order to understand how it got there.

Blueshift: The shortening of the frequency of light waves toward the blue end of the visible light spectrum as they travel towards an observer; most commonly used to describe movement of stars towards Earth.

Boiling point: The temperature at which a substance changes from a liquid to a gas or vapor.

Bond: The force that holds two atoms together.

Bone joint: A place in the body where two or more bones are connected.

Bone marrow: The spongy center of many bones in which blood cells are manufactured.

Bone tissue: A group of similar cells in the bone with a common function.

Bony fish: The largest group of fish, whose skeleton is made of bone.

Boreal: Northern.

Botany: The branch of biology involving the scientific study of plant life.

Braided rivers: Wide, shallow rivers with multiple channels and pebbly islands in the middle.

Buoyancy: The tendency of a liquid to exert a lifting effect on a body immersed in it.

By-product: A secondary substance produced as the result of a physical or chemical process, in addition to the main product.

Calcium carbonate: A substance that is secreted by a mollusk to create the shell it lives in.

Calibration: To standardize or adjust a measuring instrument so its measurements are correct.

Cambium: The tissue below the bark that produces new cells, which become wood and bark.

Camouflage: Markings or coloring that help hide an animal by making it blend into the surrounding environment.

Cancellous bone: Also called spongy bone, the inner layer of a bone that has cells with large spaces in between them filled with marrow.

Canning: A method of preserving food using airtight, vacuum-sealed containers and heat processing.

Capillary action: The tendency of water to rise through a narrow tube by the force of adhesion between the water and the walls of the tube.

Caramelization: The process of heating sugars to the point at which they break down and lead to the formation of new compounds.

Carbohydrate: A compound consisting of carbon, hydrogen, and oxygen found in plants and used as a food by humans and other animals.

Carbonic acid: A weak acid that forms from the mixture of water and carbon dioxide.

Carnivore: A meat-eating organism.

Carotene: Yellow-orange pigment in plants.

Cartilage: The connective tissue that covers and protects the bones.

Cartilaginous fish: The second largest group of fish whose skeleton is made of cartilage

Cast: In paleontology, the fossil formed when a mold is later filled in by mud or mineral matter.

Catalase: An enzyme found in animal liver tissue that breaks down hydrogen peroxide into oxygen and water.

Catalyst: A compound that starts or speeds up the rate of a chemical reaction without undergoing any change in its own composition.

Caudal fin: Tail fin of a fish used for fast swimming.

Cave: Also called cavern, a hollow or natural passage under or into the ground large enough for a person to enter.

Celestial bodies: Describing planets or other objects in space.

Cell membrane: The layer that surrounds the cell, but is inside the cell wall, allowing some molecules to enter and keeping others out of the cell.

Cell theory: All living things have one or more similar cells that carry out the same functions for the living process.

Cell wall: A tough outer covering over the cell membrane of bacteria and plant cells.

Cells: The basic unit for living organisms; cells are structured to perform highly specialized functions.

Centrifugal force: The apparent force pushing a rotating body away from the center of rotation.

Centrifuge: A device that rapidly spins a solution so that the heavier components will separate from the lighter ones.

Centripetal force: Rotating force that moves towards the center or axis.

Cerebral cortex: The outer layer of the brain.

Channel: A shallow trench carved into the ground by the pressure and movement of a river.

Chemical change: The change of one or more substances into other substances.

Chemical energy: Energy stored in chemical bonds.

Chemical property: A characteristic of a substance that allows it to undergo a chemical change. Chemical properties include flammability and sensitivity to light.

Chemical reaction: Any chemical change in which at least one new substance is formed.

Chemosense: A sense stimulated by specific chemicals that cause the sensory cell to transmit a signal to the brain.

Chitin: Substance that makes up the exoskeleton of crustaceans.

Chlorophyll: A green pigment found in plants that absorbs sunlight, providing the energy used in photosynthesis, or the conversion of carbon dioxide and water to complex carbohydrates.

Chloroplasts: Small structures in plant cells that contain chlorophyll and in which the process of photosynthesis takes place.

Chromatography: A method for identifying the components of a substance based on their characteristic colors.

Chromosome: A structure of DNA found in the cell nucleus.

Cilia: Hairlike structures on olfactory receptor cells that sense odor molecules.

Circuit: The complete path of an electric current including the source of electric energy.

Circumference: The distance around a circle.

Clay: Type of soil comprising the smallest soil particles.

Cleavage: The tendency of a mineral to split along certain planes.

Climate: The average weather that a region experiences over a long period.

Coagulation: The clumping together of particles in a mixture, often because the repelling force separating them is disrupted.

Cohesion: Attraction between like substances.

Cold blooded: When an animals body temperature rises or falls to match the environment.

Collagen: A protein in bone that gives the bone elasticity.

Colloid: A mixture containing particles suspended in, but not dissolved in, a dispersing medium.

Colony: A mass of microorganisms that have been bred in a medium.

Colorfast: The ability of a material to keep its dye and not fade or change color.

Coma: Glowing cloud of gas surrounding the nucleus of a comet.

Combustion: Any chemical reaction in which heat, and usually light, is produced. It is commonly the burning of organic substances during which oxygen from the air is used to form carbon dioxide and water vapor.

Comet: An icy body orbiting in the solar system, which partially vaporizes when it nears the Sun and develops a diffuse envelope of dust and gas as well as one or more tails.

Comet head: The nucleus and the coma of a comet.

Comet nucleus: The core or center of a comet. (Plural: Comet nuclei.)

Comet tail: The most distinctive feature of comets; comets can display two basic types of tails: one gaseous and the other largely composed of dust.

Compact bone: The outer, hard layer of the bone.

Complete metamorphosis: Metamorphosis in which a larva becomes a pupa before changing into an adult form.

Composting: The process in which organic compounds break down and become dark, fertile soil called humus.

Compression: A type of force on an object where the object is pushed or squeezed from each end.

Concave: Hollowed or rounded inward, like the inside of a bowl.

Concave lens: A lens that is thinner in the middle than at the edges.

Concentration: The amount of a substance present in a given volume, such as the number of molecules in a liter.

Condensation: The process by which a gas changes into a liquid.

Conduction: The flow of heat through a solid.

Conductivity: The ability of a material to carry an electrical current.

Conductor: A substance able to carry an electrical current.

Cones: Cells in the retina that can perceive color.

Confined aquifer: An aquifer with a layer of impermeable rock above it where the water is held under pressure.

Coniferous: Refers to trees, such as pines and firs, that bear cones and have needle-like leaves that are not shed all at once.

Conservation of energy: The law of physics that states that energy can be transformed from one form to another, but can be neither created nor destroyed.

Constellations: Patterns of stars in the night sky. There are eighty-eight known constellations.

Continental drift: The theory that continents move apart slowly at a predictable rate.

Contract: To shorten, pull together.

Control experiment: A set-up that is identical to the experiment but is not affected by the variable that will be changed during the experiment.

Convection: The circulatory motion that occurs in a gas or liquid at a nonuniform temperature owing to the variation of its density and the action of gravity.

Convection current: A circular movement of a fluid in response to alternating heating and cooling.

Convex: Curved or rounded outward, like the outside of a ball.

Convex lens: A lens that is thicker in the middle than at the edges.

Coprolites: The fossilized droppings of animals.

Coriolis force: A force that makes a moving object appear to travel in a curved path over the surface of a spinning body.

Corona: The outermost atmospheric layer of the Sun.

Corrosion: An oxidation-reduction reaction in which a metal is oxidized (reacted with oxygen) and oxygen is reduced, usually in the presence of moisture.

Cotyledon: Seed leaves, which contain the stored source of food for the embryo.

Crater: An indentation caused by an object hitting the surface of a planet or moon.

Crest: The highest point reached by a wave.

Cross-pollination: The process by which pollen from one plant pollinates another plant of the same species.

Crust: The hard outer shell of Earth that floats upon the softer, denser mantle.

Crustacean: A type of arthropod characterized by hard and thick skin, and having shells that are jointed. This group includes the lobster, crab, and crayfish.

Crystal: Naturally occurring solid composed of atoms or molecules arranged in an orderly pattern that repeats at regular intervals.

Crystal faces: The flat, smooth surfaces of a crystal.

Crystal lattice: The regular and repeating pattern of the atoms in a crystal.

Cultures: Microorganisms growing in prepared nutrients.

Cumulonimbus cloud: The parent cloud of a thunderstorm; a tall, vertically developed cloud capable of producing heavy rain, high winds, and lightning.

Current: The flow of electrical charge from one point to another.

Currents: The horizontal and vertical circulation of ocean waters.

Cyanobacteria: Oxygen-producing, aquatic bacteria capable of manufacturing its own food; resembles algae.

Cycles: Occurrence of events that take place on a regular, repeating basis.

Cytology: The branch of biology concerned with the study of cells.

Cytoplasm: The semifluid substance inside a cell that surrounds the nucleus and other membrane-enclosed organelles.

Decanting: The process of separating a suspension by waiting for its heavier components to settle out and then pouring off the lighter ones.

Decibel (dB): A unit of measurement for the amplitude of sound.

Deciduous: Plants that lose their leaves during some season of the year, and then grow them back during another season.

Decompose: To break down into two or more simpler substances.

Decomposition: The breakdown of complex molecules of dead organisms into simple nutrients that can be reutilized by living organisms.

Decomposition reaction: A chemical reaction in which one substance is broken down into two or more substances.

Deficiency disease: A disease marked by a lack of an essential nutrient in the diet.

Degrade: Break down.

Dehydration: The removal of water from a material.

Denaturization: Altering an enzyme so it no longer works.

Density: The mass of a substance divided by its volume.

Density ball: A ball with the fixed standard of 1.0 gram per milliliter, which is the exact density of pure water.

Deoxyribonucleic acid (DNA): Large, complex molecules found in the nuclei of cells that carry genetic information for an organism's development; double helix. (Pronounced DEE-ox-see-rye-bo-noo-klay-ick acid)

Dependent variable: The variable in an experiment whose value depends on the value of another variable in the experiment.

Deposition: Dropping of sediments that occurs when a river loses its energy of motion.

Desert: A biome with a hot-to-cool climate and dry weather.

Desertification: Transformation of arid or semiarid productive land into desert.

Dewpoint: The point at which water vapor begins to condense.

Dicot: Plants with a pair of embryonic seeds that appear at germination.

Diffraction: The bending of light or another form of electromagnetic radiation as it passes through a tiny hole or around a sharp edge.

Diffraction grating: A device consisting of a surface into which are etched very fine, closely spaced grooves that cause different wavelengths of light to reflect or refract (bend) by different amounts.

Diffusion: Random movement of molecules that leads to a net movement of molecules from a region of high concentration to a region of low concentration.

Disinfection: Using chemicals to kill harmful organisms.

Dissolved oxygen: Oxygen molecules that have dissolved in water.

Distillation: The process of separating liquids from solids or from other liquids with different boiling points by a method of evaporation and condensation, so that each component in a mixture can be collected separately in its pure form.

DNA fingerprinting: A technique that uses DNA fragments to identify the unique DNA sequences of an individual.

DNA replication: The process by which one DNA strand unwinds and duplicates all its information, creating two new DNA strands that are identical to each other and to the original strand.

DNA (deoxyribonucleic acid): Large, complex molecules found in nuclei of cells that carry genetic information for an organism's development.

Domain: Small regions in iron that possess their own magnetic charges.

Dominant gene: A gene that passes on a certain characteristic, even when there is only one copy (allele) of the gene.

Doppler effect: The change in wavelength and frequency (number of vibrations per second) of either light or sound as the source is moving either towards or away from the observer.

Dormant: A state of inactivity in an organism.

Dorsal fin: The fin located on the back of a fish, used for balance.

Double helix: The shape taken by DNA (deoxyribonucleic acid) molecules in a nucleus.

Drought: A prolonged period of dry weather that damages crops or prevents their growth.

Dry cell: A source of electricity that uses a non-liquid electrolyte.

Dust tail: One of two types of tails a comet may have, it is composed mainly of dust and it points away from the Sun.

Dye: A colored substance that is used to give color to a material.

Dynamic equilibrium: A situation in which substances are moving into and out of cell walls at an equal rate.

Earthquake: An unpredictable event in which masses of rock suddenly shift or rupture below Earth's surface, releasing enormous amounts of energy and sending out shockwaves that sometimes cause the ground to shake dramatically.

Eclipse: A phenomenon in which the light from a celestial body is temporarily cut off by the presence of another.

Ecologists: Scientists who study the interrelationship of organisms and their environments.

Ecosystem: An ecological community, including plants, animals and microorganisms, considered together with their environment.

Efficiency: The amount of power output divided by the amount of power input. It is a measure of how well a device converts one form of power into another.

Effort: The force applied to move a load using a simple machine.

Elastomers: Any of various polymers having rubbery properties.

Electric charge repulsion: Repulsion of particles caused by a layer of negative ions surrounding each particle. The repulsion prevents coagulation and promotes the even dispersion of such particles through a mixtures.

Electrical energy: Kinetic energy resulting from the motion of electrons within any object that conducts electricity.

Electricity: A form of energy caused by the presence of electrical charges in matter.

Electrode: A material that will conduct an electrical current, usually a metal; used to carry electrons into or out of a battery.

Electrolyte: Any substance that, when dissolved in water, conducts an electric current.

Electromagnetic spectrum: The complete array of electromagnetic radiation, including radio waves (at the longest-wavelength end), microwaves, infrared radiation, visible light, ultraviolet radiation, X rays, and gamma rays (at the shortest-wavelength end).

Electromagnetism: A form of magnetic energy produced by the flow of an electric current through a metal core. Also, the study of electric and magnetic fields and their interaction with charges and currents.

Electron: A subatomic particle with a single negative electrical change that orbits the nucleus of an atom.

Electroplating: The process of coating one metal with another metal by means of an electrical current.

Electroscope: A device that determines whether an object is electrically charged.

Element: A pure substance composed of just one type of atom that cannot be broken down into anything simpler by ordinary chemical means.

Elevation: Height above sea level.

Elliptical: An orbital path which is egg-shaped or resembles an elongated circle.

Elongation: The percentage increase in length that occurs before a material breaks under tension.

Embryo: The seed of a plant, which through germination can develop into a new plant.

Embryonic: The earliest stages of development.

Endothermic reaction: A chemical reaction that absorbs heat or light energy, such as photosynthesis, the production of food by plant cells.

Energy: The ability to cause an action or to perform work.

Entomology: The study of insects.

Environmental variables: Nonliving factors such as air temperature, water, pollution, and pH that can affect processes that occur in nature and in an experiment.

Enzyme: Any of numerous complex proteins produced by living cells that act as catalysts, speeding up the rate of chemical reactions in living organisms.

Enzymology: The science of studying enzymes.

Ephemerals: Plants that lie dormant in dry soil for years until major rainstorms occur.

Epicenter: The location where the seismic waves of an earthquake first appear on the surface, usually almost directly above the focus.

Equilibrium: A balancing or canceling out of opposing forces, so that an object will remain at rest.

Erosion: The process by which topsoil is carried away by water, wind, or ice action.

Ethnobotany: The study of how cultures use plants in everyday life.

Eukaryotic: Multicellular organism whose cells contain distinct nuclei, which contain the genetic material. (Pronounced yoo-KAR-ee-ah-tic)

Euphotic zone: The upper part of the ocean where sunlight penetrates, supporting plant life, such as phytoplankton.

Eutrophication: The process by which high nutrient concentrations in a body of water eventually cause the natural wildlife to die.

Evaporation: The process by which liquid changes into a gas.

Exoskeleton: A hard outer covering on animals, which provide protection and structure.

Exothermic reaction: A chemical reaction that releases heat or light energy, such as the burning of fuel.

Experiment: A controlled observation.

Extremophiles: Bacteria that thrive in environments too harsh to support most life forms.

False memory: A memory of an event that never happened or an altered memory from what happened.

Family: A group of elements in the same column of the periodic table or in closely related columns of the table. A family of chemical compounds share similar structures and properties.

Fat: A type of lipid, or chemical compound used as a source of energy, to provide insulation and to protect organs in an animal body.

Fat-soluble vitamins: Vitamins such as A, D, E, and K that can be dissolved in the fat of plants and animals.

Fault: A crack running through rock as the result of tectonic forces.

Fault blocks: Pieces of rock from Earth's crust that press against each other and cause earthquakes when they suddenly shift or rupture from the pressure.

Fault mountain: A mountain that is formed when Earth's plates come together and cause rocks to break and move upwards.

Fermentation: A chemical reaction in which enzymes break down complex organic compounds (for example, carbohydrates and sugars) into simpler ones (for example, ethyl alcohol).

Filament: In a flower, stalk of the stamen that bears the anther.

Filtration: The mechanical separation of a liquid from the undissolved particles floating in it.

Fireball: Meteors that create an intense, bright light and, sometimes, an explosion.

First law of motion (Newton's): An object at rest or moving in a certain direction and speed will remain at rest or moving in the same motion and speed unless acted upon by a force.

Fish: Animals that live in water who have gills, fins, and are cold blooded.

Fixative: A substance that mixes with the dye to hold it to the material.

Flagella: Whiplike structures used by some organisms for movement. (Singular: flagellum.)

Flammability: The ability of a material to ignite and burn.

Flower: The reproductive part of a flowering plant.

Fluid: A substance that flows; a liquid or gas.

Fluorescence: The emission of visible light from an object when the object is bombarded with electromagnetic radiation, such as ultraviolet rays. The emission of visible light stops after the radiation source has been removed.

Focal length: The distance from the lens to the point where the light rays come together to a focus.

Focal point: The point at which rays of light converge or from which they diverge.

Focus: The point within Earth where a sudden shift or rupture occurs.

Fold mountain: A mountain that is formed when Earth's plates come together and push rocks up into folds.

Food webs: Interconnected sets of food chains, which are a sequence of organisms directly dependent on one another for food.

Force: A physical interaction (pushing or pulling) tending to change the state of motion (velocity) of an object.

Forensic science: The application of science to the law and justice system.

Fortified: The addition of nutrients, such as vitamins or minerals, to food.

Fossil: The remains, trace, or impressions of a living organism that inhabited Earth more than ten thousand years ago.

Fossil fuel: A fuel such as coal, oil, or natural gas that is formed over millions of years from the remains of plants and animals.

Fossil record: The documentation of fossils placed in relationship to one another; a key source to understand the evolution of life on Earth.

Fracture: A mineral's tendency to break into curved, rough, or jagged surfaces.

Frequency: The rate at which vibrations take place (number of times per second the motion is repeated), given in cycles per second or in hertz (Hz). Also, the number of waves that pass a given point in a given period of time.

Friction: A force that resists the motion of an object, resulting when two objects rub against one another.

Front: The area between air masses of different temperatures or densities.

Fuel cell: A device that uses hydrogen as the fuel to produce electricity and heat with water as a byproduct.

Fulcrum: The point at which a lever arm pivots.

Fungi: Kingdom of various single-celled or multicellular organisms, including mushrooms, molds, yeasts, and mildews, that do not contain chlorophyll.

Funnel cloud: A fully developed tornado vortex before it has touched the ground.

Fusion: Combining of nuclei of two or more lighter elements into one nucleus of a heavier element; the process stars use to produce energy to produce light and support themselves against their own gravity.

Galaxy: A large collection of stars and clusters of stars containing anywhere from a few million to a few trillion stars.

Gastropod: The largest group of mollusks; characterized by a single shell that is often coiled in a spiral. Snails are gastropods.

Gene: A segment of a DNA (deoxyribonucleic acid) molecule contained in the nucleus of a cell that acts as a kind of code for the production of some specific protein. Genes carry instructions for the formation, functioning, and transmission of specific traits from one generation to another.

Generator: A device that converts mechanical energy into electrical energy,

Genetic engineering: A technique that modifies the DNA of living cells in order to make them change its characteristics. Also called genetic modification.

Genetic material: Material that transfers characteristics from a parent to its offspring.

Geology: The study of the origin, history and structure of Earth.

Geothermal energy: Energy from deep within Earth.

Geotropism: The tendency of roots to bend toward Earth.

Germ theory of disease: The theory that disease is caused by microorganisms or germs, and not by spontaneous generation.

Germination: First stage in development of a plant seed.

Gibbous moon: A phase of the Moon when more than half of its surface is lighted.

Gills: Special organ located behind the head of a fish that takes in oxygen from the water.

Glacier: A large mass of ice formed from snow that has packed together and which moves slowly down a slope under its own weight.

Global warming: Warming of Earth's atmosphere as a result of an increase in the concentration of gases that store heat, such as carbon dioxide.

Glucose: A simple sugar broken down in cells to produce energy.

Gnomon: The perpendicular piece of the sundial that casts the shadow.

Golgi body: An organelles that sorts, modifies, and packages molecules.

Gravity: Force of attraction between objects, the strength of which depends on the mass of each object and the distance between them.

Greenhouse effect: The warming of Earth's atmosphere due to water vapor, carbon dioxide, and other gases in the atmosphere that trap heat radiated from Earth's surface.

Greenhouse gases: Gases that absorb infrared radiation and warm the air before the heat energy escapes into space.

Greenwich Mean Time (GMT): The time at an imaginary line that runs north and south through Greenwich, England, used as the standard for time throughout the world.

Groundwater: Water that soaks into the ground and is stored in the small spaces between the rocks and soil.

Group: A vertical column of the periodic table that contains elements possessing similar chemical characteristics.

Hardwood: Wood from angiosperm, mostly deciduous, trees.

Heartwood: The inner layers of wood that provide structure and have no living cells.

Heat: A form of energy produced by the motion of molecules that make up a substance.

Heat capacity: The measure of how well a substance stores heat.

Heat energy: The energy produced when two substances that have different temperatures are combined.

Heliotropism: The tendency of plants to turn towards the Sun throughout the day.

Herbivore: A plant-eating organism.

Hertz (Hz): The unit of measurement of frequency; a measure of the number of waves that pass a given point per second of time.

Heterogeneous: Different throughout.

Heterotrophs: Organisms that cannot make their own food and that must, therefore, obtain their food from other organisms.

High air pressure: An area where the air is cooler and more dense, and the air pressure is higher than normal.

Hippocampus: A part of the brain associated with learning and memory.

Homogenous: The same throughout.

Hormones: Chemicals produced in the cells of plants and animals that control bodily functions.

Hue: The color or shade.

Humidity: The amount of water vapor (moisture) contained in the air.

Humus: Fragrant, spongy, nutrient-rich decayed plant or animal matter.

Hydrologic cycle: Continual movement of water from the atmosphere to Earth's surface through precipitation and back to the atmosphere through evaporation and transpiration.

Hydrologists: Scientists who study water and its cycle.

Hydrology: The study of water and its cycle.

Hydrometer: An instrument that determines the specific gravity of a liquid.

Hydrophilic: A substance that is attracted to and readily mixes with water.

Hydrophobic: A substance that is repelled by and does not mix with water.

Hydropower: Energy produced from capturing moving water.

Hydrotropism: The tendency of roots to grow toward a water source.

Hypertonic solution: A solution with a higher concentration of materials than a cell immersed in the solution.

Hypha: Slender, cottony filaments making up the body of multicellular fungi. (Plural: hyphae)

Hypothesis: An idea in the form of a statement that can be tested by observation and/or experiment.

Hypotonic solution: A solution with a lower concentration of materials than a cell immersed in the solution.

Igneous rock: Rock formed from the cooling and hardening of magma.

Immiscible: Incapable of being mixed.

Imperfect flower: Flowers that have only the male reproductive organ (stamen) or the female reproductive organs (pistil).

Impermeable: Not allowing substances to pass through.

Impurities: Chemicals or other pollutants in water.

Inclined plane: A simple machine with no moving parts; a slanted surface.

Incomplete metamorphosis: Metamorphosis in which a nymph form gradually becomes an adult through molting.

Independent variable: The variable in an experiment that determines the final result of the experiment.

Indicator: Pigments that change color when they come into contact with acidic or basic solutions.

Inertia: The tendency of an object to continue in its state of motion.

Infrared radiation: Electromagnetic radiation of a wavelength shorter than radio waves but longer than visible light that takes the form of heat.

Inner core: Very dense, solid center of Earth.

Inorganic: Not containing carbon; not derived from a living organism.

Insect: A six-legged invertebrate whose body has three segments.

Insoluble: A substance that cannot be dissolved in some other substance.

Insulated wire: Electrical wire coated with a non-conducting material such as plastic.

Insulation: A material that is a poor conductor of heat or electricity.

Insulator: A material through which little or no electrical current or heat energy will flow.

Interference fringes: Bands of color that fan out around an object.

Internal skeleton: An animal that has a backbone.

Invertebrate: An animal that lacks a backbone or internal skeleton.

Ion: An atom or groups of atoms that carry an electrical charge—either positive or negative—as a result of losing or gaining one or more electrons.

Ion tail: One of two types of tails a comet may have, it is composed mainly of charged particles and it points away from the Sun.

Ionic conduction: The flow of an electrical current by the movement of charged particles, or ions.

Isobars: Continuous lines that connect areas with the same air pressure.

Isotonic solutions: Two solutions that have the same concentration of solute particles and therefore the same osmotic pressure.

Jawless fish: The smallest group of fishes, who lacks a jaw.

Kinetic energy: The energy of an object or system due to its motion.

Kingdom: One of the five classifications in the widely accepted classification system that designates all living organisms into animals, plants, fungi, protists, and monerans.

Labyrinth: A lung-like organ located above the gills that allows the fish to breathe in oxygen from the air.

Lactobacilli: A strain of bacteria.

Landfill: A method of disposing of waste materials by placing them in a depression in the ground or piling them in a mound. In a sanitary landfill, the daily deposits of waste materials are covered with a layer of soil.

Larva: Immature form (wormlike in insects; fishlike in amphibians) of an organism capable of surviving on its own. A larva does not resemble the parent and must go through metamorphosis, or change, to reach its adult stage.

Lava: Molten rock that occurs at the surface of Earth, usually through volcanic eruptions.

Lava cave: A cave formed from the flow of lava streaming over solid matter.

Leach: The movement of dissolved minerals or chemicals with water as it percolates, or oozes, downward through the soil.

Leaching: The movement of dissolved chemicals with water that is percolating, or oozing, downward through the soil.

Leavening agent: A substance used to make foods like dough and batter to rise.

Leeward: The side away from the wind or flow direction.

Lens: A piece of transparent material with two curved surfaces that bend rays of light passing through it.

Lichen: An organism composed of a fungus and a photosynthetic organism in a symbiotic relationship.

Lift: Upward force on the wings of an aircraft created by differences in air pressure on top of and underneath the wings.

Ligaments: Tough, fibrous tissue connecting bones.

Light: A form of energy that travels in waves.

Light-year: Distance light travels in one year in the vacuum of space, roughly 5.9 trillion miles (9.5 trillion kilometers).

The Local Group: A cluster of thirty galaxies, including the Milky Way, pulled together by gravity.

Long-term memory: The last category of memory in which memories are stored away and can last for years.

Low air pressure: An area where the air is warmer and less dense, and the air pressure is lower than normal.

Luminescent: Producing light through a chemical process.

Luminol: A compound used to detect blood.

Lunar eclipse: An eclipse that occurs when Earth passes between the Sun and the Moon, casting a shadow on the Moon.

Luster: A glow of reflected light; a sheen.

Machine: Any device that makes work easier by providing a mechanical advantage.

Macrominerals: Minerals needed in relatively large quantities.

Macroorganisms: Visible organisms that aid in breaking down organic matter.

Magma: Molten rock deep within Earth that consists of liquids, gases, and particles of rocks and crystals. Magma underlies areas of volcanic activity and at Earth's surface is called lava.

Magma chambers: Pools of bubbling liquid rock that are the source of energy causing volcanoes to be active.

Magma surge: A swell or rising wave of magma caused by the movement and friction of tectonic plates, which heats and melts rock, adding to the magma and its force.

Magnet: A material that attracts other like materials, especially metals.

Magnetic circuit: A series of magnetic domains aligned in the same direction.

Magnetic field: The space around an electric current or a magnet in which a magnetic force can be observed.

Magnetism: A fundamental force in nature caused by the motion of electrons in an atom.

Maillard reaction: A reaction caused by heat and sugars and resulting in foods browning and flavors.

Mammals: Animals that have a backbone, are warm blooded, have mammary glands to feed their young and have or are born with hair.

Mantle: Thick dense layer of rock that underlies Earth's crust and overlies the core; also soft tissue that is located between the shell and an animal's inner organs. The mantle produces the calcium carbonate substance that create the shell of the animal.

Manure: The waste matter of animals.

Mass: Measure of the total amount of matter in an object. Also, an object's quantity of matter as shown by its gravitational pull on another object.

Matter: Anything that has mass and takes up space.

Meandering river: A lowland river that twists and turns along its route to the sea.

Medium: A material that contains the nutrients required for a particular microorganism to grow.

Melting point: The temperature at which a substance changes from a solid to a liquid.

Memory: The process of retaining and recalling past events and experiences.

Meniscus: The curved surface of a column of liquid.

Metabolism: The process by which living organisms convert food into energy and waste products.

Metamorphic rock: Rock formed by transformation of pre-existing rock through changes in temperature and pressure.

Metamorphosis: Transformation of an immature animal into an adult.

Meteor: An object from space that becomes glowing hot when it passes into Earth's atmosphere; also called shooting star.

Meteor shower: A group of meteors that occurs when Earth's orbit intersects the orbit of a meteor stream.

Meteorites: A meteor that is large enough to survive its passage through the atmosphere and hit the ground.

Meteoroid: A piece of debris that is traveling in space.

Meteorologist: Scientist who studies the weather and the atmosphere.

Microbiology: Branch of biology dealing with microscopic forms of life.

Microclimate: A unique climate that exists only in a small, localized area.

Microorganisms: Living organisms so small that they can be seen only with the aid of a microscope.

Micropyle: Seed opening that enables water to enter easily.

Microvilli: The extension of each taste cell that pokes through the taste pore and first senses the chemicals.

Milky Way: The galaxy in which our solar system is located.

Mimicry: A characteristic in which an animal is protected against predators by resembling another, more distasteful animal.

Mineral: An inorganic substance found in nature with a definite chemical composition and structure. As a nutrient, it helps build bones and soft tissues and regulates body functions.

Mixture: A combination of two or more substances that are not chemically combined with each other and that can exist in any proportion.

Mnemonics: Techniques to improve memory.

Mold: In paleontology, the fossil formed when acidic water dissolves a shell or bone around which sand or mud has already hardened.

Molecule: The smallest particle of a substance that retains all the properties of the substance and is composed of one or more atoms.

Mollusk: An invertebrate animal usually enclosed in a shell, the largest group of shelled animals.

Molting: A process by which an animal sheds its skin or shell.

Monocot: Plants with a single embryonic leaf at germination.

Monomer: A small molecule that can be combined with itself many times over to make a large molecule, the polymer.

Moraine: Mass of boulders, stones, and other rock debris carried along and deposited by a glacier.

Mordant: A substance that fixes the dye to the material.

Mountain: A landform that stands well above its surroundings; higher than a hill.

Mucus: A thick, slippery substance that serves as a protective lubricant coating in passages of the body that communicate with the air.

Multicellular: Living things with many cells joined together.

Muscle fibers: Stacks of long, thin cells that make up muscle; there are three types of muscle fiber: skeletal, cardiac, and smooth.

Mycelium: In fungi, the mass of threadlike, branching hyphae.

N

Nanobots: A nanoscale robot.

Nanometer: A unit of length; this measurement is equal to one-billionth of a meter.

Nanotechnology: Technology that involves working and developing technologies on the nanometer (atomic and molecular) scale.

Nansen bottles: Self-closing containers with thermometers that draw in water at different depths.

Nebula: Bright or dark cloud, often composed of gases and dust, hovering in the space between the stars.

Nectar: A sweet liquid, found inside a flower, that attracts pollinators.

Neutralization: A chemical reaction in which the mixing of an acidic solution with a basic (alkaline) solution results in a solution that has the properties of neither an acid nor a base.

Neutron: A subatomic particle with a mass of about one atomic mass unit and no electrical charge that is found in the nucleus of an atom.

Newtonian fluid: A fluid that follows certain properties, such as the viscosity remains constant at a given temperature.

Niche: The specific location and place in the food chain that an organism occupies in its environment.

Noble gases: Also known as inert or rare gases; the elements argon, helium, krypton, neon, radon, and xenon, which are nonreactive gases and form few compounds with other elements.

Non-Newtonian fluid: A fluid whose property do not follow Newtonian properties, such as viscosity can vary based on the stress.

Nonpoint source: An unidentified source of pollution, which may actually be a number of sources.

Nucleation: The process by which crystals start growing.

Nucleotide: The basic unit of a nucleic acid. It consists of a simple sugar, a phosphate group, and a nitrogen-containing base. (Pronounced noo-KLEE-uh-tide.)

Nucleus: The central part of the cell that contains the DNA; the central core of an atom, consisting of protons and (usually) neutrons.

Nutrient: A substance needed by an organism in order for it to survive, grow, and develop.

Nutrition: The study of the food nutrients an organism needs in order to maintain well-being.

Nymph: An immature form in the life cycle of insects that go through an incomplete metamorphosis.

Objective lens: In a refracting telescope, the lens farthest away from the eye that collects the light.

Oceanographer: A person who studies the chemistry of the oceans, as well as their currents, marine life, and the ocean floor.

Oceanography: The study of the chemistry of the oceans, as well as their currents, marine life, and the ocean bed.

Olfactory: Relating to the sense of smell.

Olfactory bulb: The part of the brain that processes olfactory (smell) information.

Olfactory epithelium: The patch of mucous membrane at the top of the nasal cavity that contains the olfactory (smell) nerve cells.

Olfactory receptor cells: Nerve cells in the olfactory epithelium that detect odors and transmit the information to the brain.

Oort cloud: Region of space beyond our solar system that theoretically contains about one trillion inactive comets.

Optics: The study of the nature of light and its properties.

Orbit: The path followed by a body (such as a planet) in its travel around another body (such as the Sun).

Organelle: A membrane-enclosed structure that performs a specific function within a cell.

Organic: Containing carbon; also referring to materials that are derived from living organisms.

Oscillation: A repeated back-and-forth movement.

Osmosis: The movement of fluids and substances dissolved in liquids across a semipermeable membrane from an area of its greater concentration to an area of its lesser concentration until all substances involved reach a balance.

Outer core: A liquid core that surrounds Earth's solid inner core; made mostly of iron.

Ovary: In a plant, the base part of the pistil that bears ovules and develops into a fruit.

Ovule: Structure within the ovary that develops into a seed after fertilization.

Oxidation: A chemical reaction in which oxygen reacts with some other substance and in which ions, atoms, or molecules lose electrons.

Oxidation state: The sum of an atom's positive and negative charges.

Oxidation-reduction reaction: A chemical reaction in which one substance loses one or more electrons and the other substance gains one or more electrons.

Oxidizing agent: A chemical substance that gives up oxygen or takes on electrons from another substance.

Paleontologist: Scientist who studies the life of past geological periods as known from fossil remains.

Papain: An enzyme obtained from the fruit of the papaya used as a meat tenderizer, as a drug to clean cuts and wounds, and as a digestive aid for stomach disorders.

Papillae: The raised bumps on the tongue that contain the taste buds.

Parent material: The underlying rock from which soil forms.

Partial solar/lunar eclipse: An eclipse in which our view of the Sun/Moon is only partially blocked.

Particulate matter: Solid matter in the form of tiny particles in the atmosphere. (Pronounced par-TIK-you-let.)

Passive solar energy system: A solar energy system in which the heat of the Sun is captured, used, and stored by means of the design of a building and the materials from which it is made.

Pasteurization: The process of slow heating that kills bacteria and other microorganisms.

Peaks: The points at which the energy in a wave is maximum.

Pectin: A natural carbohydrate found in fruits and vegetables.

Pectoral fin: Pair of fins located on the side of a fish, used for steering.

Pedigree: A diagram that illustrates the pattern of inheritance of a genetic trait in a family.

Pelvic fin: Pair of fins located toward the belly of a fish, used for stability.

Pendulum: A free-swinging weight, usually consisting of a heavy object attached to the end of a long rod or string, suspended from a fixed point.

Penicillin: A mold from the fungi group of microorganisms; used as an antibiotic.

Pepsin: Digestive enzyme that breaks down protein.

Percolate: To pass through a permeable substance.

Perfect flower: Flowers that have both male and female reproductive organs.

Period: A horizontal row in the periodic table.

Periodic table: A chart organizing elements by atomic number and chemical properties into groups and periods.

Permeable: Having pores that permit a liquid or a gas to pass through.

Permineralization: A form of preservation in which mineral matter has filled in the inner and outer spaces of the cell.

Pest: Any living thing that is unwanted by humans or causes injury and disease to crops and other growth.

Pesticide: Substance used to reduce the abundance of pests.

Petal: Leafy structure of a flower just inside the sepals; they are often brightly colored and have many different shapes.

Petrifaction: Process of turning organic material into rock by the replacement of that material with minerals.

pH: A measure of the acidity or alkalinity of a solution referring to the concentration of hydrogen ions present in a liter of a given fluid. The pH scale ranges from 0 (greatest concentration of hydrogen ions and therefore most acidic) to 14 (least concentration of hydrogen ions and therefore most alkaline), with 7 representing a neutral solution, such as pure water.

Pharmacology: The science dealing with the properties, reactions, and therapeutic values of drugs.

Phases: Changes in the portion of the Moon's surface that is illuminated by light from the Sun as the Moon revolves around Earth.

Phloem: The plant tissue that carries dissolved nutrients through the plant.

Phosphorescence: The emission of visible light from an object when the object is bombarded with electromagnetic radiation, such as ultraviolet rays. The object stores part of the radiation energy and the emission of visible light continues for a period ranging from a fraction of a second to several days after the radiation source has been removed.

Photoelectric effect: The phenomenon in which light falling upon certain metals stimulates the emission of electrons and changes light into electricity.

Photosynthesis: Chemical process by which plants containing chlorophyll use sunlight to manufacture their own food by converting carbon dioxide and water to carbohydrates, releasing oxygen as a by-product.

Phototropism: The tendency of a plant to grow toward a source of light.

Photovoltaic cells: A device made of silicon that converts sunlight into electricity.

Physical change: A change in which the substance keeps its molecular identity, such as a piece of chalk that has been ground up.

Physical property: A characteristic that you can detect with your senses, such as color and shape.

Physiologist: A scientist who studies the functions and processes of living organisms.

Phytoplankton: Microscopic aquatic plants that live suspended in the water.

Pigment: A substance that displays a color because of the wavelengths of light that it reflects.

Pili: Short projections that assist bacteria in attaching to tissues.

Pistil: Female reproductive organ of flowers that is composed of the stigma, style, and ovary.

Pitch: A property of a sound, determined by its frequency; the highness or lowness of a sound.

Plant extract: The juice or liquid essence obtained from a plant by squeezing or mashing it.

Plasmolysis: Occurs in walled cells in which cytoplasm, the semifluid substance inside a cell, shrivels and the membrane pulls away from the cell wall when the vacuole loses water.

Plates: Large regions of Earth's surface, composed of the crust and uppermost mantle, which move about, forming many of Earth's major geologic surface features.

Platform: The horizontal surface of a bridge on which traffic travels.

Pnematocysts: Stinging cells.

Point source: An identified source of pollution.

Pollen: Dust-like grains or particles produced by a plant that contain male sex cells.

Pollinate: The transfer of pollen from the male reproductive organs to the female reproductive organs of plants.

Pollination: Transfer of pollen from the male reproductive organs to the female reproductive organs of plants.

Pollinator: Any animal, such as an insect or bird, that transfers the pollen from one flower to another.

Pollution: The contamination of the natural environment, usually through human activity.

Polymer: Chemical compound formed of simple molecules (known as monomers) linked with themselves many times over.

Polymerization: The bonding of two or more monomers to form a polymer.

Polyvinyl acetate: A type of polymer that is the main ingredient of white glues.

Pore: An opening or space.

Potential energy: The energy of an object or system due to its position.

Precipitation: Any form of water that falls to Earth, such as rain, snow, or sleet.

Predator: An animal that hunts another animal for food.

Preservative: An additive used to keep food from spoiling.

Primary colors: The three colors red, green, and blue; when combined evenly they produce white light and by combining varying amounts can produce the range of colors.

Prism: A piece of transparent material with a triangular cross-section. When light passes through it, it causes different colors to bend different amounts, thus separating them into a rainbow of colors.

Probe: The terminal of a voltmeter, used to connect the voltmeter to a circuit.

Producer: An organism that can manufacture its own food from nonliving materials and an external energy source, usually by photosynthesis.

Product: A compound that is formed as a result of a chemical reaction.

Prokaryote: A cell without a true nucleus, such as a bacterium.

Prominences: Masses of glowing gas, mainly hydrogen, that rise from the Sun's surface like flames.

Propeller: Radiating blades mounted on a rapidly rotating shaft, which moves aircraft forward.

Protein: A complex chemical compound consisting of many amino acids attached to each other that are essential to the structure and functioning of all living cells.

Protists: Members of the kingdom Protista, primarily single-celled organisms that are not plants or animals.

Proton: A subatomic particle with a single positive charge that is found in the nucleus of an atom.

Protozoa: Single-celled animal-like microscopic organisms that live by taking in food rather than making it by photosynthesis. They must live in the presence of water.

Pulley: A simple machine made of a cord wrapped around a wheel.

Pupa: The insect stage of development between the larva and adult in insects that go through complete metamorphosis.

Radiation: Energy transmitted in the form of electromagnetic waves or subatomic particles.

Radicule: Seed's root system.

Radio wave: Longest form of electromagnetic radiation, measuring up to 6 miles (9.6 kilometers) from peak to peak.

Radioisotope dating: A technique used to date fossils, based on the decay rate of known radioactive elements.

Radiosonde balloons: Instruments for collecting data in the atmosphere and then transmitting that data back to Earth by means of radio waves.

Radon: A radioactive gas located in the ground; invisible and odorless, radon is a health hazard when it accumulates to high levels inside homes and other structures where it is breathed.

Rain shadow: Region on the side of the mountain that receives less rainfall than the area windward of the mountain.

Rancidity: Having the condition when food has a disagreeable odor or taste from decomposing oils or fats.

Reactant: A compound present at the beginning of a chemical reaction.

Reaction: Response to an action prompted by stimulus.

Recessive gene: A gene that produces a certain characteristic only two both copies (alleles) of the gene are present.

Recycling: The use of waste materials, also known as secondary materials or recyclables, to produce new products.

Redshift: The lengthening of the frequency of light waves toward the red end of the visible light spectrum as they travel away from an observer; most commonly used to describe movement of stars away from Earth.

Reduction: A process in which a chemical substance gives off oxygen or takes on electrons.

Reed: A tall woody perennial grass that has a hollow stem.

Reflection: The bouncing of light rays in a regular pattern off the surface of an object.

Reflector telescope: A telescope that directs light from an opening at one end to a concave mirror at the far end, which reflects the light back to a smaller mirror that directs it to an eyepiece on the side of the tube.

Refraction: The bending of light rays as they pass at an angle from one transparent or clear medium into a second one of different density.

Refractor telescope: A telescope that directs light through a glass lens, which bends the light waves and brings them to a focus at an eyepiece that acts as a magnifying glass.

Relative age: The age of an object expressed in relation to another like object, such as earlier or later.

Relative density: The density of one material compared to another.

Rennin: Enzyme used in making cheese.

Resistance: A partial or complete limiting of the flow of electrical current through a material. The common unit of measure is the ohm.

Respiration: The physical process that supplies oxygen to living cells and the chemical reactions that take place inside the cells.

Resultant: A force that results from the combined action of two other forces.

Retina: The light-sensitive part of the eyeball that receives images and transmits visual impulses through the optic nerve to the brain.

Ribosome: A protein composed of two subunits that functions in protein synthesis (creation).

Rigidity: The amount an object will deflect when supporting a weight. The less it deflects for a given amount of weight, the greater its rigidity.

River: A main course of water into which many other smaller bodies of water flow.

Rock: Naturally occurring solid mixture of minerals.

Rods: Cells in the retina that are sensitive to degrees of light and movement.

Root hairs: Fine, hair-like extensions from the plant's root.

Rotate: To turn around on an axis or center.

Runoff: Water that does not soak into the ground or evaporate, but flows across the surface of the ground.

S

Salinity: The amount of salts dissolved in water.

Saliva: Watery mixture with chemicals that lubricates chewed food.

Sand: Granular portion of soil composed of the largest soil particles.

Sapwood: The outer wood in a tree, which is usually a lighter color.

Saturated: In referring to solutions, a solution that contains the maximum amount of solute for a given amount of solvent at a given temperature.

Saturation: The intensity of a color.

Scanning tunneling microscope: A microscope that can show images of surfaces at the atomic level by scanning a probe over a surface.

Scientific method: Collecting evidence and arriving at a conclusion under carefully controlled conditions.

Screw: A simple machine; an inclined plane wrapped around a cylinder.

Scurvy: A disease caused by a deficiency of vitamin C, which causes a weakening of connective tissue in bone and muscle.

Sea cave: A cave in sea cliffs, formed most commonly by waves eroding the rock.

Second law of motion (Newton's): The force exerted on an object is proportional to the mass of the object times the acceleration produced by the force.

Sediment: Sand, silt, clay, rock, gravel, mud, or other matter that has been transported by flowing water.

Sedimentary rock: Rock formed from compressed and solidified layers of organic or inorganic matter.

Sedimentation: A process during which gravity pulls particles out of a liquid.

Seed crystal: Small form of a crystalline structure that has all the facets of a complete new crystal contained in it.

Seedling: A small plant just starting to grow into its mature form.

Seismic belt: Boundaries where Earth's plates meet.

Seismic waves: Vibrations in rock and soil that transfer the force of an earthquake from the focus into the surrounding area.

Seismograph: A device that detects and records vibrations of the ground.

Seismology: The study and measurement of earthquakes.

Seismometer: A seismograph that measures the movement of the ground.

Self-pollination: The process in which pollen from one part of a plant fertilizes ovules on another part of the same plant.

Semipermeable membrane: A thin barrier between two solutions that permits only certain components of the solutions, usually the solvent, to pass through.

Sensory memory: Memory that the brain retains for a few seconds.

Sepal: The outermost part of a flower; typically leaflike and green.

Sexual reproduction: A reproductive process that involves the union of two individuals in the exchange of genetic material.

Shear stress: An applied force to a give area.

Shell: A region of space around the center of the atom in which electrons are located; also, a hard outer covering that protects an animal living inside.

Short-term memory: Also known as working memory, this memory was transferred here from sensory memory.

Sidereal day: The time it takes for a particular star to travel around and reach the same position in the sky; about four minutes shorter than the average solar day.

Silt: Medium-sized soil particles.

Simple machine: Any of the basic structures that provide a mechanical advantage and have no or few moving parts.

Smog: A form of air pollution produced when moisture in the air combines and reacts with the products of fossil fuel combustion. Smog is characterized by hazy skies and a tendency to cause respiratory problems among humans.

Softwood: Wood from coniferous trees, which usually remain green all year.

Soil: The upper layer of Earth that contains nutrients for plants and organisms; a mixture of mineral matter, organic matter, air, and water.

Soil horizon: An identifiable soil layer due to color, structure, and/or texture.

Soil profile: Combined soil horizons or layers.

Solar collector: A device that absorbs sunlight and collects solar heat.

Solar day: Called a day, the time between each arrival of the Sun at its highest point.

Solar eclipse: An eclipse that occurs when the Moon passes between Earth and the Sun, casting a shadow on Earth.

Solar energy: Any form of electromagnetic radiation that is emitted by the Sun.

Solubility: The tendency of a substance to dissolve in some other substance.

Soluble: A substance that can be dissolved in some other substance.

Solute: The substance that is dissolved to make a solution and exists in the least amount in a solution, for example sugar in sugar water.

Solution: A mixture of two or more substances that appears to be uniform throughout except on a molecular level.

Solvent: The major component of a solution or the liquid in which some other component is dissolved, for example water in sugar water.

Specific gravity: The ratio of the density of a substance to the density of pure water.

Specific heat capacity: The energy required to raise the temperature of 1 kilogram of the substance by 1 degree Celsius.

Speleologist: One who studies caves.

Speleology: Scientific study of caves and their plant and animal life.

Spelunkers: Also called cavers, people who explore caves for a hobby.

Spiracles: The openings on an insects side where air enters.

Spoilage: The condition when food has taken on an undesirable color, odor, or texture.

Spore: A small, usually one-celled, reproductive body that is capable of growing into a new organism.

Stalactite: Cylindrical or icicle-shaped mineral deposit projecting downward from the roof of a cave. (Pronounced sta-LACK-tite.)

Stalagmite: Cylindrical or icicle-shaped mineral deposit projecting upward from the floor of a cave. (Pronounced sta-LAG-mite.)

Stamen: Male reproductive organ of flowers that is composed of the anther and filament.

Standard: A base for comparison.

Star: A vast clump of hydrogen gas and dust that produces great energy through fusion reactions at its core.

Static electricity: A form of electricity produced by friction in which the electric charge does not flow in a current but stays in one place.

Stigma: Top part of the pistil upon which pollen lands and receives the male pollen grains during fertilization.

Stomata: Pores in the epidermis (surface) of leaves.

Storm: An extreme atmospheric disturbance, associated with strong damaging winds, and often with thunder and lightning.

Storm chasers: People who track and seek out storms, often tornadoes.

Stratification: Layers according to density; applies to fluids.

Streak: The color of the dust left when a mineral is rubbed across a rough surface.

Style: Stalk of the pistil that connects the stigma to the ovary.

Subatomic: Smaller than an atom. It usually refers to particles that make up an atom, such as protons, neutrons, and electrons.

Sublime: The process of changing a solid into a vapor without passing through the liquid phase.

Substrate: The substance on which an enzyme operates in a chemical reaction.

Succulent: Plants that live in dry environments and have water storage tissue.

Sundial: A device that uses the position of the Sun to indicate time.

Supersaturated: Solution that is more highly concentrated than is normally possible under given conditions of temperature and pressure.

Supertaster: A person who is extremely sensitive to specific tastes due to a greater number of taste buds.

Supplements: A substance intended to enhance the diet.

Surface area: The total area of the outside of an object; the area of a body of water that is exposed to the air.

Surface tension: The attractive force of molecules to each other on the surface of a liquid.

Surface water: Water in lakes, rivers, ponds, and streams.

Suspension: A temporary mixture of a solid in a gas or liquid from which the solid will eventually settle out.

Swim bladder: Located above the stomach, takes in air when the fish wants to move upwards and releases air when the fish wants to move downwards.

Symbiosis: A pattern in which two or more organisms live in close connection with each other, often to the benefit of both or all organisms.

Synthesis reaction: A chemical reaction in which two or more substances combine to form a new substance.

Synthesize: To make something artificially, in a laboratory or chemical plant, that is generally not found in nature.

Synthetic: A substance that is synthesized, or manufactured, in a laboratory; not naturally occurring.

Synthetic crystals: Artificial or manmade crystals.

Taiga: A large land biome mostly dominated by coniferous trees.

Taste buds: Groups of taste cells located on the papillae that recognize the different tastes.

Taste pore: The opening at the top of the taste bud from which chemicals reach the taste cells.

Tectonic: Relating to the forces and structures of the outer shell of Earth.

Tectonic plates: Huge flat rocks that form Earth's crust.

Telescope: A tube with lenses or mirrors that collect, transmit, and focus light.

Temperate: Mild or moderate weather conditions.

Temperature: The measure of the average energy of the molecules in a substance.

Tendon: Tough, fibrous connective tissue that attaches muscle to bone.

Tensile strength: The force needed to stretch a material until it breaks.

Terminal: A connection in an electric circuit; usually a connection on a source of electric energy such as a battery.

Terracing: A series of horizontal ridges made in a hillside to reduce erosion.

Testa: A tough outer layer that protects the embryo and endosperm of a seed from damage.

Theory of special relativity: Theory put forth by Albert Einstein that time is not absolute, but it is relative according to the speed of the observer's frame of reference.

Thermal conductivity: A number representing a material's ability to conduct heat.

Thermal energy: Kinetic energy caused by the movement of molecules due to temperature.

Thermal inversion: A region in which the warmer air lies above the colder air; can cause smog to worsen.

Thermal pollution: The discharge of heated water from industrial processes that can kill or injure water life.

Thiamine: A vitamin of the B complex that is essential to normal metabolism and nerve function.

Thigmotropism: The tendency for a plant to grow toward a surface it touches.

Third law of motion (Newton's): For every action there is an equal and opposite reaction.

Thorax: The middle segment of an insect body; the legs and wings are connected to the thorax.

Tides: The cyclic rise and fall of seawater.

Titration: A procedure in which an acid and a base are slowly mixed to achieve a neutral substance.

Topsoil: The uppermost layers of soil containing an abundant supply of decomposed organic material to supply plants with nutrients.

Tornado: A violently rotating, narrow column of air in contact with the ground and usually extending from a cumulonimbus cloud.

Total solar/lunar eclipse: An eclipse in which our view of the Sun/Moon is totally blocked.

Toxic: Poisonous.

Trace element: A chemical element present in minute quantities.

Trace minerals: Minerals needed in relatively small quantities.

Translucent: Permits the passage of light.

Transpiration: Evaporation of water in the form of water vapor from the stomata on the surfaces of leaves and stems of plants.

Troglobite: An animal that lives in a cave and is unable to live outside of one.

Troglophile: An animal that lives the majority of its life cycle in a cave but is also able to live outside of the cave.

Trogloxene: An animal that spends only part of its life cycle in a cave and returns periodically to the cave.

Tropism: The growth or movement of a plant toward or away from a stimulus.

Troposphere: The lowest layer of Earth's atmosphere, ranging to an altitude of about 9 miles (15 km) above Earth's surface.

Trough: The lowest point of a wave. (Pronounced trawf.)

Tsunami: A large wave of water caused by an underwater earthquake.

Tuber: An underground, starch-storing stem, such as a potato.

Tundra: A treeless, frozen biome with low-lying plants.

Turbine: A spinning device used to transform mechanical power from energy into electrical energy.

Turbulence: Air disturbance that affects an aircraft's flight.

Turgor pressure: The force that is exerted on a plant's cell wall by the water within the cell.

Tyndall effect: The effect achieved when colloidal particles reflect a beam of light, making it visible when shined through such a mixture.

Ultraviolet: Electromagnetic radiation (energy) of a wavelength just shorter than the violet (shortest wavelength) end of the visible light spectrum and thus with higher energy than the visible light.

Unconfined aquifer: An aquifer under a layer of permeable rock and soil.

Unicellular: Living things that have one cell. Protozoans are unicellular, for example.

Unit cell: The basic unit of the crystalline structure.

Universal law of gravity: The law of physics that defines the constancy of the force of gravity between two bodies.

Updraft: Warm, moist air that moves away from the ground.

Upwelling: The process by which lower-level, nutrient-rich waters rise upward to the ocean's surface.

Vacuole: An enclosed, space-filling sac within plant cells containing mostly water and providing structural support for the cell.

Van der Waals' force: An attractive force between two molecules based on the positive and negative side of the molecule.

Variable: Something that can affect the results of an experiment.

Vegetative propagation: A form of asexual reproduction in which plants are produced that are genetically identical to the parent.

Velocity: The rate at which the position of an object changes with time, including both the speed and the direction.

Veneer: Thin slices of wood.

Viable: The capability of developing or growing under favorable conditions.

Vibration: A regular, back-and-forth motion of molecules in the air.

Viscosity: The measure of a fluid's resistance to flow; its flowability.

Visible spectrum: The range of individual wavelengths of radiation visible to the human eye when white light is broken into its component colors as it passes through a prism or by some other means.

Vitamin: A complex organic compound found naturally in plants and animals that the body needs in small amounts for normal growth and activity.

Volatilization: The process by which a liquid changes (volatilizes) to a gas.

Volcano: A conical mountain or dome of lava, ash, and cinders that forms around a vent leading to molten rock deep within Earth.

Voltage: Also called potential difference; a measurement of the amount of electric energy stored in a mass of electric charges compared to the energy stored in some other mass of charges. The common unit of measure is the volt.

Voltmeter: An instrument for measuring the amperage, voltage, or resistance in an electrical circuit.

Volume: The amount of space occupied by a three-dimensional object; the amplitude or loudness of a sound.

Vortex: A rotating column of a fluid such as air or water.

Waste stream: The waste materials generated by the population of an area, or by a specific industrial process, and removed for disposal.

Water (hydrologic) cycle: The constant movement of water molecules on Earth as they rise into the atmosphere as water vapor, condense into droplets and fall to land or bodies of water, evaporate, and rise again.

Water clock: A device that uses the flow of water to measure time.

Water table: The level of the upper surface of groundwater.

Water vapor: Water in its gaseous state.

Water-soluble vitamins: Vitamins such as C and the B-complex vitamins that dissolve in the watery parts of plant and animal tissues.

Waterline: The highest point to which water rises on the hull of a ship. The portion of the hull below the waterline is under water.

Wave: A means of transmitting energy in which the peak energy occurs at a regular interval; the rise and fall of the ocean water.

Wavelength: The distance between the peak of a wave of light, heat, or other form of energy and the next corresponding peak.

Weather: The state of the troposphere at a particular time and place.

Weather forecasting: The scientific predictions of future weather patterns.

Weathered: Natural process that breaks down rocks and minerals at Earth's surface into simpler materials by physical (mechanical) or chemical means.

Wedge: A simple machine; a form of inclined plane.

Weight: The gravitational attraction of Earth on an object; the measure of the heaviness of an object.

Wet cell: A source of electricity that uses a liquid electrolyte.

Wetlands: Areas that are wet or covered with water for at least part of the year.

Wheel and axle: A simple machine; a larger wheel(s) fastened to a smaller cylinder, an axle, so that they turn together.

Work: The result of a force moving a mass a given distance. The greater the mass or the greater the distance, the greater the work involved.

Xanthophyll: Yellow pigment in plants.

Xerophytes: Plants that require little water to survive.

Xylem: Plant tissue consisting of elongated, thick-walled cells that transport water and mineral nutrients. (Pronounced ZY-lem.)

Yeast: A single-celled fungi that can be used to as a leavening agent.

Acid Rain

Did you know that acid rain can also be acid snow, acid fog, or even acid dust? Acid rain is a form of precipitation that is significantly more acidic than neutral water. The pH scale offers a way to compare the acidity of substances, including rain. pH (the abbreviation for potential hydrogen) is a measure of the acidity or alkalinity of a solution. The symbol pH refers to the concentration of hydrogen ions present in a liter of fluid. The pH scale ranges from 0 (greatest concentration of hydrogen ions and therefore most acidic) to 14 (least concentration of hydrogen ions and therefore most alkaline). An alkaline solution is also called a base. The number 7 represents a neutral solution, such as pure water.

Water with a pH of 4 is 10 times more acidic than water with a pH of 5. A pH of 4 is 100 times more acidic than a pH of 6. So you can see that a small increase or decrease in pH makes a big difference in acid levels.

How does acid get in rain? Normal rainfall is slightly acidic, with a pH of about 5.6. Rain with a pH below 5.6 is considered to be acid rain. Acid rain is created when smoke and fumes from burning fossil fuels—coal, oil, and natural gas—rise into the air. The smoke and fumes come from oil- and coal-fired power plants, factory smokestacks, and automobile exhaust.

The main toxic (poisonous) chemicals in this pollution are sulfur dioxide and nitrogen oxides. These chemicals react with sunlight and moisture in the air to produce rain or snow that is a mild solution of sulfuric acid and nitric acid. Some of the pollutant particles fall to the ground as acid dust. When acid rain falls, this dust dissolves in the water, further increasing the rain's acidity.

Why is acid rain a problem? Acid rain can make lakes and streams so toxic that nothing can live there. Amphibians and the young of most

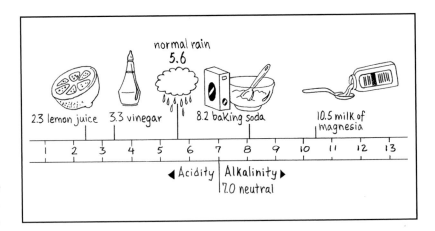

normal rain
5.6

2.3 lemon juice   3.3 vinegar   8.2 baking soda   10.5 milk of magnesia

1 2 3 4 5 6 7 8 9 10 11 12 13

◄ Acidity | Alkalinity ►
7.0 neutral

The pH scale shows the acidity and alkalinity of liquids.
GALE GROUP.

The taller the smokestacks, the longer acid rain stays in the air and the farther it is likely to travel.
PHOTO RESEARCHERS INC.

fish are sensitive to acidity, so they are the first to die. With water at a pH of 5.0, most fish eggs are unable to hatch. If the pH level continues to drop, adult animals begin to die. Experiment 1 will help you determine how sensitive brine shrimp are to acid rain.

Acidity kills plants in the water, too, thus upsetting the food chain. Even plant-eating fish that can tolerate low pH levels are soon unable to find enough to eat. With few plant-eating fish able to survive, the fish-eating fish go hungry, too.

Acid rain can slowly kill whole forests by dissolving the toxic metals in soil and rock. In their dissolved form, these metals damage tree roots. Acid rain also dissolves nutrients in the soil and washes them away before the trees and plants can use them. In addition, acid rain burns tree leaves and needles and wears away their protective coatings, leaving them unable to produce enough food energy to meet the trees' needs. Viruses, fungi, and pests can then easily finish off the weakened trees. Experiment 2 will help you determine how acid rain affects plant growth.

Along with harming plants and life, acid rain can also damage manmade structures. Many buildings are made of limestone. Limestone is a type of rock that primarily contains calcium carbonate. Statues are often made from marble, a hard substance that is also composed of calcium carbonate. Acids in the rain react with the calcium and slowly dissolve the material. In Experiment 3, you will test how acid rain can affect structures.

Trees take a long time to recover from damage caused by acid rain. PHOTO RESEARCHERS INC.

What can be done? Acid rain was first identified in 1852 by an English chemist named Robert Angus Smith. He suggested that factories that burned coal were sending sulfur dioxide into the air. Since then, the world has gained many more factories—and many more sources of air pollution.

Fortunately, scientists have found ways to wash the sulfur out of coal before it is burned and to wash the sulfur out of smoke before it leaves the smokestacks. In addition, new vehicles must now have a device called a catalytic converter, which uses filters and chemicals to change carbon monoxide and other air pollutants into carbon dioxide

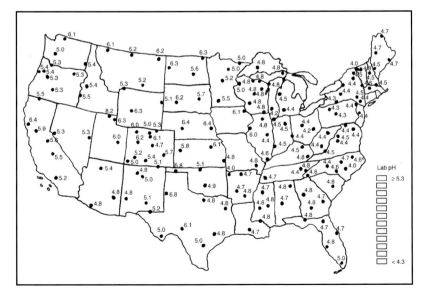

pH levels in the United States. GALE GROUP.

WORDS TO KNOW

Acid rain: A form of precipitation that is significantly more acidic than neutral water, often produced as the result of industrial processes and pollution.

Alkaline: Having a pH of more than 7.

Amphibians: Animals that live both on land and in water.

Base: A water-soluble compound that when dissolved in water makes an alkaline, or basic, solution with a pH of more than 7.

Control experiment: A set-up that is identical to the experiment but is not affected by the variable that will be changed during the experiment.

Fossil fuel: A fuel such as coal, oil, or natural gas that is formed over millions of years from the remains of plants and animals.

Hypothesis: An idea in the form of a statement that can be tested by observation and/or experiment.

Ion: An atom or groups of atoms that carry an electrical charge—either positive or negative—as a result of losing or gaining one or more electrons.

Neutralization: A chemical process in which the mixing of an acidic solution with a basic (alkaline) solution results in a solution that has the properties of neither an acid nor a base.

pH: A measure of the acidity or alkalinity of a solution referring to the concentration of hydrogen ions present in a liter of a given fluid. The pH scale ranges from 0 (greatest concentration of hydrogen ions and therefore most acidic) to 14 (least concentration of hydrogen ions and therefore most alkaline), with 7 representing a neutral solution, such as pure water.

Toxic: Poisonous.

Variable: Something that might affect the results of an experiment.

and water. This device nearly eliminates the nitrogen oxide released by cars' exhaust systems.

Lime, which is a natural base, can be added to streams and lakes to neutralize their acidity. Neutralization is a chemical process in which an acidic solution is mixed with a basic (alkaline) solution, resulting in a solution that is neutral—it has the properties of neither an acid nor a base. However, neutralizing streams and lakes is expensive and must continue as long as acid rain keeps falling.

Scientists are also researching more ways to use sources of energy that do not pollute the air, including solar power. We all can help reduce acid rain by reducing our own use of fossil fuels and by learning more about the effects of acid rain.

EXPERIMENT 1

Acid Rain and Animals: How does acid rain affect brine shrimp?

Purpose/Hypothesis In this experiment, you will use vinegar, which is an acid, to gradually lower the pH level of water containing brine shrimp. (As the pH level drops, acidity increases.) You will measure the changing pH level and observe how the shrimp react.

Before you begin, make an educated guess about the outcome of this experiment based on your knowledge of acid rain. This educated guess, or prediction, is your hypothesis. A hypothesis should explain these things:

- the topic of the experiment
- the variable you will change
- the variable you will measure
- what you expect to happen

A hypothesis should be brief, specific, and measurable. It must be something you can test through observation. Your experiment will prove or disprove whether your hypothesis is correct. Here is one possible hypothesis for this experiment: "All the brine shrimp will be dead by the time the pH level of the water reaches 4.5."

In this case, the variable you will change is the pH level of the water, and the variable you will measure is the number of brine shrimp that remain alive. You expect them all to die by the time the pH level reaches 4.5.

You will also set up a control experiment. It will be identical to the "real" experiment, except that the pH level will remain the same in the control water and decrease in the experimental water.

After each pH decrease in the experimental water, you will estimate the number of brine shrimp that remain alive in the experimental and the control water. If the shrimp in the experimental water are all dead by the time the pH reaches 4.5, while most remain alive in the control water, you will know your hypothesis is correct.

What Are the Variables?

Variables are anything that might affect the results of an experiment. Here are the main variables in this experiment:

- the size and health of the brine shrimp
- the number of brine shrimp in a given amount of water
- the temperature of the water
- the kind and amount of food the brine shrimp receive
- the pH level of the water

In other words, the variables in this experiment are everything that might affect the survival of the brine shrimp. If you change more than one variable, you will not be able to tell which variable had the most effect on the shrimps' survival.

Level of Difficulty Moderate, because of the time involved.

Materials Needed

- 1 tablespoon of live brine shrimp (Brine shrimp are sold as fish food at tropical and saltwater fish shops. The clerk will measure 1 tablespoon of shrimp, which contains several hundred shrimp, and pour it into a container of water.)
- 2 wide-mouth jars
- distilled water at room temperature (or tap water that has been in an open container overnight to allow the chlorine in it to evaporate)
- 2 small, clear containers
- 2 labels and a marker
- litmus paper and a color scale
- white vinegar
- measuring spoons
- a stirrer
- 2 medicine droppers
- 1 package dry yeast
- Optional: small aquarium pump with two outlets and plastic tubing

Approximate Budget $5 for the brine shrimp, litmus paper, and yeast. (The other materials should be available in most households.)

Timetable One week.

Step-by-Step Instructions

1. Fill both glass jars half-full of water.
2. Use the two small, clear containers to divide the brine shrimp into two equal portions.
3. Pour one portion of shrimp into each of the jars. Rinse the small containers. Label one jar *Control* and one *Experiment.*
4. Dip a different strip of litmus paper into each jar, check the color scale, and record the beginning pH level of each jar on a chart like the one illustrated.

5. Use the following steps to take a sample of water from each jar and estimate the number of live shrimp in it:

a. Gently stir the water in the experimental jar until the shrimp are distributed evenly.

b. Quickly use a medicine dropper to take out a sample of water and shrimp.

c. Deposit the sample in one of the clear containers.

d. Count or estimate the number of live brine shrimp in it.

e. Record the number on your chart.

f. Pour the sample back into the same jar.

g. Rinse the dropper and container.

h. Complete the same process with the control jar.

6. Use the other medicine dropper to slowly add 2 tablespoons (30 ml) of vinegar to the experimental jar. Again measure and record the pH level in that jar. Do not add vinegar to the control jar.

7. Place both jars in a warm, lighted place where they will not receive direct sun. Add a pinch of dry yeast to both jars as food for the brine shrimp.

8. Optional: Attach a length of plastic tubing to each outlet on the aquarium pump. Insert one of the tubes into each jar so it rests on the bottom of the jar. Start the pump, which will keep the water gently moving and increase its oxygen content.

9. Each day for a week:

a. Add another pinch of dry yeast to both jars.

b. Add 2 more tablespoons of vinegar to the experimental jar.

Record of Live Brine Shrimp					
	Mon.	Tues.	Wed.	Thurs.	Fri.
Experiment Jar	pH:	pH:	pH:	pH:	pH:
	No. of Shrimp:	No. of Shrimp:	No. of Shrimp:	No. of Shrimp:	No. of Shrimp:
Control Jar	pH:	pH:	pH:	pH:	pH:
	No. of Shrimp:	No. of Shrimp:	No. of Shrimp:	No. of Shrimp:	No. of Shrimp:

Step 4: Recording chart for Experiment 1. GALE GROUP.

Step 5d: Brine shrimp in a small, clear container. GALE GROUP.

Troubleshooters' Guide

Below are some problems that may arise during this experiment, some possible causes, and ways to remedy the problems.

Problem: All or nearly all the brine shrimp died in both jars.

Possible causes:

1. The shrimp were "old." The fish shop might have kept those shrimp for some time without feeding them. Try again with a fresh batch of shrimp.

2. The water had too much chlorine or other chemicals in it. Try again with water from a different source or let the water sit longer before using it.

3. The yeast polluted the water. Try again, feeding the shrimp much less yeast or not at all.

4. The water became too cold or too hot. Make the necessary adjustments and try again.

Problem: Very few of the shrimp died in the experimental jar.

Possible cause: The pH did not reach a toxic level. Continue the experiment, further decreasing the pH level of the experimental water.

c. Measure and record the pH levels of both jars.

d. Repeat Step 5 to monitor how many live brine shrimp remain in both jars. If no live brine shrimp remain in the experimental jar before the end of the week, end the experiment.

Summary of Results Use the data on your chart to create a line or bar graph of your findings. Then study your chart and graph and decide whether your hypothesis was correct. At what pH level did the brine shrimp in the experimental jar start to die in greater numbers? At what level were they all dead? Did most of the shrimp in your control jar survive until the end of the week? Write a paragraph summarizing your findings and explaining whether they supported your hypothesis.

Change the Variables To vary this experiment, consider these possibilities:

- Try hatching your own brine shrimp from eggs bought at a pet shop. The hatched shrimp will be very small, but cheap, available, and plentiful. Or use a plankton net to collect small aquatic organisms from pond water. You may need to use a microscope to monitor them during the experiment.

- Change the water temperature. Put two jars of water with a pH of 4.8 (mildly acid rain) under different temperature conditions to see if the shrimp tolerate acid rain better at higher or lower temperatures.

- Change the type of acid by using lemon juice. It is more acidic than vinegar and will cause the pH level to drop more quickly.

EXPERIMENT 2

Acid Rain and Plants: How does acid rain affect plant growth?

Purpose/Hypothesis In this experiment, you will use cuttings of plants that are easy to grow, such as ivy, philodendron, begonia, or coleus. You will place two cuttings in water with a pH level of 7.0, which is neutral, and two cuttings in water with a pH of 4.0, which is in the range of acid rain. Your goal is to determine how the acidity affects the growth of roots.

Before you begin, make an educated guess or hypothesis about the outcome of this experiment based on your understanding of acid rain. This educated guess, or prediction, is your hypothesis. A hypothesis should explain these things:

- the topic of the experiment
- the variable you will change
- the variable you will measure
- what you expect to happen

A hypothesis should be brief, specific, and measurable. It must be something you can test through observation. Your experiment will prove or disprove whether your hypothesis is correct. Here is one possible hypothesis for this experiment: "Cuttings placed in water with a pH level of 4.0 will not grow any roots, while cuttings in water with a pH of 7.0 will begin to grow roots during the experiment."

In this case, the variable you will change is the pH level of the water, and the variable you will measure is the amount of roots that grow. You expect no roots to grow in the water with a pH level of 4.0.

The cuttings in the water with a pH of 7.0 serve as a control experiment, allowing you to observe root growth when the pH of the water remains neutral. After the two-week period of the experiment, if the cuttings in the neutral water have grown roots, but those in the acid water have not, you will know your hypothesis is correct.

Level of Difficulty Moderate, because of the time involved.

What Are the Variables?

Variables are anything that might affect the results of an experiment. Here are the main variables in this experiment:

- the type, size, and health of the plant cuttings
- the air temperature where the jars of cuttings are placed
- the amount of sun the cuttings receive
- the pH level of the water

In other words, the variables in this experiment are everything that might affect the growth of roots. If you change more than one variable, you will not be able to tell which one had the most effect on root growth.

How to Experiment Safely

Be careful in handling glass jars.

Materials Needed

- 4 small, clear jars
- 4 labels and a marker
- 2 large water containers
- water
- litmus paper and a color scale
- white vinegar
- baking soda
- measuring cups and spoons
- a stirrer
- 2 cuttings each of two easily grown plants, such as ivy, philodendron, begonia, or coleus (Make sure each cutting has the same number of leaves and same amount of stem.)

Approximate Budget $5 for the plants and litmus paper. (Ask friends, neighbors, or family members for cuttings so you will not need to buy plants, and the other materials should be available in most households.)

Timetable Two weeks to observe plant growth.

Step-by-Step Instructions

1. Label the four small jars in this way: (name of plant 1), neutral; (name of plant 1), acid; (name of plant 2), neutral; (name of plant 2), acid.
2. Pour 2 cups of water into each of the large containers.
3. Use the litmus paper and a litmus color scale to measure the pH level of the neutral or control container. It should be 7.0. If it is higher, add a drop or two of vinegar, stir, and check it again. If it is lower than 7.0, sprinkle in a little baking soda, stir, and check again. Repeat until the color scale shows that the pH level is 7.0.
4. Pour 1 tablespoon (15 ml) of vinegar into the acid or experimental container, stir, and check the pH level. It should be 4.0. If it is higher or lower, add vinegar or baking soda, as in Step 3.
5. Nearly fill the two small jars labeled *Neutral* with the neutral water. Then pour the same amount of acid water into the two

Step 6: Plant cuttings in labeled jars of water. GALE GROUP.

small jars labeled *Acid.* Label and save any leftover water so you can keep the small jars full of water with the correct pH level.

6. Place the four plant cuttings in their labeled jars. Make sure the stem and part of the lowest leaf is under water.

7. Place all four jars in a warm, sunny place.

8. Create a chart like the one illustrated. Draw each cutting to show how it looked at the beginning.

9. For the next two weeks:

a. Every day, make sure all cuttings are still in the water. Add more acid or neutral water to replace any that evaporates. (Be careful to add the right kind to each cup.)

b. Every other day, check the pH of the water in each cup, and use vinegar or baking soda to adjust it so it is 7.0 or 4.0.

c. Every day, record any changes or growth on the chart. Clearly show any roots that grow longer or branch out, leaves that grow larger, and the emergence of new leaves.

Summary of Results Study the drawings on your chart and decide whether your hypothesis was correct. Did both cuttings in acid water not

Step 8: Recording chart for Experiment 2. GALE GROUP.

Record of Plant Growth

Week 1	Mon.	Tues.	Wed.	Thurs.	Fri.
Acid, Plant 1 Drawing:					
Acid, Plant 2 Drawing:					
Neutral, Plant 1 Drawing:					
Neutral, Plant 2 Drawing:					

Week 2	Mon.	Tues.	Wed.	Thurs.	Fri.
Acid, Plant 1 Drawing:					
Acid, Plant 2 Drawing:					
Neutral, Plant 1 Drawing:					
Neutral, Plant 2 Drawing:					

Troubleshooters' Guide

Below are some problems that may arise during this experiment, some possible causes, and ways to remedy the problems.

Problem: None of the cuttings grew.

Possible causes:

1. The cuttings were infected with insects, fungus, or something else. Try the experiment again with fresh cuttings from different plants. Use different jars or wash the old jars well.

2. The cuttings were from old, woody sections of the plant. Try cuttings from the growing tips of the plants.

3. The cuttings did not receive enough sun or became too cold or too hot. Perhaps their stems did not remain in the water. Try again, placing the cups in a warm (not hot) place where they will receive several hours of sun every day. Check to make sure the stems remain underwater.

Problem: All of the cuttings grew about the same amount.

Possible causes:

1. The pH of the water in the acid jars might not have remained at 4.0. Try the experiment again, carefully checking the pH levels during the observation period.

2. Perhaps both kinds of plants are tolerant of acid water. That would mean your hypothesis is incorrect for these kinds of plants.

grow at all? Or did they grow some, but less than those in neutral water? Was the cutting of one plant more tolerant of acid water than the cutting of the other plant? Did both cuttings in neutral water grow as you expected? Write a paragraph summarizing your findings and explaining whether they supported your hypothesis.

Change the Variables Here are some ways you can vary this experiment:

- Use different kinds of plants.
- Water potted plants with acid and neutral water and compare their leaf and stem growth and appearance, general health, and frequency of blooming, if applicable, over time.
- Use water with different pH levels, such as 5.0, 4.0, and 3.0 to determine if growth decreases with each increase in acidity.

EXPERIMENT 3

Acid Rain: Can acid rain harm structures?

Purpose/Hypothesis In this experiment, you will observe how acid rain can harm buildings, statues, and other structures. The acid you will be using is vinegar, which is about 5% acid. Vinegar is slightly more acidic than acid rain, but acid rain works its reaction over a period of years and this experiment will only take about a week. You will test vinegar's effect on two different forms of structural materials: marble and limestone. For the limestone, you will use chalk, which is a type of limestone. You can determine if some of the materials dissolve by noting the weight and appearance. By weighing the materials both before and after they are exposed to vinegar, you can measure the effect of acid on structures.

Before you begin, make an educated guess about the outcome of this experiment based on your knowledge of acid rain. This educated guess, or prediction, is your hypothesis. A hypothesis should explain these things:

- the topic of the experiment
- the variable you will change
- the variable you will measure
- what you expect to happen

A hypothesis should be brief, specific, and measurable. It must be something you can test through further investigation. Your experiment will prove or disprove whether your hypothesis is correct. Here is one possible hypothesis for this experiment: "Acid will wear away some of the materials, causing the substances to weigh less after they are immersed in acid."

In this case, the variable you will change is the acidity. The variable you will measure is the appearance and weight of the material.

Conducting a control experiment for each material will help you isolate the variable and measure the changes in the dependent variable. Only one variable will change between the control and your experiment. In this experiment, you will have two controls: one for the marble and one for the limestone (chalk). For the controls, you will use distilled water.

Level of Difficulty Moderate.

Materials Needed

- crushed marbles (the size of small pebbles), available from a craft or home garden store
- white chalk
- gram scale
- wax paper
- 4 small jars with lids
- distilled water
- white vinegar
- spoons

What Are the Variables?

Variables are anything that might affect the results of an experiment. Here are the main variables in this experiment:

- the temperature of the solution
- the room temperature
- the size of the materials
- the shape of the materials

In other words, the variables in this experiment are everything that might affect the rate at which the materials dissolve. If you change more than one variable at the same time, you will not be able to tell which variable had the most effect on the chalk and marble.

How to Experiment Safely

Make sure the experiment is well labeled and stored somewhere safe. Wash your hands after setting up and finishing the experiment.

Approximate Budget $8 (assuming gram scale is a household item).

Timetable 20 minutes setup; about ten minutes daily for five to 10 days.

Step-by-Step Instructions

1. Label each of the jars: "Marble," "Marble Control," "Limestone," and "Limestone Control."
2. Make a chart listing the materials, starting weight, ending weight, and appearance. (See chart).
3. Place a sheet of wax paper on the gram scale and weight out 2 grams of the crushed marble. (You can use less but make sure to note the exact weight in your chart.) Carefully pour into the jar labeled "Marble."
4. Weigh another 2 grams of the marble and pour into the Control jar.
5. Break the chalk into roughly 1-inch (2.5 centimeters) pieces.
6. Using a fresh piece of wax paper, weigh 2 grams of the chalk and place in the jar labeled "Limestone." Weigh out another 2 grams and place in the Control jar.
7. In both control jars, cover the chalk and marble with distilled water.
8. In both experimental jars, cover the chalk and marble with vinegar.
9. After four days, note the appearance of the materials and solutions in your chart. Does the chalk look smaller? Does the vinegar appear cloudy?
10. After a minimum of a week, when it looks like the acid has affected the material, carefully scoop out the marble and chalk onto separate sheets of wax paper. You may need to rinse them off. Scoop out the control marble and chalk too. Make sure to keep track of the test and control materials! You can either label the wax papers or keep the material next to the labeled jar.
11. Let the marble and chalk pieces dry overnight.
12. When completely dry, weigh each of the materials and note the results.

Step 2: The recording chart for Experiment 3. ILLUSTRATION BY TEMAH NELSON.

	Starting Weight	Ending Weight	Appearance
Marble			
Marble control			
Limestone			
Limestone control			

Summary of Results Examine your results and note the appearance of each of the materials. Calculate the difference between the starting and ending weights. Compare the chalk and marble to the controls. How did the acid from the vinegar affect the materials? Was your hypothesis correct?

Change the Variables There are several ways you can alter the variables in this experiment. You can try different materials, such as metals. Dolomite is a rock that is similar to limestone. You can also vary the strength of the acid. For a weaker acid, more similar to acid rain, add water to the vinegar. For a stronger acid, you can carefully boil away some of the vinegar's water, leaving more of the acid.

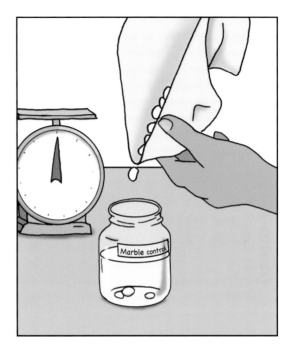

Design Your Own Experiment

How to Select a Topic Relating to this Concept You can explore many other aspects of acid rain. Consider what puzzles you about this topic. For example, what would happen if you added vinegar or another acid to a jar of water with limestone (calcium carbonate) gravel in the bottom? Lime is a base that can neutralize acid, so would the pH level of the water still drop with the limestone in there?

How does ground lime affect plants that have been damaged by acid rain? Will they begin growing well again if lime neutralizes the soil? What if lime is applied first and then the plants are watered with acid rain? Will the lime protect them? How does acid rain affect the germination of seeds? Which plants are more tolerant of acid rain than others?

Check the Further Readings section and talk with your science teacher or school or community media specialist to start gathering information on acid rain questions that interest you.

Steps in the Scientific Method To do an original experiment, you need to plan carefully and think

Step 3: Carefully pour into the jar labeled "Marble.&rdquo ILLUSTRATION BY TEMAH NELSON.

Step 7: The controlled jars are filled with distilled water. The experimental jars are filled with vinegar. ILLUSTRATION BY TEMAH NELSON.

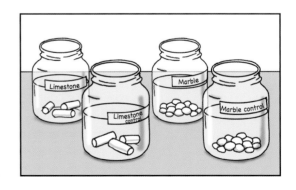

Troubleshooter's Guide

Below is a problem that may arise during this experiment, a possible cause, and a way to remedy the problem.

Problem: The marble weighed the same, even after ten days.

Possible cause: Marble is a much harder material than chalk. The pieces may have been too large to dissolve. Try again with marble pieces that are more finely crushed.

Problem: There was no notable difference in the weight of the chalk, even though it appears smaller.

Possible cause: The chalk may still contain some of the liquid it absorbed, which would add weight. Set the chalk aside in a warm area for another day, then weigh again.

things through. Otherwise, you might not be sure what question you are answering, what you are or should be measuring, or what your findings prove or disprove.

Here are the steps in designing an experiment:

- State the purpose of—and the underlying question behind—the experiment you propose to do.

- Recognize the variables involved, and select one that will help you answer the question at hand.

- State a testable hypothesis, an educated guess about the answer to your question.

- Decide how to change the variable you selected.

- Decide how to measure your results.

Recording Data and Summarizing the Results In the two acid rain experiments, your raw data might include not only charts of brine shrimp survival rates and root growth, but also drawings or photographs of these changes.

If you display your experiment, limit the amount of information you offer, so viewers will not be overwhelmed by detail. Make clear your beginning question, the variable you changed, the variable you measured, the results, and your conclusions. Viewers—and judges at science fairs—will want to see how your experiment was set up. You might include photographs or drawings of the steps of the experiment. Viewers will want to know what materials you used, how long each step took, and other basic information.

Related Projects You can undertake a variety of projects related to acid rain. For example, you might explore how acid rain affects buildings, statues, and other outdoor structures. Which kinds of stone are most susceptible to damage from acid rain? How do people fare in regions with highly acidic rain? Do they have more respiratory problems?

For More Information

Edmonds, Alex. *A Closer Look at Acid Rain.* Brookfield, CT: Copper Beech Books, 1997. Examines the causes of acid rain; its effects on plants, lakes, and human health; and ways to tackle the problem.

Gutnik, Martin. *Experiments That Explore Acid Rain.* Brookfield, CT: Millbrook Press, 1992. Outlines projects and experiments dealing with acid rain.

Parks, Peggy J. *Acid Rain.* Detroit, MI: KidHaven Press, 2006. Explanation and effects of acid rain.

Rainis, Kenneth. *Environmental Science Projects for Young Scientists.* New York: Franklin Watts, 1994. Outlines detailed projects easily completed by middle school students.

U.S. Environmental Protection Agency. "Acid Rain." http://www.epa.gov/acidrain (accessed on January 17, 2008).

The sulphur in acid rain reacts with the limestone in statues, forming a powder that easily washes away. PHOTO RESEARCHERS INC.

2

Adhesives

An adhesive is any substance that binds or adheres objects together. Adhesives are generally out of sight, but they are all around us. They are holding together the pages of a book, the wood in furniture, and the cardboard in food packages. Adhesives are also a part of modern technologies, such as airplanes, sports equipment, and electronics. And as the development of adhesives continues to improve, they are increasingly becoming a part of products and structures.

Nature's sticky stuff Before the development of synthetic (man-made) adhesives, people used natural adhesives. Many animals and plants have sticky substances. Historians have found evidence that about 3,000 years ago Egyptians made an early form of paper called papyrus (pronounced pa-PI-rus) with a natural starch, like flour. Manuscripts were bound with egg whites. Letters were sealed with beeswax.

Humans aren't the only organisms that use adhesives. The gecko, for example, can produce an adhesive on its feet that it uses to climb vertically. The natural adhesive of this lizard is so strong it can support the gecko's weight but it can also detach itself from the surface easily.

Beetles and other insects also produce natural adhesives. Researchers study the natural adhesives on animals to develop similar synthetic adhesives.

Glue it on The manufacturing of modern glues began about the turn of the nineteenth century. The understanding and development of polymers helped advance the manufacturing of glues. Glues are polymers, long chains of molecules made up of smaller, repeating molecules. Both natural and synthetic polymers are all around us. Plastics are a type of synthetic polymer. Natural polymers include silk and rubber, along with other sticky substances in nature.

How glues cause materials to bond to one another depends upon the glue polymer. In modern day, there are a variety of glue types. Some examples of commonly used glues include:

The gecko can produce an adhesive on its feet that it uses to climb vertically. AP PHOTO/ KEYSTONE, STEFFEN SCHMIDT.

- All purpose white glue, which is commonly used in schools and homes, is a substance called polyvinyl acetate (PVA). PVA is a water-based glue that bonds many different types of surfaces together.
- Cyanoacrylate glues are also known as superglue. A small amount of this glue will form an extremely strong bond.
- Contact cement is a rubber-based glue that can have both a lighter and stronger bond, depending upon how it is applied.
- Epoxies come as two parts that must be mixed together. One part causes the other part to link together in crosslinks and harden, resulting in an extremely strong bond.

One way that glue bonds surfaces together is through a chemical change. Glue can cause the molecules to become attracted to one another. This attractive force is referred to as a van der Waals' force. Named after Dutch scientist Johannes Diderik van der Waals (1837–1923), the van der Waals forces relates to the attraction between molecules that have a positive and negative end.

The water molecule, for example, is made up of two hydrogen atoms and an oxygen atom. It has a positive hydrogen side and a negative oxygen side. Because opposite charges attract, the hydrogen side of one water molecule is attracted to the negative side of another oxygen molecule. Even though these forces are relatively weak, when millions of separate van der Waals forces occur in millions of water molecules it can form a bond.

The PVA glue molecule also has positive charges on one side and negative on the other. If the glue and surface molecules are close to one another a bond can form.

Another way glue works is by mechanical bonding. When glue is spread on a surface it seeps into all the tiny pores and cracks of the material. When the glue hardens, a bond is formed.

PVA works mainly by evaporation. After spreading it on the surface, the water evaporates and the chemicals bonds to one another. The

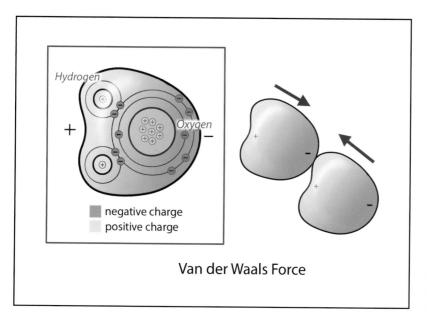

The van der Waals forces relates to the attraction between molecules that have a positive and negative end. ILLUSTRATION BY TEMAH NELSON.

cyanoacrylate glues also depend on water. Cyanoacrylate molecules begin lining up into chains when they come into contact with water. When the molecules can no longer move, the glue is hard.

Behind the tape Another form of familiar adhesive is tape. Tapes are relatively new to the adhesive world, with the first tapes developed in the 1800s. Masking tape was invented in the 1920s. Soon after came the first transparent tape. In modern day, there are a wide variety of tapes of all stickiness levels.

There are two parts to what makes a tape adhere: the backing material and the adhesive. The adhesive in tapes is also a form of polymer. Unlike glues, which are liquid and harden over time, tape adhesives are solid and remain solid. When pressure is applied to the tape, van der Waals forces are at work and there is stickiness.

Tape adhesives are also distinct from glue because a piece of tape can be removed. Some tapes have strong adhesives that can hold a lot of weight and withstand force. These tapes are removable, but they can cause harm the surface of the taped material. Packing tape, for example, can hold a box together, but when it is peeled away it also likely remove some of the cardboard.

When glue is spread on a surface it seeps into all the tiny pores and cracks of the material. ILLUSTRATION BY TEMAH NELSON.

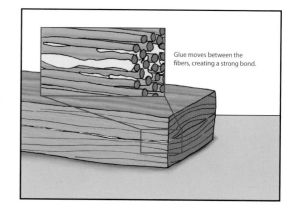

Glue moves between the fibers, creating a strong bond.

WORDS TO KNOW

Adhesive: A substance that bonds or adheres two substances together.

Control experiment: A setup that is identical to the experiment, but is not affected by the variable that acts on the experimental group.

Hypothesis: An idea in the form of a statement that can be tested by observation and/or experiment.

Polyvinyl acetate: A type of polymer that is the main ingredient of white glues.

Polymer: Chemical compound formed of simple molecules (known as monomers) linked with themselves many times over.

Synthetic: Something that is made artificially, in a laboratory or chemical plant, but is generally not found in nature.

Variable: Something that can affect the results of an experiment

Van der Waals' force: An attractive force between two molecules based on the positive and negative side of the molecule.

Other tapes were developed with light adhesives so they are easily removed without harming the surface. Sticky notes are an example of this type of adhesive. They stick where they are placed and can be removed without a trace of the stickiness.

Adhesives are a wide and fascinating group of materials. What kind of adhesives do you have questions about? You will have an opportunity to explore both glues and tapes in the following two experiments.

Sticky notes use a light adhesive so that the item they are attached to is not damaged when the note is removed. AP PHOTO/JIM MONE.

EXPERIMENT 1

Material Adhesion: How do various glues adhere to different materials?

Purpose/Hypothesis How glues adhere to materials depend upon both the properties of the glue and the material. Metals, plastics, and wood each have unique properties. Wood, for example, has tiny pores that the glue moves into.

In this experiment, you will use three types of glue: rubber cement, a white glue, and a "super" glue. The materials you can glue together are wood, plastic, and metal (aluminum foil). By gluing each material to itself, you can determine what glues adhere to which materials.

Experiment Central, 2nd edition

Do you think one glue will adhere to all the materials?

To begin the experiment, use what you have learned about adhesives and glue to make a guess about what glue will adhere to what materials. This educated guess, or prediction, is your hypothesis. A hypothesis should explain these things:

- the topic of the experiment
- the variable you will change
- the variable you will measure
- what you expect to happen

A hypothesis should be brief, specific, and measurable. It must be something you can test through observation. Your experiment will prove or disprove whether your hypothesis is correct. Here is one possible hypothesis for this experiment: "The super glue will adhere all materials to one another; the white glue will only bond wood together; and the rubber cement will not bond to any of the materials."

In this case, the variable you will change for each glue is the type of materials being glued together. The variable you will measure is whether there is a bond between the materials.

Level of Difficulty Moderate. (This experiment requires monitoring over several hours.)

Materials Needed

- white glue, such as an all purpose school glue or wood glue
- rubber cement, acid-free, craft
- cyanoacrylate glue, such as Superglue or Krazy clue, select a glue that says it will not bond to skin instantly
- strips of wood, about 0.125 inch (0.32 centimeter) thick and 1 foot (30 centimeter) long (available at craft stores)
- aluminum foil

What Are the Variables?

Variables are anything that might affect the results of an experiment. Here are the main variables in this experiment:

- the air temperature
- the temperature of the glue
- the material being glued
- the amount of glue

In other words, the variables in this experiment are everything that might affect the bond between the materials. If you change more than one variable at a time, you will not be able to determine which variable had the most effect on whether the materials adhere to one another.

Step 5: Starting with the white glue, use the cotton swabs to spread the glue on the wood. Press the wood together firmly and note the time. ILLUSTRATION BY TEMAH NELSON.

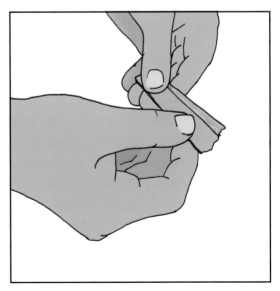

How to Experiment Safely

Make sure you purchase the cyanoacrylate glue that states it will not bind instantly to skin. Although this type of cyanoacrylate glue will not bind instantly, it can still bond to skin and cause irritation. Have an adult help you wipe the cyanoacrylate glue on the materials. Be careful not to get the glue on your skin. If you do so, immediately follow the instructions on the glue.

- plastic, from a container or bottle
- scissors
- cotton swabs
- wax paper or paper towels

Approximate Budget $10.

Timetable 30 minutes to set-up; approximately 45 minutes to monitor results over at least a 12-hour period.

Step-by-Step Instructions

1. Break the long wood strip into six pieces, each about 2 inches (5 centimeters) long.
2. Cut the plastic into six pieces, each about 2 inches long and approximately matching the width of the wood strips.
3. Tear six pieces of aluminum foil, each about 2 inches long and approximately matching the width of the wood strips.
4. Set all the materials on wax paper or paper towels to protect the surface.
5. Starting with the white glue, use the cotton swabs to spread the glue on the wood. Press the wood together firmly and note the time.
6. One by one, use the white glue to contine gluing a piece of each material to every other material. You will have three test pieces for each glue: wood to wood; plastic to plastic; and aluminum foil to aluminum foil.
7. Repeat Steps 5 and 6, using first the rubber cement and then the cyanoacrylate glue. See illustration.
8. Wait 15 minutes and test the adhesive bond between the materials. Gently try to move one of the pieces. Does one piece of aluminum foil peel back? If one of the pieces is not bonded, press the pieces back together and set it down. If any of the pieces are bonded, write down the results in a chart and note the approximate time it took.

Step 7: Repeat Steps 5 and 6, using first the rubber cement and then the cyanoacrylate glue. ILLUSTRATION BY TEMAH NELSON.

9. Wait 15 minutes and test the adhesive bond between the materials. Gently try to move one of the pieces. Does one piece of aluminum foil peel back? If one of the pieces is not bonded, press the pieces back together and set it down. If any of the pieces are bonded, write down the results in a chart and note the approximate time it took.

10. Continue checking the adhesive bonds between the materials every 30 minutes over the next two to three hours. When the materials are bonded together note the time on a chart and you do not have to test them anymore.

11. Allow the materials that have not bonded to sit overnight or for a 12-hour period before you test adhesion for the final time.

Summary of Results Study the results of your chart. Did one type of glue bond to all of the materials? Was there a glue that only bonded to one type of material? Consider how the properties of plastic, wood, and aluminum foil may have interacted with the glue. Write a paragraph summarizing and explaining your findings.

Troubleshooter's Guide

It's common for experiments to not work exactly as planned but it can often offer a learning experience. Below are some problems that may arise during this experiment, some possible causes, and ways to remedy the problems.

Problem: The wood pieces did not bond to anything.

Possible causes: The pieces may have needed more pressure when forming a bond. Try gluing two wooden pieces together and use a weight to press them together. You can use a heavy book or pot. Place a strip of wax paper between the pieces and the weight so as not to get any glue on the heavy item.

Problem: The foil and plastic keep slipping apart when I test them.

Possible causes: You may have applied too much glue to the surface and peeling them apart causes them to slip. Try it again, applying less glue. Once you know the general amount of time it takes for the materials to set, wait until that time period before you test the bond.

Change the Variables There are several ways you can change the variables in this experiment. One way is by focusing on one glue type. Rubber cement, for example, is available in several types and can be applied in different ways. Wiping the adhesive to each side of the material and pressing the materials together can give a stronger bond. You can test this bond on all the materials. You can also focus on one type of material. There are many kinds of woods, plastics, and metals. Can the white glue bond certain woods together but not others?

What Are the Variables?

Variables are anything that might affect the results of an experiment. Here are the main variables in this experiment:

- the environmental conditions
- the amount of time in each environmental condition
- the type of paper
- the material the adhesive is stuck to
- the age of the adhesive
- the strength of the fan
- the type of paper bag
- the type of bottle used to test strength

In other words, the variables in this experiment are everything that might affect the adhesion. If you change more than one variable at the same time, you will not be able to tell which variable had the most effect on the adhesive properties.

EXPERIMENT 2

Adhesives in the Environment: Will different environmental conditions affect the properties of different adhesives?

Purpose/Hypothesis There are adhesives developed for strength and others that are meant to have a weak adhesive. Sticky notes, for example, was a completely new type of adhesive when it was developed in the 1960s. The removable paper will adhere where it is placed and is easily removed. Tape made for painting is another adhesive that can be removed without a trace. All adhesives are designed to work in certain environmental conditions.

This experiment explores how temperature and the environment affect adhesives. You will use two types of adhesives: the low-strength sticky note, and a tape with a strong adhesive. You will expose each adhesives to a cold, hot, and humid environment. By comparing how the adhesive "sticks" both before and after each environmental change, you can measure how the environment affects the properties of each adhesive.

Before you begin, make an educated guess about the outcome of this experiment based on your knowledge of adhesives and the environmental conditions. This educated guess, or prediction, is your hypothesis. A hypothesis should explain these things:

- the topic of the experiment
- the variable you will change
- the variable you will measure
- what you expect to happen

A hypothesis should be brief, specific, and measurable. It must be something you can test through further investigation. Your experiment will prove or disprove whether your hypothesis is correct. Here is one possible hypothesis for this experiment: "The cold and heat will change the adhesive properties of the low-adhesive material but not the tape with the strong adhesive."

Materials needed.
ILLUSTRATION BY TEMAH
NELSON.

In this case, the variable you will change is the environmental conditions for each adhesive, one at a time. The variable you will measure is the adhesion properties, as compared to the unchanged adhesive material.

Level of Difficulty Moderate (there are a lot of steps to this experiment; to simplify, you can test adhesive strength for only hot and cold conditions, leaving out the humidity).

Materials Needed

- sticky notes
- tape with a strong adhesive, such as Duct, packing, or masking tape
- paper
- fan
- 3 blocks of wood, the same type of wood
- clamp
- 3 small paper bags (lunch bags work well)
- 2-liter plastic bottle

How to Experiment Safely

Be careful when working with the heat lamp after it has been turned on and use caution with the boiling water. Part of this experiment can be messy. If you have a workbench or other movable bench you may want to clamp the block of wood outside.

- funnel
- heat lamp, or a warm, sunny day
- large container or garbage can
- freezer
- scissors
- tall pot, such as a soup pot
- chest grater, strainer, or other metal item with holes in it that can sit on the top of the pot

Timetable 1 to 2 hours working time; approximately 3 hours total time.

Step-by-Step Instructions Testing adhesive strength under "normal" environmental conditions.

1. Sticky note: Stick one note on a piece of paper and place the paper directly in front of the fan. Use the tape measure to measure how far the paper is from the fan.
2. Turn the fan on to the highest setting and hold the paper for 30 seconds and turn off the fan.
3. If the sticky adhesive did not hold the note in place during the 30 seconds, move the paper 1 to 2 inches (2–5 centimeter) farther away from the fan. Sticky on a fresh sticky note, turn the fan on and repeat. Continue moving the paper back until the sticky note does not blow away. If the sticky does not blow away, move the paper 1 to 2 inches closer to the fan. Continue moving the paper forward until the sticky cannot move any more before it blows away.
4. When you have the distance that the sticky adhesive keeps the note on the paper, note distance on a chart.
5. Tape: Tape the paper bag to the bottom half of the piece of wood. Note the size and direction you tape the bag.
6. Clamp the piece of wood to a work bench, chair, or other sturdy item. Make sure the clamp is not touching the bag.
7. Set the empty bottle inside the bag. The bottle should be slightly higher than the bag. You may need to cut the top of the bag with the scissors.

Steps 2 and 3: Stick one note on a piece of paper and place the paper directly in front of the fan. Turn the fan on to the highest setting and hold the paper for 30 seconds.

ILLUSTRATION BY TEMAH NELSON.

8. If you are working inside, set a large container or garbage can underneath the bag/bottle. Place the funnel in the bottle.

9. Carefully add ¼ cup (about 2 ounces) of water to the bottle, being careful not to drip any water on the bag. Continue adding water in ¼ cup increments, remembering to note how much water you are adding. When the tape can no longer support the bottle, write down the amount of weight the tape held.

Setup for adhesive strength under warm environmental conditions.

1. Place a new sticky note on a fresh piece of paper.

2. Tape a new paper bag to the wood block in the same direction and using the same length of tape as the normal environmental trial.

3. If it is a hot day outside and the sun is out, place both the paper and wood (with the attached bag) out in the sun. If you are working indoors, place both items under the heat lamp.

Setup for adhesive strength under cold environmental conditions.

Place a new sticky note on a fresh piece of paper.

Tape a new paper bag to a wood block in the same direction and using the same length of tape as the normal environmental trial.

Place both items in the freezer.

Setup for adhesive strength under humid environmental conditions.

1. Place a new sticky note on a fresh piece of paper.

2. Tape a new paper bag to a wood block in the same direction and using the same length of tape as the normal environmental trial.

3. Fill the pot about a quarter way with water and bring to a boil.

4. Remove the pot from the heat and allow it to cool for one to two minutes. Carefully set the cheese grater (or other item) on top of the pot.

5. Place the paper with the sticky and the wood block with the bag on top of the grater with the tape facing upwards.

Testing adhesive strength.

Steps 5–9: Tape a paper bag to the bottom half of the piece of wood and clamp the piece of wood to a chair. Set the empty bottle inside the bag and insert the funnel. Add ¼ cup (about 2 ounces) of water to the bottle.
ILLUSTRATION BY TEMAH NELSON.

Troubleshooter's Guide

Here are some problems that may arise during this experiment, some possible causes, and ways to remedy the problems.

Problem: The bag keeps breaking when the water is poured in.

Possible cause: The funnel might be too narrow and you may be dripping water onto the bag, which would weaken the bag. Have a helper hold the funnel upright while you carefully pour. You may also need a larger funnel. Repeat the tests.

Problem: The tape and sticky completely peeled off when it was placed above the hot water.

Possible causes: There may have been too much steam. Try it again, allowing the pot to cool another couple minutes before placing the adhesives over the pot.

Wait approximately three hours.

Sticky note: Hold the paper with the sticky that was under the hot environmental conditions in front of the fan. Use your chart and tape measure to determine where the paper should be (it should be the same distance as it was in the normal environmental conditions). Again, turn the fan on the highest setting for 30 seconds and note if the sticky adhesive holds.

Repeat this step with the sticky note that was undergoing cold conditions and then the humid conditions.

Tape: Use your chart to determine how much weight the tape should hold. Repeat the setup in Steps 7 and 8 for each block of wood, carefully pouring in the water.

After testing the adhesives that underwent hot, cold, and humid conditions, note the results on a chart.

Summary of Results Examine your data and compare the results of the tests with your hypothesis. Did your hypothesis prove true? How did the adhesive undergoing each of the different environmental conditions compare to the normal condition? Was there one environment that affected the adhesive the most? Compare each of the two adhesives against one another. Consider why it might be important for different adhesives to withstand certain types of environments. You may want to write a summary of your results.

Change the Variables Variables you can change in this experiment include:

- Changing the type of adhesives to determine if there are patterns to environmental conditions and the strength of the tape.
- Change the material the adhesive adheres to.
- Focus on one environmental condition and measure at what point the environment breaks down the adhesive.

Design Your Own Experiment

How to Select a Topic Relating to this Concept You make use of adhesives every day. Think about what interests you about adhesion and what questions you have. Do you want to know about how the materials play a role in adhesion? Or how synthetic glues differ from natural glues? Make a list of all the types of adhesives and where they are applied.

Check the Further Readings section and talk with your science teacher to learn more about adhesives. Because adhesives are so diverse, there are many different types of scientists who work with them. Ask family, teachers, and friends if they know someone who works a lot with adhesives. It could be a carpenter or researcher.

Steps in the Scientific Method To do an original experiment, you need to plan carefully and think things through. Otherwise, you might not be sure what question you are answering, what you are or should be measuring, or what your findings prove or disprove.

Here are the steps in designing an experiment:

- State the purpose of—and the underlying question behind—the experiment you propose to do.
- Recognize the variables involved and select one that will help you answer the question at hand.
- State your hypothesis, an educated guess about the answer to your question.
- Decide how to change the variable you selected.
- Decide how to measure your results.

Recording Data and Summarizing the Results Your data should include charts and graphs such as the one you did for these experiments. They should be clearly labeled and easy to read. You may also want to include photographs and drawings of your experimental setup and results, which will help other people visualize the steps in the experiment.

If you are preparing an exhibit, you may want to display your results, such as any experimental setup you designed. If you have completed a nonexperimental project, explain clearly what your research question was and illustrate your findings.

Related Projects You can use the materials around you to think of projects related to adhesives. They are in furniture, school supplies, and many products that you purchase. You could examine how adhesives play a role in everyday products. If you are interested in natural adhesives, you can make your own and test the adhesives against commercial brands.

Consider the adhesive properties of tape. Sticky notes and envelopes, for example, make use of adhesives. What makes their adhesive properties unique and why are they important? How does waterproofing play a role in choosing the right adhesive? You could also experiment with what materials can remove adhesives.

For More Information

Roach, John. "Gecko, Mussel Powers Combined in New Sticky Adhesive." *National Geographic News.* July 18, 2007, http://news.nationalgeographic.com/news/2007/07/070718-geckel-glue.html (accessed on April 1, 2008).

This to That. http://www.thistothat.com (accessed on April 1, 2008). Suggestions on what glue to use to adhere one material to another, along with trivia facts and glue news briefs.

Fix-It Club. "Glues." *HowStuffWorks.* http://home.howstuffworks.com/glues.htm (accessed on April 1, 2008). Explanation of how different types of glues adhere.

VanCleave, Janice. *Janice VanCleave's 204 Sticky, Gloppy, Wacky and Wonderful Experiments.* Hoboken, NJ: J. Wiley, 2002.

Weiss, Malcolm E. *Why glass breaks, rubber bends, and glue sticks: how everyday materials work.* New York: Harcourt Brace Jovanovich, 1977.

3

Air

Even though you cannot feel it, see it, or smell it, air surrounds you and extends far upward for miles. Air is a mixture of gases, mainly nitrogen and oxygen, with about four times as much nitrogen as oxygen. With few exceptions, all living things on Earth need air to survive. It is what makes all flight possible, from airplanes to birds. It allows fuels to burn and it shields Earth from the sun's harmful rays. Air is also what gives us our weather patterns. Air's temperature, pressure, density, and volume all create the weather.

Surrounded by air All the air that covers Earth is called the atmosphere. Earth's gravity holds the atmosphere in place around our planet. The atmosphere is a blanket of air over 600 miles (1,000 kilometers) high. Scientists have divided the atmosphere into five layers, according to differences in the temperature of the air. The layer closest to Earth is called the troposphere. The troposphere extends about 9 miles upward (15 kilometers). It contains almost all of what makes up Earth's weather, including clouds, rain, and snow.

Like any gas, air has pressure, mass, and a temperature. Air is composed of 78% nitrogen, 21% oxygen, 0.9% argon, and the remaining 0.1% a handful of other gases, including carbon dioxide. The molecules in air's gases are constantly flying around at high speeds. This air can feel completely still because there are billions of individual molecules zipping in all directions. When the molecules travel in one direction, it results in wind.

Oh, the pressure Winds begin with differences in air pressure. Air always moves from areas of high pressure to low pressure. The greater the difference in pressures, the stronger the wind's force.

Air's pressure is caused by the weight of the air in Earth's atmosphere pushing down on the air below. Air in the troposphere has the highest pressure of all the layers. The air at the top of the atmosphere has little weight above it to push it down, so its pressure is less. The air at the

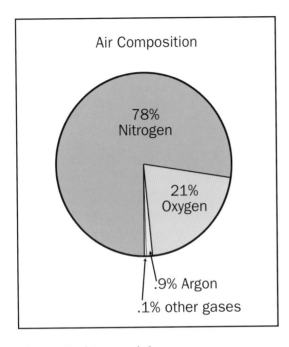

Air Composition

78%
Nitrogen

21%
Oxygen

.9% Argon

.1% other gases

The air on Earth is composed of several different gases. GALE GROUP.

bottom of the atmosphere is being pushed down by the hundreds of miles of air above it. This results in air low to the ground having more pressure than air high in the atmosphere. The air pressing down on you weighs about 1 ton (0.9 metric ton). You cannot feel this pressure because you are supported by equal air pressure on all sides, and your body is filled with gases and liquid that push back with equal pressure.

Meteorologists, or people who study weather, measure air pressure with a barometer. Changes in the air pressure or barometric pressure occur during changes in the weather. The mercury barometer uses the heavy liquid metal mercury, which is about 14 times heavier or denser than water. An empty glass tube with the upper end closed is inserted into a dish of mercury. The height of the column of mercury in the glass tube is controlled by the air pressing down on the mercury in the dish. Normal air pressure lifts the mercury to a height of about 30 inches (760 millimeters). When air pressure falls, the air does not push on the mercury in the dish as much, and the column of mercury falls. When air pressure increases, the column of mercury will rise. In general, falling air pressure means that clouds and rains or snow are likely. Rising air pressure signals that clear weather is likely.

In the mid 1600s Italian mathematician Evangelista Torricelli (1608–47) designed the first barometer to prove that air had weight and pressure. Then in 1648 French philosopher and mathematician Blaise Pascal (1632–62) hypothesized that air pressure decreased with altitude. He sent his brother-in-law up to the peak of a mountain in France with a barometer. The column of mercury dropped lower and lower the higher he went. Today, the international unit of pressure is called the Pascal, in his honor.

Changing densities Quick changes in the weather are caused by movements of large bodies of air called air masses. Air masses usually cover very large areas. All the air in an air mass has nearly the same properties. When two air masses that have different densities meet, they mix slowly and form an area between them called a front.

The density of an air mass is related to its pressure and temperature. Air density is the amount of matter or mass in a specific volume. Increasing the temperature of a gas pushes its molecules farther apart. When the sun heats up the air, the space between the molecules increases and the hot air expands. The air becomes less dense and has less pressure. When the temperature of air decreases its molecules move closer together and the air contracts. The air becomes more dense and has greater pressure.

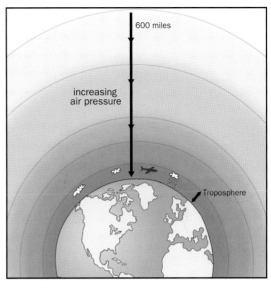

Air presses down from the upper atmosphere, causing more pressure in the layer closest to Earth, the troposphere. GALE GROUP.

There are three main types of fronts: cold fronts, warm fronts, and occluded fronts. A cold front forms when a cold air mass meets and pushes under a warm air mass. Violent storms are associated with a cold front. Fair, cool weather usually follows. A warm front forms when a mass of warm air moves into a cold air mass. Rain and showers usually accompany a warm front. Hot, humid weather usually follows. An occluded front happens when a cold front catches up and merges with a warm front. An occluded front often brings heavy rain.

The closer air lies to the surface of Earth, the denser it is because there are more molecules of air compressed into a smaller volume. The troposphere

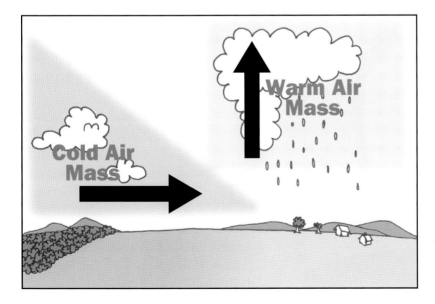

A cold front occurs when a cold air mass meets and pushes under a warm air mass. GALE GROUP.

layer is so compressed that it contains about 80% of the air found in the entire atmosphere by mass. The higher up in the atmosphere someone goes, the less dense the air. When mountain climbers trek up high mountains, they often need to bring tanks of oxygen with them because the air is less dense and contains less oxygen for them to breathe.

The up-and-down movement of air due to different densities is called convection currents. When the air becomes less dense it rises upward through the denser, cool air above it. As this warm air moves through the cold air it cools off, becomes more dense again, and eventually sinks back to the bottom.

When mountain climbers trek up high mountains, they often bring tanks of oxygen with them because the air contains less oxygen for them to breathe.

AP/WIDE WORLD PHOTOS.

The up-and-down movement of air due to different densities is called convection currents.

GALE GROUP.

air cools

cool
dense
air sinks

warm
light air
rises

air warms up

heat source

EXPERIMENT 1

Air Density: Does warm air take up less room than cool air?

Purpose/Hypothesis Density is the mass of anything divided by the volume it occupies. As the temperature of a given mass of air increases, its volume expands and the air gets less dense as a result—same mass, but larger volume, means less dense. As the temperature of a given mass of air decreases, its volume contracts and the air gets more dense. In this experiment, you will examine the density of air by causing a mass of air in a closed container to become both more and less dense by changing the temperature. To see these changes you will place a balloon over the open end of a bottle. When the trapped air expands, the balloon should get bigger; when the air contracts, the balloon should get smaller.

Before you begin, make an educated guess about the outcome of this experiment based on your knowledge of air density. This educated guess, or prediction, is your hypothesis. A hypothesis should explain these things:

WORDS TO KNOW

Air: Gaseous mixture that covers Earth, composed mainly of nitrogen (about 78%) and oxygen (about 21%) with lesser amounts of argon, carbon dioxide, and other gases.

Air density: The ratio of the mass of a substance to the volume it occupies.

Air mass: A large body of air that has similar characteristics.

Air pressure: The force exerted by the weight of the atmosphere above a point on or above Earth's surface.

Atmosphere: Layers of air that surround Earth.

Barometer: An instrument for measuring atmospheric pressure, used especially in weather forecasting.

Control experiment: A setup that is identical to the experiment, but is not affected by the variable that acts on the experimental group.

Convection currents: Circular movement of a gas in response to alternating heating and cooling.

Front: The area between air masses of different temperatures or densities.

Hypothesis: An idea in the form of a statement that can be tested by observation and/or experiment.

Meteorologists: Professionals who study Earth's atmosphere and its phenomena, including weather and weather forecasting.

Troposphere: The lowest layer of Earth's atmosphere, ranging to an altitude of about 9 miles (15 km) above Earth's surface.

Variable: Something that can affect the results of an experiment.

- the topic of the experiment
- the variable you will change
- the variable you will measure
- what you expect to happen

A hypothesis should be brief, specific, and measurable. It must be something you can test through further investigation. Your experiment will prove or disprove whether your hypothesis is correct. Here is one possible hypothesis for this experiment: "As the air gets warmer and less dense it will cause the the balloon to get larger; as the air gets cooler and less dense it will cause the balloon to get smaller."

In this case, the variable you will change is the temperature of the air inside the bottle by warming and cooling the outside of the bottle. The variable you will measure is the balloon's circumference.

Conducting a control experiment will help you isolate each variable and measure the changes in the dependent variable. Only one variable will

What Are the Variables?

Variables are anything that might affect the results of an experiment. Here are the main variables in this experiment:

- thickness of the plastic bottles
- material the balloons are made from

In other words, the variables in this experiment are everything that might affect the density of the air. If you change more than one variable at the same time, you will not be able to tell which variable had the most effect on air density.

change between the control and the experimental trials. Your control experiment will not heat or cool the air in the bottles.

Level of Difficulty Easy.

Materials Needed

- 2 rubber balloons
- ice
- hot water
- 2 plastic bottles, such as plastic soda bottles
- 2 containers that go at least midway up the sides of the bottles (one should be heatproof)

Approximate Budget $2.

Timetable 15 minutes.

Steps 3 and 4: Heat causes the air in the bottle to warm; ice causes the air in the bottle to cool. GALE GROUP.

Step-by-Step Instructions

1. Place a balloon over the mouth of each plastic bottle. Leave one bottle out as your control.
2. Fill up one container with very hot water. Fill up the other container with a little ice and some cold water.
3. Place the experimental bottle in the container of cold water and hold it there for roughly one minute. (Another option is to place the bottle in a freezer for one minute.) Note the size of the balloon compared to the control balloon.
4. Place the experimental bottle in the container of hot water for one minute. (Another option is to carefully hold the bottle under running hot tap water.) Note the size of the balloon compared to the control balloon.

5. Again, place the experimental bottle in the pan of cold water and hold for 30 seconds.

Summary of Results Examine how much the balloon grew or shrunk in your experiment. Was your hypothesis correct? How did the size of the experimental balloon compare to the control balloon? Did the experimental balloon shrink more or at a different rate the second time you placed it in the cold water? Draw a picture of the results of your experiment and write a brief summary.

EXPERIMENT 2

Convection Currents: How can rising air cause weather changes?

Purpose/Hypothesis Convection currents occur as rising gas carries heat upward and the cooler gas is brought downward. In the atmosphere, convection currents rise above warm areas on Earth's surface. These rising air currents produce differences in air pressure, which cause changes in the weather. Small convection currents can produce winds and rain. Larger convection currents can cause severe thunderstorms and hurricanes.

When convection occurs in an enclosed container, the currents help distribute the heat throughout the container. The entire process is driven by the differences in air density. In this experiment, you will create a convection current in a closed container and look at the air's actions. You will cool the air in one glass jar and warm the air in another. Visible smoke from an incense stick will go into the warm jar. Then you will observe what occurs to the movements of the smoke.

Before you begin, make an educated guess about the outcome of this experiment based on your knowledge of air convection. This educated guess, or prediction, is your hypothesis. A hypothesis should explain these things:

> ### How to Experiment Safely
>
> Have an adult present when working with the hot water.

> ### Troubleshooter's Guide
>
> Below is a problem that may arise during this experiment, some possible causes, and some ways to remedy the problems.
>
> **Problem:** Nothing happened to the balloon.
>
> **Possible cause:** Your water may not have been hot or cold enough. You may also not given enough time to allow the air temperature to change. Try the experiment again, placing your bottles deeper into the hot and cold water.
>
> **Possible cause:** Your balloon may have a slight leak. Try the experiment again with a new balloon.

What Are the Variables?

Variables are anything that might affect the results of an experiment. Here are the main variables in this experiment:

- The amount of smoke
- The temperature of the warm air
- The temperature of the cold air

In other words, the variables in this experiment are everything that might affect the movement of the smoke. If you change more than one variable at the same time, you will not be able to tell which variable had the most effect on the convection currents.

- the topic of the experiment
- the variable you will change
- the variable you will measure
- what you expect to happen

A hypothesis should be brief, specific, and measurable. It must be something you can test through further investigation. Your experiment will prove or disprove whether your hypothesis is correct. Here is one possible hypothesis for this experiment: "Air in the warmer container will rise, pushing the cold air above it downward, and creating movement of the smoke."

In this case, the variable you will change is the temperature of the air in the glass jar. The variable you will measure is the visible movement of the smoke.

Conducting a control experiment will help you isolate each variable and measure the changes in the dependent variable. Only one variable will change between the control and the experimental trial. Your control experiment will use jars that have not been heated or cooled.

Level of Difficulty Easy/Moderate (the experiment is simple, but working with burning incense increases the difficulty level).

Materials Needed

- four glass jars of equal size with equal-sized openings (mayonnaise jars work well; you do not need the lids)
- incense stick (do not use smokeless incense)
- matches
- small piece of thick paper (big enough to cover the opening of the jars)
- lamp with at least a 100-watt bulb
- black piece of paper or cardstock about the size of the jars
- access to freezer or cold-water bath

Approximate Budget $5.

Timetable 20 minutes.

Step-by-Step Instructions

1. Place one jar in the freezer or cold-water bath for about five minutes.

2. While the first jar is cooling, run hot water over the outside of the second jar.

3. When about three minutes have passed, turn on the lamp and position the warm jar upside down in front it. Fold the black paper in half and lean it closely against the side of the jar opposite the lamp to help heat the air.

4. After five minutes, take the jar out of the freezer or cold-water bath and have the small piece of thick paper nearby. (You may need to wipe off the outside of the jar so that you can see inside it.)

5. Light the stick of incense, lift up the warm jar (with the opening still facing downward), and hold the burning incense underneath the opening of the warm jar. The incense stick should give off black smoke. Blow out the incense stick and capture any remaining black smoke inside the warm jar.

6. Quickly place the small piece of thick paper firmly over the opening in the warm jar to hold the smoke inside. Turn the warm jar right side up while you hold the thick paper in place. Turn the cold jar upside down and set it directly on top of the warm jar so their openings line up exactly and the thick piece of paper is between them.

7. Lift the cold jar slightly and pull the paper out from between the jars. Observe what happens to the smoke.

8. For the control experiment, repeat Steps 5 through 7 with two room-temperature glass jars. Note the results.

Summary of Results Was your hypothesis correct? Compare the results between the movement in the air of the control jars and the cold and warm jars. Use arrows to draw what was happening to both the cold and warm air in the jars. What do you hypothesize would occur if the

Step 6: Turn the warm jar right side up while you hold the thick paper in place. Turn the cold jar upside down and set it directly on top of the warm jar so their openings line up exactly and the thick piece of paper is between them. GALE GROUP.

Troubleshooter's Guide

Below is a problem that may arise during this experiment, a possible cause, and a way to remedy the problem.

Problem: No black smoke was visible.

Possible cause: You may have used a smokeless incense stick. Try purchasing another type and repeating the experiment.

cold jar was placed on the bottom and the warm jar was placed on top of it. Write a brief description of how air of different temperatures causes weather change.

Modify the Experiment You can experiment with convection currents in air without matches in a simple test that illustrates the principles behind hot air balloons. You will need at least two black balloons, string, and a hot, sunny day. Blow up both balloons about half way. Knot the balloons and tie a piece of string about 4 feet (1.2 meters) long to the knot. Place one balloon in a basement or air conditioned room where the air is cool. Place the second balloon outside in the sun and tie the string to something on the ground. Make a note whether both balloons lie on the ground. Leave the balloons alone for several hours.

Look at the balloon outside. Is it still on the ground? It will rise if the air inside the balloon is lighter than the surrounding air. Untie the outside balloon and place it next to the balloon that is sitting in the cool room. What happens? Does the balloon with the warmer air rise? Observe the two balloons for several minutes, as the hot air balloon cools. You can try the experiment again with varying size balloons or at higher outside temperatures.

Design Your Own Experiment

How to Select a Topic Relating to this Concept Whenever you step outside you are feeling the effects of air's properties and movement. Consider what types of weather-related topics are of interest to you. Watch the weather forecast carefully and write down what terms and pictures look interesting to you.

Check the Further Readings section and talk with your science teacher to learn more about air properties and weather. As you consider possible experiments, make sure to discuss them with your science teacher or another adult before trying them.

Steps in the Scientific Method To do an original experiment, you need to plan carefully and think things through. Otherwise, you might not be sure what question you are answering, what you are or should be measuring, or what your findings prove or disprove.

Here are the steps in designing an experiment:

- State the purpose of—and the underlying question behind—the experiment you propose to do.
- Recognize the variables involved and select one that will help you answer the question at hand.
- State your hypothesis, an educated guess about the answer to your question.
- Decide how to change the variable you selected.
- Decide how to measure your results.

Recording Data and Summarizing the Results In any experiment you conduct, you should look for ways to clearly convey your data. You can do this by including charts and graphs for the experiments. They should be clearly labeled and easy to read. You may also want to include

The less-dense hot air in a hot air balloon allows it to rise high above the ground. © DUOMO/ CORBIS.

photographs and drawings of your experimental setup and results, which will help others visualize the steps in the experiment. You might decide to conduct an experiment that lasts several months. In this case, include pictures or drawings of the results taken at regular intervals.

If you are preparing an exhibit, you may want to display your results, such as any experimental setup you designed. If you have completed a nonexperimental project, explain clearly what your research question was and illustrate your findings.

Related Projects There are many related projects you can undertake related to air and the weather. Because air is not visible to the naked eye, there are instruments that enable people to "see" how the air reacts. To explore air temperature, you could make a radiometer, an instrument that uses reflection and absorption to measure the sun's rays. A radiometer will allow you to see how the sun's energy causes the warm air to move. You could also make a barometer to measure air pressure. By watching changes in the barometer, you can observe how varying air pressures result in changes in the weather.

To further explore convection, you can make a convection box as another way to see how air currents with clashing temperatures act. The cyclical process of convection currents also occurs in liquids, which follow the same density rules as gases. Warm water, less dense than cold water, rises to the surface as the cooler water sinks to the bottom. The results cause currents in the water. You can examine convection currents in bodies of water by adding drops of different food colorings to the hot and cold water.

For More Information

"Atmospheric science resources." *USA Today.* December 19, 2001. http:// www.usatoday.com/weather/wworks0.htm#pressure (accessed February 26, 2008). Graphics and clear text that explains various weather phenomena.

Elsom, Derek. *Weather Explained.* New York: Henry Holt and Company, 1997. From basic weather and air questions to weather extremes, this book answers how weather forms, with lots of colorful pictures.

Met Office. *Secondary Students.* http://www.metoffice.gov.uk/education/ secondary/students/index.html (accessed February 26, 2008). Information on weather topics, including air masses and fronts.

Wright, David. "How Much Does the Sky Weigh?" *Chain Reaction.* http:// chainreaction.asu.edu/weather/digin/wright.htm (accessed February 26, 2008). Article on air and its pressure with ideas for experiments.

4

Air and Water Pollution

Air or water that is contaminated with impurities is described as polluted. The contamination is the pollution. Directly or indirectly, the overwhelming majority of pollution results from human activity, yet nature can also release pollutants. Pollution usually is in the form of gas, liquid, and solid materials; it results from anything that alters the natural environment, such as a temperature shift and noise. Air and water pollution has become a significant problem since the growth of cities, industry, and travel in the late nineteenth century.

All life on Earth depends on air and water to live and grow. Pollution of these substances harms and destroys plants, animals, and microscopic organisms. It causes health problems and death in humans. Pollution upsets the natural cycles on which all life depends, causing a ripple effect that can harm organisms hundreds of miles away from the pollutant. For example, pollutants in a body of water can harm the sea life and poison the plants that depend on the water. In turn, surrounding animals that depend on the plants for food and shelter, such as birds, will need to either move to another location or die. Water and air pollution also destroy Earth's natural beauty.

What you can't see ... Air is essential for life on Earth. It provides oxygen for animals and carbon dioxide for plants. It encircles Earth to form its atmosphere, protecting the planet against harmful rays and causing its weather. Air pollution comes in the form of gases—such as nitrogen dioxide, sulfur dioxide, and carbon monoxide—as well as solid and liquid particles called particulate matter. Measuring about 0.0001 inch (0.0025 millimeters, also called 2.5 microns) in diameter, particulate matter is small enough to be suspended, or float, in the air.

There are several major categories of air pollution produced by humans. Pollutants include the gases nitrogen dioxide, sulfur dioxide, and carbon monoxide, along with lead pollution and particulate matter.

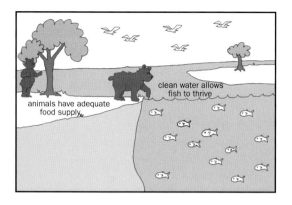

Clean air and water support a healthy life cycle for all organisms. GALE GROUP.

Gases: In most industrial nations the majority of air pollution comes from the automobile. The exhaust in cars and trucks releases carbon monoxide, carbon dioxide, nitrogen oxides, and sulfur dioxide. Automobiles, especially diesel vehicles, also release smoke particles. The burning of fossil fuels—such as gas, oil, and coal—is also a major source of air pollution. Power plants that burn coal and oil release nitrogen oxides, sulfur oxides, carbon dioxide, and particles. Various industrial processes also produce large amounts of these pollutants.

Scientists generally agree that the greenhouse effect, also called global warming, comes from the buildup of carbon dioxide, methane, and other gases in the atmosphere. The increased levels of carbon dioxide and other greenhouse gases trap heat close to Earth, resulting in an overall increase in temperature. This warmer climate could produce extreme weather events, such as droughts and floods, raise the sea level, and alter the life populations.

Another planetwide effect of air pollution is the breakdown of the layer of air in Earth's upper atmosphere. The upper atmosphere protects people and animals from dangerous ultraviolet rays produced by the Sun. In humans, exposure to ultraviolet rays is linked to skin cancer and harm to the immune system. Chlorofluorocarbon (CFC) gases are one of the main pollutants that bore holes in Earth's upper atmosphere.

Lead: Lead is a toxic or lethal metal that was once a common component of gasoline, paints, and various industrial processes. Unleaded gasoline and paint, along with improvements in industrial processes, have brought about a decrease in the release of lead in the air. Especially harmful to young children, lead can slow down mental development, and can harm the kidneys, liver, nervous system, and other organs.

Air and water pollutants can affect a wide variety of surrounding life. GALE GROUP.

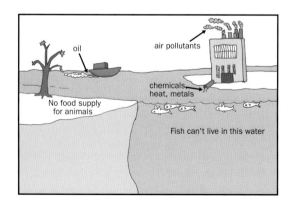

Particulates: Particulate matter varies in size. Larger particles settle near their source after a few minutes in the air; small particles can remain in the air for several days and spread over a wide area. Particles that are especially small can cause health problems in humans and animals.

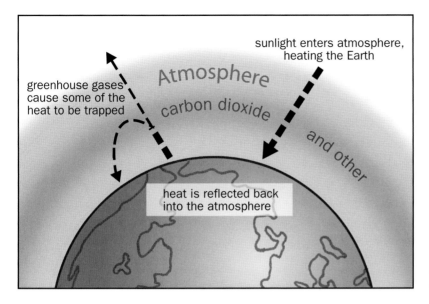

Carbon dioxide and other gases trap heat close to Earth, causing a warming in Earth's climate. GALE GROUP.

Particles enter the respiratory system and penetrate deeply into the lungs. Brief exposure can result in symptoms ranging from coughing to a sore throat. Long-term exposure can cause asthma and congestion.

Suspended particles in the atmosphere are seen as dust, smoke, soot, and haze. These particles can also cause smog. Smog is a type of large-scale outdoor pollution caused by reactions between strong sunlight and different pollutants, primarily automobile exhaust and industrial emissions. Smog appears as a haze over wide areas.

Smog often worsens in warm temperatures when a thermal inversion can occur. In a thermal inversion, a layer of warm air traps the cool air close to Earth. When this happens the polluted air cannot rise and disperse into the atmosphere. The pollution can build up to dangerous levels. In 1952, thermal inversion caused a London smog that killed over four thousand people. In the United States, Los Angeles, California, is the city most profoundly affected by smog, according to a 2009 American Lung Association report.

In a thermal inversion, a layer of warm air traps the cool air close to Earth. When this happens the polluted air cannot rise and disperse into the atmosphere, causing pollution to build up to dangerous levels. GALE GROUP.

Smog appears as a haze over large areas. Here, the skyline of New York City is wrapped in a veil of smog. NATIONAL ARCHIVES AND RECORDS ADMINISTRATION.

Pollutants from nature Air inside homes can also become polluted. Trapped in an enclosed area, indoor pollution can cause people serious health problems because of the large amount of time people spend indoors. Cigarette smoke, cooking and heating appliances, paints, and some cleaning products are all possible sources of indoor pollution. Radon, an odorless natural gas released from the ground, is another possible pollutant. Radon can enter buildings through cracks and can seep into basements of homes. Lung cancer is one health effect of radon.

Radon is an example of a natural pollutant. Other types of naturally occurring pollutants include erupting volcanoes, which produce large amounts of sulfur oxides and particulate matter. Some microorganisms that break down plant material also release methane gas, a contributor to the greenhouse effect. Among the places these microorganisms live is in cows' stomachs to help with their digestion. When the cows belch, methane gas gets released.

Sickly water About 70% of Earth is covered by the ocean, which makes up almost all the water on the planet. All life on Earth needs water to survive. Oceans, rivers, lakes, and other bodies of water hold a rich diversity of animal, plant, and microscopic life that organisms in both the water and on land depend upon to live. Oil, pesticides, fertilizers, litter, wastes, heat, and toxic chemicals are several major sources of water pollution. Polluted water kills sea life and causes disease in humans.

Oils: While oil spills from cargo ships make headline news, these accidents make up only a fraction of the oil released into the oceans. The majority of oil in North American waters comes from industry and road runoff, along with boating. Other sources of oil pollution include drilling, shipping, and improper disposal of oil waste. Oils are also released naturally from eroding rocks at the bottom of the ocean.

The impact of oil on marine life depends upon the amount of oil, where it is located, and the amount of toxic chemicals in the oil. Oils spills form a visible film on the water called an oil slick. Oil in a slick sticks to birds, fish, and plants, blocking their breathing and possibly causing death. The reduced food supply can have a long-term impact for whole ecosystems. Oils also wash up on beaches and other human recreational areas. Researchers are working to discover how the steady, relatively small release of oil affects ocean and human life.

Chemicals: Chemical water pollutants are substances not naturally occurring in the waters. Industrial compounds, such as sulfur and nitrogen oxides, along with herbicides and pesticides are common chemicals released into the waters. Rainwater can carry chemicals from the land into waterways. Heavy metals, such as copper, lead, and mercury, enter the water from industries, automobile exhaust, mines, and even natural soil.

An oil-soaked bird washes up on a beach in northern Spain in November 2002, after a tanker leaked 3,000 tons of oil off the western coast of Spain before eventually sinking. AP/WIDE WORLD

Heat: When hot water is poured into a cooler body of water it is called thermal pollution. All life forms have a range of temperature in which they can live. If the water temperature is outside of that range it will upset and kill organisms. Thermal pollution is common near factories and power plants, where water is heated to high temperatures. Although the water is cooled before it is added to natural bodies of water, it often remains hotter than the natural water. Thermal pollution is also caused by the removal of trees and vegetation that shade bodies of waters.

Natural substances: Upsetting the balance of nutrients can also pollute the waters in a process called eutrophication. Nitrates and phosphates are natural nutrients that plants such as algae use for growth. Fertilizers and untreated sewage can contain many of these nutrients. Rain washes the nutrients into bodies of water where they accumulate and stimulate algae growth. The algae grow more rapidly than fish can eat them, causing two major effects. When the algae die it causes decomposing organisms to thrive, depleting the water of oxygen. The lack of oxygen causes fish and surrounding plants to die. Also, the abundance of algae

The sun's rays pass through clean water. Plants produce oxygen that sea life need to live.

sunlight passes through water

plants produce oxygen that sea life need to live

sunlight cannot pass through water

overgrowth of algae causes depletion of oxygen

sea life cannot live in water

The process of eutrophication depletes the water of oxygen and blocks needed sunlight, causing fish and plant life to die. GALE GROUP.

clog the waters and block sunlight for the plants underneath. These plants, which provide food and shelter for sea life, then die.

Solid matter: Along with blemishing water's natural beauty, litter can significantly harm sea life. Litter is often made of plastic, which takes hundreds of years to break down. Birds and fishes can mistake such litter for food. When enough litter is consumed, the animal's intestines become blocked and it dies. Plastic bags can also suffocate small sea life. Plastic fishing lines and other debris can entangle seabirds and other life. Some estimates put the number of plastic-related deaths at two million seabirds and 100,000 marine mammals each year.

Pollution prevention In the mid-to-late 1900s, the U.S. government began to enact regulations on pollutants that have helped clear much of the waters and air. In 1970 the Clean Air Act established standards for air quality and emissions. The act required automobile manufacturers to produce cars that use unleaded fuel, which has reduced pollutants, and to install pollution-control devices on the exhaust. Factories, incinerators, and power plants were also required to install pollution-control mechanisms. In the 1970s the Safe Water Drinking Act and the Clean Water Act were enacted. These acts set water standards for public water systems and established regulations for the discharge of pollutants into waters.

Other governments also have enacted regulations against releasing pollutants. Companies have developed improved methods to clean up pollution, such as a genetically modified type of bacteria that eats oil from oil spills. As almost all pollutants are the result of human activity, there are multiple ways that individuals can help reduce pollutants. Producing less garbage by recycling, not littering, avoiding disposing of oil or oil-related products down the drain, and driving less and using a car that conserves fuel are a few ways that one person can reduce air and water pollutants.

WORDS TO KNOW

Control experiment: A setup that is identical to the experiment, but is not affected by the variable that affects the experimental group.

Eutrophication: The process by which high nutrient concentrations in a body of water eventually cause the natural wildlife to die.

Greenhouse effect: The warming of Earth's atmosphere due to water vapor, carbon dioxide, and other gases in the atmosphere that trap heat radiated from Earth's surface.

Hypothesis: An idea in the form of a statement that can be tested.

Particulate matter: Solid matter in the form of tiny particles in the atmosphere. (Pronounced par-TIK-you-let.)

Pollution: The contamination of the natural environment, usually through human activity.

Radon: A radioactive gas located in the ground; invisible and odorless, radon is a health hazard when it accumulates to high levels inside homes and other structures where it is breathed.

Smog: A form of air pollution produced when moisture in the air combines and reacts with the products of fossil fuel combustion. Smog is characterized by hazy skies and a tendency to cause respiratory problems among humans.

Thermal inversion: A region in which the warmer air lies above the colder air; can cause smog to worsen.

Thermal pollution: The discharge of heated water from industrial processes that can kill or injure water life.

Variable: Something that can affect the results of an experiment.

EXPERIMENT 1

Pollutant Bioindicators: Can lichens provide clues to an area's air pollution?

Purpose/Hypothesis Lichens are organisms that are extremely sensitive to air pollution. These life forms are actually two types of organisms living in partnership: fungi and either a green algae or a blue-green bacterium. Lichens grow on rocks, buildings, and on trees. These organisms receive virtually all their water and nutrients from the air. Lichens are especially sensitive to certain air pollutants, such as sulfur dioxide. When lichens are exposed to these pollutants they will die. Automobile emissions and some industrial processes can produce these pollutants. Because of this, scientists use lichens as indicators of pollution, or bioindicators.

The quantity, diversity, and colors of the lichens all provide evidence of the area's pollutants. These organisms are colored red, orange, yellow, gray, black, brown, and green. When lichens are affected by pollutants, they turn from their usual color and can peel away from the surface they

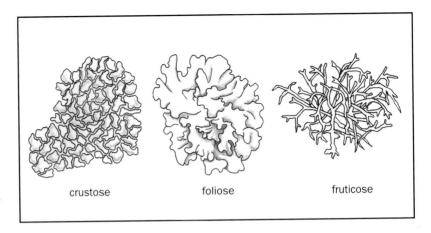

crustose   foliose   fruticose

There are three main types of lichens. GALE GROUP.

live on. There are three main types of lichens: Fruticose lichens look like miniature 1-inch (25-mm) tall shrubs or lettuce leaves and hang from branches; foliose lichens appear like flat leafs; and crustose lichens sit closely to their surface and appear crustlike. The crustose lichens are the most resistant to air pollution, and are often seen in cites. Fruticose lichens are the most sensitive to pollutants.

In this experiment you will measure an area's air pollution by using lichens as the bioindicator. You will choose three different areas and randomly select three trees of similar sizes in each area. You may need to look at pictures of the different types of lichens before you begin. By placing a transparent grid over the tree you can count the amount and type of lichens covering each tree.

Before you begin, make an educated guess about the outcome of this experiment based on your knowledge of air pollution and lichens. This educated guess, or prediction, is your hypothesis. A hypothesis should explain these things:

- the topic of the experiment
- the variable you will change
- the variable you will measure
- what you expect to happen

A hypothesis should be brief, specific, and measurable. It must be something you can test through further investigation. Your experiment will prove or disprove whether your hypothesis is correct. Here is one possible hypothesis for this experiment: "There will be fewer and less diversity in the lichens living near high traffic and/or industrial areas than the lichens in more remote areas."

In this case, the variable you will change is the location. The variable you will measure is the quantity and type of lichens.

Level of Difficulty Moderate.

Materials Needed

- three locations (sites) of different environments; all should have trees (example: a city street, in a park, near a school parking lot)
- trees in each area, of the same or similar species (kinds)
- magnifying glass
- ball of string or twine
- tape measure
- transparent piece of grid paper (1×1 inch squares work well, or slightly larger squares)
- marking pen
- partner (optional but helpful)

Approximate Budget $5.

Timetable 2.5 hours (including travel time).

Step-by-Step Instructions

1. Create a chart for each area, listing "Tree 1," "Tree 2," and "Tree 3" across the top columns. Label the rows: "Fruticose," "Foliose," "Crustose," "Bark," and "Other."
2. Choose a tree at random in the first area of study. The tree should have lichen growing on it. Circle the string around the trunk at a height that you can comfortably observe, such as 3 feet (0.9 meters).
3. Tie a knot in the string and cut. Mark the string with a 1 or one mark.
4. Starting at the marked line, place the transparency directly below the string. Count and note the squares covered by

What Are the Variables?

Variables are anything that might affect the results of an experiment. Here are the main variables in this experiment:

- the location
- types of trees
- the size of trees

In other words, the variables in this experiment are everything that might affect the growth of lichens. If you change more than one variable at the same time, you will not be able to tell which variable had the most effect on inhibiting lichen growth.

How to Experiment Safely

If studying trees near the road, be careful of traffic. Try to conduct your experiment during a low-traffic time of the week and day; and ask an adult to accompany you to a high-traffic area.

Troubleshooter's Guide

Below is a problem that may arise during this experiment, some possible causes, and some ways to remedy the problem.

Problem: All the lichen looked the same.

Possible cause: It is possible that much of the lichen was the same, especially if the sites were close to one another. To categorize lichens it is also helpful to refer to reference material. If possible, take a book out of the library with pictures of the different types of lichen and repeat the experiment, using the photographs as a guide.

each group of lichens, bare bark, and other life forms, such as moss. You may want to use the magnifying glass. Have your partner write down the results for each grid. Continue this along the tree until you have made a complete circle. Repeat the process above the string.

5. Add up the numbers of squares covered by each lichen, bark, and any other growth and then note those numbers on the chart.

6. Also note the color of the lichens on the chart.

7. Repeat this process with two more randomly chosen trees nearby at the same site. For each tree, tie a fresh piece of string at the same height. Mark the second string with a 2 or two marks and the third tree with a 3 or three marks.

8. At the second site, use the three pieces of string that are marked. Try to measure three trees that have roughly the same circumference as each of the trees at the first site. Again, note the types of lichens and the number of squares each fills.

9. Repeat the process at the third site, choosing three trees randomly that are roughly the same diameter.

Summary of Results Calculate the average numbers for each site. Use the averages of your data to create a graph of the three sites. How do the numbers of lichens compare between the sites? Is your hypothesis correct? For the same type of lichens, is there a difference in their colors? Determine if there was one dominant type of lichen in each area. How does that dominant type compare to the lichens in the other two areas? Examine the possible pollutants in each area. Write a brief summary of your findings and analysis.

Step 4: Count the squares that each type of lichen, plain bark, and other life form(s) takes up on the tree. GALE GROUP.

Change the Variables To change the variables in this experiment you can focus on one location and measure the lichens on different trees. You can focus on specific parts of the trees also, such as a shady or sunny section. You can also concentrate your research on different pollutants, such as automobile exhaust and industrial processes. You can then find areas where you observe each pollutant occurring, and determine its effect on the lichen.

EXPERIMENT 2

Eutrophication: The effect of phosphates on water plants.

Purpose/Hypothesis Phosphorus is a vital nutrient that both plants and people need. Plants use phosphorus for converting sunlight into energy, cell growth, and reproduction. Organisms usually take in phosphorous in the form of phosphate, a phosphorous compound. Because they promote plant growth, phosphates are one of the nutrients in many agricultural and garden fertilizers. Many dishwasher detergents add phosphates to reduce spotting on glasses and dishes. Laundry detergents can contain phosphates to soften the water.

In this experiment, you will explore how an excess of phosphates can affect life in lakes, streams, and oceans. When too many nutrients accumulate in a body of water, it can spark eutrophication. This process begins with the growth of algae. Algae are simple water plants that are found near the surface of waters. There are many types of algae, and sea life depends upon them for food. In waters, phosphorous is naturally present in low concentrations, as algae require only small amounts of it to live.

In this experiment you will add phosphates to healthy water plants that are living in water with a natural amount of algae. You will add two different concentrations of the phosphate and then observe their effect on the plant. By observing the water plants daily you will be able to determine the effect of the phosphate.

Before you begin, make an educated guess about the outcome of this experiment based on your knowledge of water pollution and eutrophication. This educated guess, or prediction, is your hypothesis. A hypothesis should explain these things:

- the topic of the experiment
- the variable you will change
- the variable you will measure
- what you expect to happen

What Are the Variables?

Variables are anything that might affect the results of an experiment. Here are the main variables in this experiment:

- the type of plant
- the soap
- the quantity of soap
- the environmental conditions (sunlight, air temperature, water temperature, etc.)

In other words, the variables in this experiment are everything that might affect the growth of the plants. If you change more than one variable at the same time, you will not be able to tell which variable had the most effect on how the algae affected the plants' health.

A hypothesis should be brief, specific, and measurable. It must be something you can test through further investigation. Your experiment will prove or disprove whether your hypothesis is correct. Here is one possible hypothesis for this experiment: "Water with the highest concentrations of phosphates will cause the algae to clog the waters and cause the plants to die."

In this case, the variable you will change is the amount of phosphate added to the water. The variable you will measure is the plant's health. To measure the plants health you can observe its height, color, root structure, and leaves.

Conducting a control experiment will help you isolate each variable and measure the changes in the dependent variable. Only one variable will change between the control and the experimental setup, and that is the amount of phosphate-soap added to the water. The control in this experiment will be to add no additive to the plant's water.

Note: When making a solid/liquid solution, it is standard to use weight/weight (grams/grams) or weight/volume (grams/milliliters). With water, 1 gram of water equals 1 milliliter. In this experiment, teaspoons and tablespoons are used to measure the solid.

Level of Difficulty Easy.

Materials Needed

- three small water plants of the same type with roots; elodea work well (available at pet shops)
- pond water (preferred) or water that plants were living in: collect enough to fill each of the jars about three-quarters full
- three glass jars, large enough to hold plants
- detergent with high phosphate content (preferably, a detergent with 7% or higher phosphate content)
- masking tape
- marking pen
- measuring spoons

Approximate Budget $8.

Timetable 20 minutes to set up; five minutes daily for about 10 days.

Step-by-Step Instructions

1. Label the jars "High Phosphate," "Low Phosphate," and "Control." Fill each jar with the pond water.
2. Create a chart with "Day 1," "Day 5," and "Day 10" written across the top and the jar labels written down the side.
3. Measure out 1 tablespoon of the detergent and mix into the High Phosphate water.
4. Measure out 1 teaspoon of the detergent and mix into the Low Phosphate water.
5. Place one of the plants in each of the three jars. Do not add detergent to the Control jar.
6. Fill in the physical description of the plant and water for Day 1 on the chart.
7. Place the three jars in the same sunny location.
8. Observe each plant's health and its water daily for about 10 days (time will vary depending on the amount of algae in the control water and the amount of sun).
9. On Day 5 and Day 10, note in a chart the color of the water for each jar and any physical properties of the plant.

Summary of Results Examine the results of your data chart. Hypothesize how phosphates would have different effects in shallow and slow-moving waters compared to that of deep and flowing waters. In which types of water would sea life be the most in danger? Many states now limit the use of phosphates in their detergents. You can research if your state has regulations on phosphate usage and calculate how those amounts compare to the amount used in your experiment.

Measure the water color and plant health at Day 1, Day 5, and Day 10. GALE GROUP.

Change the Variables There are several ways that you can alter this experiment. Try using different brands of detergent, either dishwashing or laundry. You can use the same amount of

Troubleshooter's Guide

Below is a problem that may arise during this experiment, some possible causes, and some ways to remedy the problem.

Problem: The water in the experiment jars remained the same as the Control.

Possible cause: You may not have collected enough algae to foster growth. Try to find a pond in your area or use water from another shop. Repeat the experiment with this new water.

Possible cause: Algae grow best in a sunny environment. It also might look like nothing is growing when they will suddenly bloom. Make sure the jars are in a sunny window and continue your observations.

detergent in the water and place the jars in varying environments, by placing them in a hot- or cold-water bath (you will have to change it daily). Will a cool, sunny environment stimulate algae growth more than a warm, sunny environment? You can also change the type of water plant that you use.

Modify the Experiment This experiment measures how water pollution can harm sea life. You can make this experiment more challenging by experiment with methods of cleaning up water pollution and the affected sea life.

The water pollution you used in this experiment dissolved in water. For you to better see and test cleaning water pollution, you can pollute the water with oil. Pluck several leaves from the water plants and place them in a container of water. You may want to add other plant life to each container, such as grasses, along with feathers. Pour about a quarter-cup of oil into the container, and gently move it back and forth several times.

Collect cotton cloth, string, paper towels, tubing, straws, and liquid soap. Try to remove as much oil as you can with the tools you have collected. Tubing can contain the oil; cloth can absorb it; straws can pull it up, and string can collect it. You may need to conduct several tests before you find a technique that you find effective. When you have cleaned up the pollution as best you can, carefully remove the "organisms" and note how each is affected by the oil. What happens if you gently rub drops of soap on the sea life? Experiment with methods of removing the pollution from the organisms. Could the same techniques be practiced on actual organisms? Consider how soap may affect sea plants, birds, and animals.

Design Your Own Experiment

How to Select a Topic Relating to this Concept Air and water pollution is all around, no matter what your location. To think of a topic, you can first observe the pollution in the waters, cities, and roadways. Think about methods of measuring the air and water pollution. Check the Further Readings section and talk with your science teacher to learn more about air pollution. You may also want to explore any companies in your area that measure pollutants.

Steps in the Scientific Method To conduct an original experiment, you need to plan carefully and think things through. Otherwise, you might not be sure what question you are answering, what you are or should be measuring, or what your findings prove or disprove.

Here are the steps in designing an experiment:

- State the purpose of—and the underlying question behind—the experiment you propose to do.
- Recognize the variables involved and select one that will help you answer the question at hand.
- State your hypothesis, an educated guess about the answer to your question.
- Decide how to change the variable you selected.
- Decide how to measure your results.

Recording Data and Summarizing the Results Your data should include charts and graphs such as the one you did for these experiments. They should be clearly labeled and easy to read. You may also want to include photographs and drawings of your experimental setup and results, which will help other people visualize the steps in the experiment.

If you are preparing an exhibit, you may want to display your results, such as any experimental setup you designed. If you have completed a nonexperimental project, explain clearly what your research question was and illustrate your findings.

Related Projects Projects related to air and water pollution include examining their effect on organisms. You can visit a lake or stream in your area and collect water samples to determine its pollutants, then compare that to its plant and animal life. You can collect samples of particulate matter in the air by hanging papers smeared with petroleum jelly. After collecting the data, you can compare the test sites to the animal and plant life in the area. For a research project, you could examine how pollutants affect people's health and determine if those health problems are correlated to locations with high levels of pollution. Other projects include examining methods that scientists have developed to clean up pollutants. Taking a look at pollution around the world and its impact is another area of exploration.

For More Information

"Loveable Lichens." *Earthlife.* http://www.earthlife.net/lichens/intro.html (accessed on March 19, 2008) Photos and information on all types of lichens.

Macmillian Encyclopedia of Science: The Environment. New York: Macmillan Publishing USA, 1997. Covers all aspects of our environment and how pollution affects it.

Spilsbury, Louise. *Environment at Risk: The Effects of Pollution.* Chicago: Raintree, 2006. Information and case studies of the effects of pollution.

"Students and Teachers." *NOAA's Office of Response and Restoration.* response.restoration.noaa.gov/kids/kids.html (accessed on March 19, 2008) Information and activities on oil spills.

U.S. Environmental Protection Agency. "Air." *EPA Student Center.* http://www.epa.gov/students/air.htm (accessed on March 19, 2008) A comprehensive web site with links and information on a wide range of environmental issues including air pollution, air quality standards, and more.

5

Animal Defenses

If you've ever smelled the odor of a skunk or been hissed at by a cat, you've experienced an animal defense. Animals have developed a lot of clever defenses to protect them from harm. When attacked by a predator, an animal can run away or fight. Some types of defenses protect the animal from ever being seen by predators (the attacking animal). Other defenses defend the animal when it is attacked.

Playing dead In general, meat-eating animals don't like to eat animals that they find dead. An animal that is dead could be carrying disease and cause illness. The opossum uses this instinct as a defensive strategy. When threatened or wanting to avoid an attack, the opossum can fall down and play dead. Its tongue rolls out, eyes become glazed and it releases a foul odor. The predator might sniff or poke the opossum but it lies completely still. After the would-be predator leaves, the opossum returns to "life." Several types of snakes also use the play–dead defense.

Blending into the scene One way to avoid danger is to avoid being spotted by a predator. Camouflage is the markings or colors that blend in to the environment. Most animals exhibit some type of camouflage and "blending in" is a common animal defense. The green color of many insects matches leaves; the brown earth tones of deer, squirrels, and other woodland animals matches the woods colors; the patterns and stripes of animals, such as a zebra, break up the animal's shape so a predator does not identify it.

Many insects, mammals, and birds have colors or patterns that match the natural environment so well they are hard to spot, even when you know they are there. At night, the colorful parrot fish covers itself with a dark substance that it makes while breathing. The protective coat shields the parrot fish from its predators. The skin of mossy frogs has the same colors, bumps, and texture as the moss that they live in. A leaf frog features bumps over its eyes and a pointed nose, taking on the color

WORDS TO KNOW

Camouflage: A coating that allows an animal to blend in to its surrounding environment.

Ecosystem: An ecological community, including plants, animals and microorganisms, considered together with their environment.

Hypothesis: An idea in the form of a statement that can be tested by observation and/or experiment.

Mimicry: A characteristic in which an animal is protected against predators by resembling another, more distasteful animal.

Predator: An animal that hunts another animal for food.

Variable: Something that can affect the results of an experiment.

and shape of a leaf. The walking stick insect can easily be mistaken for a twig from its appearance and its stillness.

In camouflage, an animal appears as something in its environment. When animals appear as another, more-dangerous or inedible animal, it is called mimicry.

The skunk can omit a strong, foul odor when in danger. AP PHOTO/PHIL COALE.

Often one type of animal will take on the appearance of a poisonous, similar animal. There are butterflies in the Amazon that take on the appearance of poisonous butterflies. Several species of harmless snakes have the bright red, yellow, and black strips as the venomous (poisonous) coral snake. Some animals simply don't want to have predators think they taste good. A type of butterfly in Brazil has developed the appearance of another butterfly species that tastes foul.

There are also animals that can mimic the appearance of animals that are different species. Several types of jumping spiders mimic ants. One of these spiders is the same size, shape, and color as a weaver ant, which has a sharp bite and painful venom. The mimic octopus gets its nickname from its ability to take on the appearance of several venomous ocean creatures, including a lionfish and sea snake.

The smell that scares When an animal is struck with a bad odor, it is usually not going to enjoy eating. After a skunk has tried to scare or move away from a threat, it defends itself with a smelly spray. The odor is so strong and foul it can cause nausea. The skunk will often aim for the face of the predator because the spray can also sting. Weasels, bedbugs, and snakes are other animals that use foul odors to ward off predators.

Wild and strange defenses There are many other defense strategies animals have evolved. The horned lizards are ant-eating lizards in North America. When attacked or threatened, the lizard shoots blood out of the tear ducts in its eyes. The blood contains substances that make it foul tasting. Having an imposing look is the defense strategy for several animals, including the puffer fish. When the puffer fish is threatened, it can increase up to three times its size by gulping water.

The electric eel is one of several animals that defends itself with a jolt of electricity when a predator attacks. Octopi and cuttlefish are just two marine animals that squirt out a black ink for defense.

The electric eel uses a jolt of electricity when a predator attacks. GEORGE GRALL. NATIONAL GEOGRAPHIC, GETTY IMAGES.

PROJECT 1

Camouflage: Does an animal's living environment relate to the color of the animal life?

Purpose/Hypothesis How an animal defends itself is strongly influenced by its living environment. A wide variety of animals use camouflage as a form of defense. The purpose of this project is to observe the camouflage that small animals use in one isolated outside environment. The area you choose could be the bark of a tree, a grassy patch, leaves, or a stretch of dirt. You will record the animal colors living in that particular environment. You will then compare the percentage of animals living in the first environment to animals living in another type of habitat.

Depending upon the environment, common animals you can look for include butterflies, stick insects, moths, beetles, grasshoppers, frogs, rabbits, squirrels, and crickets.

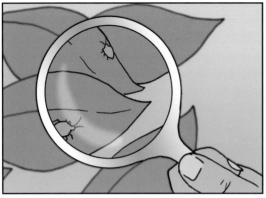

A wide variety of animals use camouflage as a form of defense. ILLUSTRATION BY TEMAH NELSON.

Use a similar chart to compare the two environments. ILLUSTRATION BY TEMAH NELSON.

	Habitat 1 (color)		Habitat 2 (color)	
	Organisms	color	Organisms	color
1.				
2.				
3.				
4.				
5.				
6.				
7.				
8.				
9.				
10.				

Level of Difficulty Moderate. (This project requires careful observation and patience.)

Materials Needed

- camera (optional)
- magnifying glass (optional)
- paper and pencil
- a nice day

Approximate Budget $0.

Timetable Varies widely, depending upon the area, animals, and number of animals you want to locate.

Step-by-Step Instructions

1. Once you decide on a specific habitat, spend some time looking for insects or other small animals that live in that environment. When you spot an insect or other animal, write down the insect— or describe it if you don't know it's name—and note its color. You may want to use a magnifying glass. If you have a camera, take a picture of each organism you find.

2. Continue looking for small animals until you have located at least five to 10 different organisms living in the environment you selected. In some environments, this may take time and careful attention. Remember, some animals might be camouflaged!

3. Determine the percent of organisms that are the color of its surrounding environment. (You can determine the percent by dividing the number of organisms that were a certain color by the total number of organisms located.)

4. Repeat the entire process for another environment, which is a different color. Again, try to located at least five to 10 organisms.

Summary of Results Compare the percent of insects the color of the first environment to the percent in the second environment. If you took pictures, compare the pictures of the animals in each environment. Does the color of the environment predict the color of the organisms that live there? You may want to chart your results. You could also use your notes or pictures to try and identify any unknown animals.

EXPERIMENT 2

Ladybug Threats: How do ladybugs defend themselves when they feel threatened?

Purpose/Hypothesis In this experiment, you will determine how ladybugs defend themselves when they sense a threat. Ladybugs have three methods of defense that help keep them safe. The distinct red color of a ladybug is in itself a defense mechanism. Many animals instinctively know not to eat bright colors organisms because they are often poisonous (many red berries, for example). Ladybugs also can give off a foul odor when threatened and this helps to keep their predator away. Lastly, ladybugs will "play dead" when approached by a potential predator or when unsure of their surroundings. Many insects and animals will not eat dead things and so they move away from the ladybug. In time, the ladybug will resume its activity.

You will test different stimuli on the ladybug that it may see as threatening or unknown, and then observe how the ladybugs defend themselves. For the stimuli, you will expose the ladybugs to light, air movement, gentle nudging, vibrations, and sound. You can then observe its reactions for each.

Before you begin the experiment, make an educated guess about the outcome based on your knowledge of animal defenses and ladybugs. This educated guess, or prediction, is your hypothesis. A hypothesis should explain these things:

How to Experiment Safely

Never touch the insects/animals or disturb their living environment; simply observe them.

Troubleshooter's Guide

Not locating enough organisms in each environment is the major problem that can occur in this project. Finding organisms can take patience and care. Many animals are more active in the beginning and end of the day, rather than during midday. If you are having trouble locating organisms, look for the organisms another time in the day, such as early morning. You could also try searching in another place, using the same environment.

What Are the Variables?

Variables are anything that might affect the results of an experiment. Here are the main variables in this experiment:

- light intensity the ladybug is exposed to
- wind movement
- movement the ladybug experiences
- physical proximity to object
- physical proximity to another insect
- sound intensity in the background

In other words, the variables in this experiment are everything that might effect the reaction of the ladybug to various situations. If you change more than one variable, you will not be able to tell which variable had the most effect on the reaction of the ladybug.

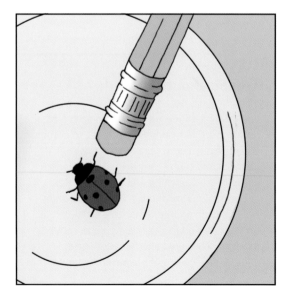

Step 8: Approach the ladybug with the pencil and note the reaction. ILLUSTRATION BY TEMAH NELSON.

- the topic of the experiment
- the variable you will change
- the variable you will measure
- what you expect to happen

A hypothesis should be brief, specific, and measurable. It must be something you can test through observation. Your experiment will prove or disprove your hypothesis. Here is one possible hypothesis for this experiment: "The ladybug will play dead when it is in a threatening or unknown situation."

In this case, the variables you will change are situations that may be perceived as threatening or unknown to the ladybug. The variable you will measure is the reaction of the ladybug to these various new situations.

Level of Difficulty Moderate.

Materials Needed

- 3–5 ladybugs, found or purchased from local nursery or online
- plastic container with cover, approximately 5 to 7 inches (13–18 centimeter) long
  - flashlight
  - 1–2 ants, caterpillars, inchworms, or spiders (found)
  - 1 pencil

Approximate Budget $10–15 if you have to purchase ladybugs; $0 if you can find the bugs.

Timetable Approximately one hour.

Step-by-Step Instructions

1. Place two ladybugs in the plastic container with lid. If one of the ladybugs flies away, replace it with another.
2. Observe and note the ladybugs behavior for several minutes. Wait for them to

become comfortable in their new environment and move around slightly.

3. Shine a flashlight into the plastic container. Note whether the ladybugs react to the change in light.

4. Wait about two to three minutes until the ladybugs resume activity.

5. Lift off the lid of the container and blow softly onto one or both of the ladybugs. Note the reaction. Change the intensity of your breath, blowing slightly harder. Note whether the reaction of the ladybug change as well.

6. After waiting for ladybugs to resume activity (two to three minutes) introduce another insect (ant, caterpillar, inchworm, spider) into the box. Note the reaction of the ladybugs. Be careful that the insect does not actually attack the ladybug (if so, remove the insect).

7. Remove the second type of insect and again, wait for the ladybugs to resume normal activity.

8. Without poking the ladybug, approach it with the pencil and note reaction. Gently nudge the ladybug with the pencil and note its reaction. Repeat this on the second ladybug.

9. Wait several minutes until both ladybugs resumes activity.

10. Try clapping your hands at different sound intensities close to the ladybug. Start with a soft clap and increase to a loud noise. Note which, if any, sound intensity appears to threaten the ladybug and note its reaction.

11. Wait several minutes until the ladybugs resumes normal activity.

12. Try gently shaking the container with the ladybug in it. Does this sudden movement cause the ladybug to react?

Summary of Results Study the observations of the ladybugs' reactions to various situations and decide whether your hypothesis was correct. In what situation did the ladybug appear to feel threatened and how did it react? If it played dead, how long did it take for it to start moving

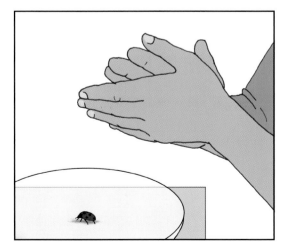

Step 10: Clap your hands at different sound intensities close to the ladybug. ILLUSTRATION BY TEMAH NELSON.

Troubleshooter's Guide

Below is the main problem that may occur during this project and ways to remedy the problem.

Problem: Ladybug doesn't play dead.

Possible cause: The ladybugs may not feel threatened. Sometimes there is safety in numbers and ladybugs may feel more vulnerable by themselves. Separate ladybugs from one another and try various scenarios with one ladybug.

Possible cause: You may have tested possibly very old or sick ladybugs. Try collecting new ladybugs and repeat the tests.

again? Write a summary of your results. You may want to include pictures.

Change the Variables Here are some ways you can vary this experiment:

- Test other stimuli that may be potentially threatening to the ladybug, such as strong smells (onion or garlic).
- Alter the environment: Conduct the experiment outside in the ladybugs' natural environment, as opposed to a plastic container.
- Change the insect: For example the pill bug, a common insect found in soil, will curl itself into a ball when it senses danger.

Design Your Own Experiment

How to Select a Topic Relating to this Concept As you think about experiments and projects relating to animal defenses, consider animals that are familiar to you. What are some behaviors of cats, dogs, and fish? Consider animals that you have seen in zoos or in the movies.

Check the Further Readings section and talk with your science teacher to start gathering information on animal defense questions that interest you. You may want to speak with people who are knowledgeable about different types of animals. As you consider possible experiments, be sure to discuss them with your science teacher or another knowledgeable adult before trying them. Remember that some animals can be dangerous and you should never provoke any animal. Work with someone familiar with the animal and plan how you will care for or handle any animal that you collect or purchase.

Steps in the Scientific Method To conduct an original experiment, you need to plan carefully and think things through. Otherwise, you might not be sure what question you are answering, what you are or should be measuring, or what your findings prove or disprove.

Here are the steps in designing an experiment:

- State the purpose of—and the underlying question behind—the experiment you propose to do.
- Recognize the variables involved, and select one that will help you answer the question at hand.
- State a testable hypothesis, an educated guess about the answer to your question.
- Decide how to change the variable you selected.
- Decide how to measure your results.

Recording Data and Summarizing the Results The most important part of the experiment is the information gathered from it. Think of how you can share your results with others. Charts, graphs, and diagrams of the progress and results of the experiments are helpful in informing others about an experiment. You may also want to take photographs.

Related Experiments Many experiments or projects with animals can be made through simple observation. You may want to observe how different animals species interact with one another when they feel threatened or excited. You can observe the interactions between dogs, cats, squirrels, and other familiar animals, or you can observe the behavior of insect interactions. You could also observe the many camouflage adaptations animals have by visiting a local zoo or aquarium. You could conduct a research project on one type of animal that lives in your area or are curious about.

For More Information

"Camouflage." *BBC: Walking with Beasts.* http://www.abc.net.au/beasts/fossilfun/camouflage/camouflage.swf (accessed on May 11, 2008). An interactive game on animal camouflage.

"Exploring Mammals." *Natural History Museum.* http://www.nhm.org/mammals/home.html (accessed on May 31, 2008). Information on animal behavior and defenses.

Kaner, Etta. *Animal Defenses: How Animals Protect Themselves.* Toronto, ON: Kid's Can Press, 1999.

National Geographic. *Animals,* http://animals.nationalgeographic.com (accessed on May 11 2008). Information on animal features, with pictures and video.

6

Annual Growth

Did you ever measure your height to see how much taller you were than the year before? This change is your annual growth. In humans, annual growth depends on factors such as your age (babies grow at a faster rate than teenagers) and your genes (which make sure your growth pattern is similar to that of your parents and grandparents). How can we determine the annual growth of other organisms, and what factors can we find that affect their growth?

Trees are probably the tallest living organisms you will see in your life. Yet most trees around you grew from seeds no larger than the eraser on a pencil. The process by which these tiny seeds become trees is fascinating and easy to observe, when you know what to look for.

How does a tree grow? A tree grows in two ways. The tips of its branches and tips of its roots contain cells that reproduce, making the tree taller and its roots deeper. Another layer of dividing cells increases the width of the tree's trunk little by little, increasing its support and providing a route for water to reach the upper branches. While a tree is alive, scientists can determine its growth rate by measuring the change in its diameter and also by observing the patterns of new growth on branches and twigs. When a tree has fallen or been cut down, scientists can learn much about the tree's growth throughout its life and can even learn about changes in climate and soil composition long ago by examining the growth rings inside the main trunk.

The growth rings that are visible on a tree stump result from the tree's cycle of growth and dormancy. The interior of a tree's trunk contains special tube-like vertical cells called xylem, which function as a vital part of the tree's water-transport system. Each year, new xylem is produced near the outer layer of bark. In the spring, when conditions are usually wettest, the tree produces large xylem cells. During the drier months of summer, the tree produces smaller xylem cells. In the winter, the tree's growth cycle

When a tree has fallen or been cut down, its annual growth rings become visible. GALE GROUP.

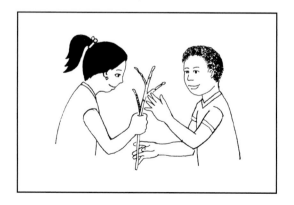

You can learn about a tree's growth pattern by observing the segments of twigs on the tree. GALE GROUP.

goes into a state of dormancy, a period of inactivity to keep its energy in reserve while water is scarce.

This alternating pattern of fast and slow growth causes the dark and light pattern of rings you can see on the tree stump. Each ring represents a growing season. Generally, a larger, more prominent ring marks a longer, wetter growing season. In this way, scientists have been able to pinpoint when climatic changes occurred long ago in a region's history. A skilled scientist with the right tools can learn even more from a tree's rings, such as when the tree experienced changes in soil composition, forest fires, and floods.

We can also learn about a tree's growth pattern by observing the segments of twigs on the tree. Each spring, the tree will put out a bud at the end of each twig. That bud forms the beginning of that year's new growth. Once the twig grows beyond the point where the bud first formed, the remnants of the bud create a scar, or ring. These rings mark off each year of the tree's growth. The most recent segment is the one closest to the end of the twig (assuming the twig has not been broken).

Some twigs exhibit growth rings going back many years. Once a growing season is completed, that season's segment will not grow any longer. The segments can give you a rough indication of how much growth a tree experienced in one season compared to other seasons. Remember that growth may not be the same from one side of a tree to the other, especially in large trees. The segment indicates most accurately how much growth occurred on that branch of the tree in a given growing season.

In the first experiment, you will compare the annual growth pattern of twigs on several trees in your area with the rainfall figures for each year. You will then determine if precipitation in your area has had a measurable effect on the trees' annual growth.

Lichens: Another kind of annual growth Have you ever noticed the patches of colorful plant life that sometimes grow on rocks and buildings? Some resemble greenish-brown stains, while others look like blotches of mold. When examined closely, some appear to be tiny forests of hairy branches. These are actually a unique and

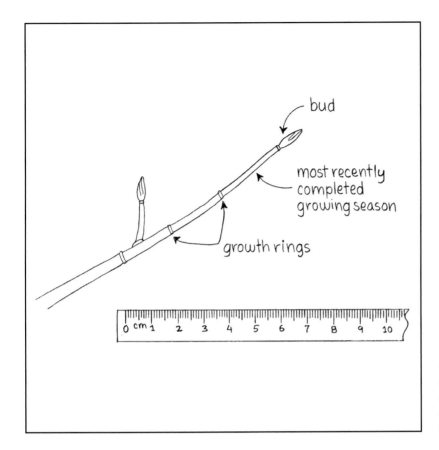

bud

most recently
completed
growing season

growth rings

*On many trees, twigs exhibit
evidence of past growing seasons
by the distance separating their
scars or annual growth rings.*
GALE GROUP.

fascinating life form called lichens. Scientists who study lichens are known as
lichenologists. One of the most renowned lichenologists was Beatrix Potter,
the author of *The Tale of Peter Rabbit.* Though better known for her children's
stories, Potter devoted much of her time to the study of lichens and produced
detailed watercolor illustrations of different lichen forms.

Lichens are far more complex than they appear. Each lichen contains
two partners, usually a fungus and an alga, that bond together in a symbiotic relationship. Symbiosis occurs when two organisms form a relationship that benefits both. By combining the advantages of fungus with the
advantages of algae, the lichen is able to survive where other organisms
would perish.

The most visible part of the typical lichen is a fungus. Fungi are plant-like
organisms that differ from true plants in that they are heterotrophs, organisms
that must get their food from other organisms. Fungi usually get their food
from dead and decaying matter. Fungi are composed of thin strands that form

Lichens are actually complex partnerships of different organisms working together.
PETER ARNOLD INC.

a network that becomes a home for the fungus's partner. That partner is usually an alga, although some lichens contain cyanobacteria instead. If you examine a cross-section of a lichen, you will usually see the alga as a thin layer of green just under the organism's top layer. Algae are tiny plants that use photosynthesis to create nutrients, making them autotrophs.

Lichens can survive harsh environments The symbiotic relationship between the fungus and the algal cells of the lichen depends on the structure and functioning of each. The fungus is capable of securing itself to inhospitable surfaces, such as bare rock or even plastic. Often, however, a fungus would not find sufficient nutrients in such a habitat. The algal cells, on the other hand, can produce food by photosynthesis, but they could not survive on their own on a bare rock. The two form a symbiotic union. The fungus provides the algae with protection from the harsh environment, while the algae provide the fungus with food.

Cyanobacteria are among the most ancient organisms on Earth. They are usually found in water, sometimes joining together in colonies. Cyanobacteria contain chlorophyll and perform photosynthesis, and thus they sometimes are found in lichens in place of algae.

Lichen growth patterns can be used to determine the age of rocks and rock formations because the rate of growth is extremely slow and regular. Lichens serve as a good indicator of air pollution levels because of their sensitivity to impurities in the atmosphere. In the second experiment, you will utilize two samples of living lichen to measure differences in air quality in different places.

EXPERIMENT 1

Tree Growth: What can be learned from the growth patterns of trees?

Purpose/Hypothesis For this experiment, you will examine and collect growth data from branches of different trees. Then you will determine whether these data correspond to the precipitation in your region. Before you begin, make an educated guess about the outcome of this experiment based on your knowledge of plant growth. This educated guess, or prediction, is your hypothesis. A hypothesis should explain these things:

- the topic of the experiment
- the variable you will change
- the variable you will measure
- what you expect to happen

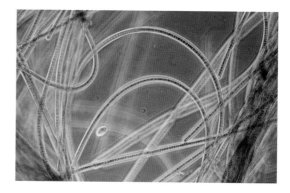

Cyanobacteria are single-celled organisms that perform photosynthesis. PHOTO RESEARCHERS INC.

A hypothesis should be brief, specific, and measurable. It must be something you can test through observation. Your experiment will prove or disprove whether your hypothesis is correct. Here is one possible hypothesis for this experiment: "The branches of trees in this area will show similar growth patterns over the past few years because they all received the same amounts of rainfall during each growing season."

In this case, the variable you will change is the type of tree, and the variable you will measure is the growth pattern over the past few years. You expect the growth patterns to be similar.

The fungus in a lichen provides a protecting structure for the algal cells, which provide food. GALE GROUP.

Level of Difficulty Moderate.

Materials Needed

- sketchbook and pencil
- ruler (one showing millimeters or sixteenths of an inch)
- pruning shears (optional)
- camera (optional)

Approximate Budget $2.

Timetable This experiment should be done in two periods of at least 15 minutes each: one period to collect and organize data, and the other to interpret the data and present the results.

WORDS TO KNOW

Alga/Algae: Single-celled or multicellular plants or plant-like organisms that contain chlorophyll, thus making their own food by photosynthesis. Algae grow mainly in water.

Autotroph: An organism that can build all the food and produce all the energy it needs with its own resources.

Chlorophyll: A green pigment found in plants that absorbs sunlight, providing the energy used in photosynthesis, or the conversion of carbon dioxide and water to complex carbohydrates.

Cyanobacteria: Oxygen-producing, aquatic bacteria capable of manufacturing its own food; resembles algae.

Dormancy: A state of inactivity in an organism.

Fungi: Kingdom of various single-celled or multicellular organisms, including mushrooms, molds, yeasts, and mildews, that do not contain chlorophyll.

Gene: A segment of a DNA (deoxyribonucleic acid) molecule contained in the nucleus of a cell that acts as a kind of code for the production of some specific protein. Genes carry instructions for the formation, functioning, and transmission of specific traits from one generation to another.

Heterotrophs: Organisms that cannot make their own food and that must, therefore, obtain their food from other organisms.

Hypothesis: An idea in the form of a statement that can be tested by observation and experiment.

Lichen: An organism composed of a fungus and a photosynthetic organism in a symbiotic relationship.

Niche: The specific location and place in the food chain that an organism occupies in its environment.

Photosynthesis: Chemical process by which plants containing chlorophyll use sunlight to manufacture their own food by converting carbon dioxide and water to carbohydrates, releasing oxygen as a by-product.

Symbiosis: A pattern in which two or more organisms live in close connection with each other, often to the benefit of both or all organisms.

Variable: Something that can affect the results of an experiment.

Xylem: Plant tissue consisting of elongated, thick-walled cells that transport water and mineral nutrients.

Step-by-Step Instructions

1. Choose branches or twigs that exhibit the visible signs of annual growth described above. Select different trees in different locations. If you use fallen branches, make sure they are recently fallen. Otherwise, you will not be sure when the most recent growth occurred. Branches that have been split or damaged, especially at the growth tip, may not provide useful results.

2. Ask your teacher or an adult before cutting any branches or twigs. Remember that any change you make to the natural environment will probably have a lasting effect, so avoid damaging trees whenever possible. If you decide to cut a branch to illustrate your project, do not cut the branch too close to the trunk or greater branch, as this could harm the tree.

3. Note the number of segments you can find on the branch you have selected. Determine which is from the most recently completed growing season and then note how many growth seasons are visible on your branch.

4. Sketch or photograph the branch. Note as much information as possible about the tree and its immediate environment. What kind of tree is it? Is it competing with other trees for water and sunlight? Might there be some other environmental factors affecting its growth, such as air pollution or drainage from parking lots or sidewalks? Check whether the tree is receiving water from an irrigation or sprinkler system. This would have a clear effect on your data, and may make an interesting comparison for your study.

5. Measure each segment and record your data. Use a chart to keep your information consistent. Your chart should look something like the illustration.

6. Once you have found and examined a number of different samples, use your data to test your hypothesis. For each sample, find the year in which the least growth occurred. Then find the year in which the greatest growth occurred. Use the different samples you have for each growing season to find an average growth for that year. Ask your teacher or librarian for help in finding annual rainfall figures for the years for which you have sample. Compare these figures to the results of your branch measurements.

What Are the Variables?

Variables are anything that might affect the results of an experiment. Here are the main variables in this experiment:

- the species of tree being examined
- the condition of the branches (damaged or not damaged, for example)
- variations in rainfall among the areas where the trees are growing
- the amount of fertilizer or other nutrients each tree receives
- other factors influencing growth, such as the amount of sunlight, level of air pollution, and the presence of disease in the trees

If you change more than one variable, you will not be able to tell which variable had the most effect on the growth patterns. Try to keep all variables the same except the one you are examining: the amount of annual growth.

How to Experiment Safely

If you choose to cut a branch or branches to illustrate your findings, be sure to ask permission before cutting. Use proper protective wear and be careful with the pruning shears.

Summary of Results Examine your results and determine whether your hypothesis is correct. Did the samples show consistently greater or lesser growth for one or more growing seasons? If so, did those years have more or less rainfall than usual?

Change the Variables You can vary this experiment by changing the variables. Instead of comparing growth seasons, try simply comparing growth rates from one type of tree to another. See if you can find which tree branches in your area exhibit the most growth in a season. Which tree branches grow the least?

Modify the Experiment In this experiment, you learned about how the growing pattern of trees is affected by the rainfall in an area. For a more in-depth understanding of tree growth, you can use the branches you collected to determine if water absorption differs among trees in the same area.

You know that water is an important source of nutrients that trees need to grow. But do all trees in the same area absorb equal amounts of available water? First, make a hypothesis. Select two of the branches you collected from two different types of trees growing in the same area. A twig from a

Tree Growth Chart

Segment number	Segment year	Length of segment
1	1998	2.3 cm
2	1997	1.9 cm
3		

Step 5: Example of tree growth recording chart. GALE GROUP.

tree with needles and a twig from a tree with large leaves would work well. Snap off two twigs (about the same size) from each of the two branches. You should have four twigs: two from one type of tree and two from another, all about the same size.

Prepare two clear measuring cups. Place the two twigs that are the same in one cup and the two other twigs in the second cup. Fill each of the cups half-full with water, leaving the top of the twigs not immersed. Make sure that the two cups contain equals amounts of water. For example, if the twigs stand slightly past a two-cup measuring cup, you may want to fill each cup with 1.5 cups of water. Write down the amount of water and mark the water line with a piece of masking tape.

Cover the tops of the cups with paper. You may need to poke the twigs through the paper so that the paper rests on the cup. Set aside for two days and then note the water level. Was the amount of water absorbed different for each type of tree? What twig absorbed the most water? Place another piece of tape at the water level and wait another day. Continue for several days or until the water is almost gone. Graph your results. What does this tell you about the water usage of different types of trees? What types of trees would fare better in a drought?

Troubleshooter's Guide

Here is a problem that may arise, a possible cause, and a way to remedy the problem.

Problem: The amount of growth varies greatly from tree to tree.

Possible cause: Different types of trees can have drastically different growth rates. Remember that you are looking for which years had the greatest and the least growth for each tree—a factor that may be consistent from tree to tree regardless of each one's growth rate.

EXPERIMENT 2

Lichen Growth: What can be learned from the environment by observing lichens?

Purpose/Hypothesis For this experiment, you will need to locate different lichens in various habitats around your school and/or home. Counting and measuring the number of lichens you find growing in different areas will give you a rough idea of the amounts of air pollution present. Lichens are nearly everywhere. You will need, however, to find samples large enough to examine and measure. In rural environments, this should not be difficult. Lichens can frequently be found on trees, dead wood, and rocks. Before you begin, make an educated guess about the outcome of this experiment based on your knowledge of lichens. This educated guess, or prediction, is your hypothesis. A hypothesis should explain these things:

What Are the Variables?

Variables are anything that might affect the results of an experiment. Here are the main variables in this experiment:

- the species of lichen being examined
- the surface on which the lichen is growing
- the amount of sunlight and rainfall the lichen receives
- the location of the lichen relative to sources of air pollution

In other words, the variables in this experiment are everything that might affect the size and numbers of the lichens. If you change more than one variable, you will not be able to tell which variable had the most effect on lichens.

- the topic of the experiment
- the variable you will change
- the variable you will measure
- what you expect to happen

A hypothesis should be brief, specific, and measurable. It must be something you can test through observation. Your experiment will prove or disprove whether your hypothesis is correct. Here is one possible hypothesis for this experiment: "Fewer and smaller lichens will grow in areas with higher levels of air pollution (near roads and factories) than in areas with cleaner air."

In this case, the variable you will change is the location of the lichens, and the variable you will measure is their number and size. You expect fewer and smaller lichens will be found near sources of air pollution.

Level of Difficulty Moderate.

Materials Needed

- sketchbook and pencil
- magnifying glass
- ruler (one showing millimeters or sixteenths of an inch)
- camera (optional)

Approximate Budget $5.

Timetable This experiment requires a commitment of several hours searching and cataloging lichens.

Step-by-Step Instructions

1. Your research for this experiment should begin in the library. It will be worthwhile to photocopy photographs and illustrations of different forms of lichen and bring this information with you when you go out looking for lichen.
2. Remember that lichens can be quite fragile. Treat lichens gently while measuring and sketching them.

3. If you are working together with a group, you might find it useful to divide the responsibilities. Have one group member sketch the lichen while others measure or write brief descriptions of the lichen's habitat. Prepare a chart on which you will record your observations for each lichen you find. Your chart should look something like the illustration.

4. Once you have found a lichen, take note on your chart of the habitat. Is the lichen growing on a tree or rock, or on some other object, such as a rusted barrel? How close is the lichen to the nearest source of air pollution? Note all other environmental factors that might affect the rate of lichen growth, such as shelter from rain and sun. Next examine the lichen itself. Describe it as clearly as possible, identifying its color, form, and texture.

5. Measure the lichen using your ruler. Lichen that grow in patches start with one tiny spore-like structure and then grow outward, like mold on bread. Therefore, try to locate the largest single sample instead of measuring two that have grown together. Measure the lichen's greatest

How to Experiment Safely

This project puts you in contact with fungus from the wild. NEVER eat any wild fungus, even one that looks familiar. Fungi that closely resemble edible mushrooms can in fact be highly toxic. Treat lichens the same way. Though some are edible, many are not. You should also wear gloves when handling the fungus.

Lichen Chart

Location of Lichen	Local Environment	Approx. Height	Approx. Width
① side of building 441 Main St.	close to major road and parking lot	9 cm	7 cm
② tree in Baldwin Park	far from roads (approx. ½ mile)	15 cm	9 cm

Step 3: Example of the lichen recording chart. GALE GROUP.

Troubleshooter's Guide

Here is a problem that may arise, a possible cause, and a way to remedy the problem.

Problem: No lichens can be found.

Possible cause: Some areas, particularly urban environments with high levels of air pollution, may not have any lichens. If you think this may be possible, check with your teacher before attempting this experiment.

horizontal length and greatest vertical length and record this data on your chart.

6. Select different sites that are more likely to show the effects of air pollution. Try to find lichens at different distances from highways, airports, or factories. Roadway intersections often produce increased pollution levels due to cars and trucks stopping and starting.

Summary of Results Examine your results and determine whether your hypothesis is correct. Did you find a consistent difference in the size (or presence) of lichens on trees closer to roads or parking lots? What other factors did you note that might be affecting lichen growth? Write a summary of your findings.

Change the Variables There are several ways you can vary this experiment. Try measuring the effect of changes on the lichen, such as treatment of sunlight and moisture, competition with other plants, or exposure to lichen-eating animals.

Design Your Own Experiment

How to Select a Topic Relating to this Concept Try growing lichen in a controlled environment. If you find lichen growing on an easily movable object, such as a piece of dead wood or a small rock, try carefully moving that rock into your classroom or laboratory. Remember that the lichen needs light and moisture. If you are able to transport lichen, you can design an experiment that will more accurately test the effects of different air qualities on the lichen.

Check the Further Readings section and talk with your science teacher or school or community media specialist to start gathering information on annual growth or lichen questions that interest you.

Steps in the Scientific Method To do an original experiment, you need to plan carefully and think things through. Otherwise, you might not be sure what question you are answering, what you are or should be measuring, or what your findings prove or disprove.

Here are the steps in designing an experiment:

- State the purpose of—and the underlying question behind—the experiment you propose to do.

- Recognize the variables involved, and select one that will help you answer the question at hand.
- State a testable hypothesis, an educated guess about the answer to your question.
- Decide how to change the variable you selected.
- Decide how to measure your results.

Recording Data and Summarizing the Results In the experiments included here and in any experiments you develop, you can try to display your data in more accurate and interesting ways. Collecting samples of the lichen you measure for your experiment will make the results more interesting to viewers. Photographs of the lichen you find can be helpful, but you may discover that careful sketches can reproduce details that are not clear in photographs.

Related Projects Projects and experiments in annual growth can reveal much about our environment that usually occurs too slowly for us to notice. Some fascinating experiments can be conducted over longer periods of time if you establish a structure for other students to follow later on. Talk with your teacher and classmates about starting a project to monitor long-term tree or lichen growth in your area. Take measurements of the circumference of the tree trunks near your school and record your data for comparison next year. Look for sources of information on tree growth in the past. Old photographs cannot provide exact measurements, but they can show roughly how much a tree has changed over a period of years or even decades.

For More Information

Arbor Day Foundation. *Fantastic Arborday.org Tree Guide.* http://www.arborday.org/trees/treeguide (accessed on January 19, 2008). Information about classification of trees.

Menninger, Edward. *Fantastic Trees.* Portland, OR: Timber Press, 1995. A fun and fascinating look at strange and little-known facts about trees.

Oregon State University. *Fantastic Lichenland.* http://ocid.nacse.org/lichenland (accessed on January 19, 2008). Information about types of lichen.

Platt, Rutherford. *1001 Questions Answered About Trees.* New York: Dover Publishing, 1992. A question-and-answer format book covering practically everything about trees.

Pollick, Steve. *Find Out Everything About Plants.* London: BBC Publishing, 1996. Contains a number of interesting and clearly illustrated project ideas on plant- and growth-related topics.

7

Bacteria

You cannot see them with the naked eye, but the world is teeming with bacteria. They live around you, inside of you, and are found in environments that would kill most every other life form. Bacteria are microbes, organisms that are so small they can only been seen with a microscope. They are the simplest, most abundant, and oldest life form on Earth, having evolved roughly 3.5 billion years ago. That beats other life forms by a long shot including dinosaurs, which only arrived on the scene 250 million years ago, and humans, who appeared a mere 2 million years ago. Scoop up a teaspoon of soil and, if you could see them, you would count about a billion bacteria.

While bacteria often make headline news as the cause of disease, the vast majority are either harmless or helpful to humans. Many bacteria live in the soil and decompose dead plants and animals. This process returns needed nutrients back into the environment, which plants and animals then use to live and grow. Other bacteria change the nitrogen gas from the air into a form of nitrogen that plants needs to survive. For humans, they are used to produce foods, such as yogurt and cheese. Humans and some animals depend on bacteria in their digestive tract to break down the plants they eat so they can process the food. Bacteria are an integral part to all life on Earth.

Wretched beasties The discovery that bacteria exist is one of the major breakthroughs in science. It began with the development of the microscope. In the late 1600s Dutch merchant and amateur scientist Antony van Leeuwenhoek (1632–1723) had built microscopes that magnified objects up to 200 times their size. While he was examining water droplets and the white matter on teeth he noted the existence of these "wretched beasties" wriggling about. Although he did not know it, this was the first recorded sighting of bacteria.

Two hundred years later researchers connected these tiny microbes to some of the deadly diseases that were sweeping through the world and killing hundreds of millions of people. For thousands of years, people did not

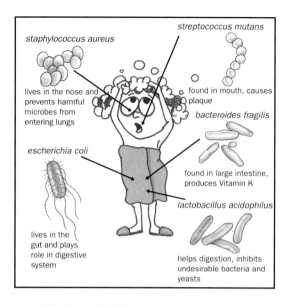

staphylococcus aureus

lives in the nose and prevents harmful microbes from entering lungs

streptococcus mutans

found in mouth, causes plaque

bacteroides fragilis

found in large intestine, produces Vitamin K

escherichia coli

lives in the gut and plays role in digestive system

lactobacillus acidophilus

helps digestion, inhibits undesirable bacteria and yeasts

The human body houses trillions of bacteria. Bacteria can cause disease if they get out of control, yet many help humans stay healthy. GALE GROUP.

Cell structure of the typical bacterium. GALE GROUP.

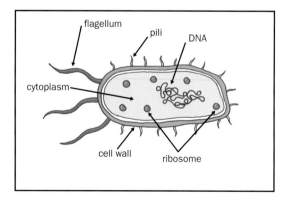

flagellum

pili

DNA

cytoplasm

cell wall

ribosome

understand the cause of disease; they often blamed a disease on evil spirits or as a punishment to the victim.

Then in the 1860s scientists Louis Pasteur (1822–1895) and Robert Koch (1843–1910) conducted a series of experiments that showed microbes could cause disease. They called their evidence the germ theory of disease. Pasteur discovered bacteria could cause food to spoil and he developed a method to destroy these bacteria, now called pasteurization. Koch isolated the individual bacteria that caused the deadly diseases anthrax, tuberculosis, and cholera. Understanding that microbes acted upon other life forms opened the door to an entirely new field of research. Scientists learned how to destroy and protect against these microbes, saving millions of lives.

What they look like There are thousands of species of bacteria, yet all share some basic features. Bacteria are single-celled organisms and fall into a category of life called prokaryotes. Prokaryotes do not have certain specialized structures in their cells and they do not have a cell nucleus, which humans have. A nucleus is a cellular compartment inside cells that surrounds DNA and other organelles. An organelle is an enclosed structure in a cell that performs a specific function, much like the role of an organ in the body.

What the typical bacteria does have is a fluid called cytoplasm inside its cell. Cytoplasm is a gooey, gel-like substance that holds everything and helps move materials around inside the cell. All the genetic information is contained in the deoxyribose nucleic acid (DNA) molecule. The DNA in bacteria sits loosely in the cytoplasm. Also located in the cytoplasm are the ribosomes. Ribosomes play a key role in translating the information from DNA into proteins.

The cytoplasm is surrounded by a simple cell membrane, which has a variety of functions, including bringing nutrients and chemicals into the cells. The cell membrane is enclosed by a rigid cell wall that provides the overall shape. Bacteria come in three basic shapes. There are bacteria shaped like rods, those that are spherical or round, and those that are helical or spiral.

Some bacteria have whiplike structures called flagella that they use to move forward. Some also have small hairlike projections from the cell surface called pili. Pili help the cell stick to surfaces or to each other.

The typical bacteria range in size from 1 to 5 micrometers (μm). One micrometer equals one millionth of a meter. Scientists use micrometers as the unit of measurement because bacteria are too small to be measured in inches or millimeters. A large clump of bacteria growing together is called a colony. A colony can have millions of individual bacteria and is visible to the naked eye.

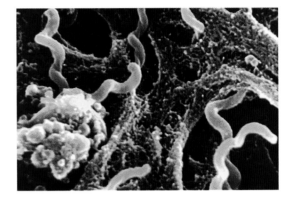

Closeup of the Leptospira *bacteria.* CUSTOM MEDICAL STOCK PHOTO

Living and eating Bacteria have survived on Earth for billions of years because they are able to adapt relatively quickly to changing environments. One of the ways they adapt is by having a speedy reproduction rate. Bacteria usually reproduce by simply dividing into two cells. All the genetic information, the DNA, is passed along to each of the cells. Sometimes bacteria reproduce sexually: one bacterium transferring part of its DNA to another bacterium. This allows bacteria to quickly create or pass along new traits that help them adapt to different environments.

Given ideal conditions, bacteria can reproduce about every twenty minutes. That means one bacterium could multiply to more than five billion in about ten hours. If all bacteria really were to reproduce this quickly, the world would soon be overtaken with these microorganisms. Luckily, in the real world, conditions are never ideal. Once there are too many bacteria in one place their food runs out, they crowd each other, and eventually they start dying.

Bacteria have a wide range of diets and living conditions. Some bacteria eat other organisms. Many of these feed off dead organisms, the waste of other organisms, or get their food from living in or on other organisms. Many of these bacteria depend on such foods as sugars, proteins, and vitamins. The bacteria in the human gut, for example, get their food from digested food. Other bacteria make their own food either from sunlight, like

Bacteria come in three basic shapes: rod, spherical or round, and spiral. GALE GROUP.

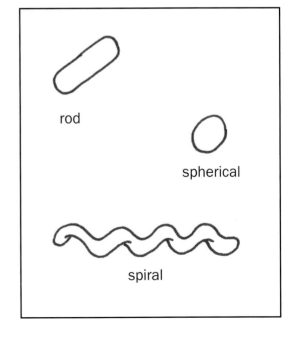

rod

spherical

spiral

Bacteria that live in extreme habitats, such as the boiling hot geysers at Yellowstone National Park, are called extremophiles.
© PAT O'HARA/CORBIS.

plants, or from different chemicals in their environment. The chemicals these bacteria use for foods are often unusual, such as iron and sulfur.

Scientists have found bacteria in practically every known locale and environment. Until the late 1960s, it was thought that no organism could survive in certain extreme environments, meaning environments that would kill other creatures such as humans. Then a researcher discovered there were bacteria living in the hot springs of Yellowstone National Park, which reached temperatures over 158°F (70°C). The bacteria that live in these extreme habitats are called extremophiles. Since that time scientists have discovered an increasing number of extremophiles. There are extremophiles that live in sub-freezing temperatures under sheets of ice; thrive in highly acidic environments; and withstand blasts of radiation thousands of times greater than the level that would kill a human.

Extremophiles are of great interest to both industry and basic research. Researchers are interested in how these organisms survive. NASA is conducting experiments on extremophiles to investigate survival in outer space. The biotechnology industry uses extremophiles to manufacture items, such as detergents, diagnostics, and food products.

Building up resistance While most bacteria are harmless or helpful to humans, there are a number of bacteria that do cause disease. Lyme

WORDS TO KNOW

Antibiotic: A substance derived from certain fungi, bacteria, and other organisms that can destroy or inhibit the growth of other microorganisms; widely used in the prevention and treatment of infectious diseases.

Antibiotic resistance: The ability of microorganisms to change so that they are not killed by antibiotics.

Bacteria: Single-celled microorganisms found in soil, water, plants, and animals that play a key role in the decay of organic matter and the cycling of nutrients. Some are agents of disease. (Singular: bacterium.)

Colony: A visible growth of microorganisms, containing millions of bacterial cells.

Control experiment: A setup that is identical to the experiment, but is not affected by the variable that acts on the experimental group.

Cytoplasm: The semifluid substance inside a cell that surrounds the nucleus and other membrane-enclosed organelles.

Deoxyribonucleic acid (DNA): Large, complex molecules found in the nuclei of cells that carry genetic information for an organism's development.

Extremophiles: Bacteria that thrive in environments too harsh to support most life forms.

Flagella: Whiplike structures used by some organisms for movement. (Singular: flagellum.)

Germ theory of disease: The theory that disease is caused by microorganisms or germs, and not by spontaneous generation.

Hypothesis: An idea in the form of a statement that can be tested by observation and/or experiment.

Nucleus, cell: Membrane-enclosed structure within a cell that contains the cell's genetic material and controls its growth and reproduction. (Plural: nuclei.)

Organelle: A membrane-enclosed structure that performs a specific function within a cell.

Pili: Short projections that assist bacteria in attaching to tissues.

Prokaryote: A cell without a true nucleus, such as a bacterium.

Ribosome: A protein composed of two subunits that functions in protein synthesis (creation).

Variable: Something that can affect the results of an experiment.

---

disease, anthrax, tuberculosis, and salmonellosis are examples of diseases caused by bacteria. Many bacterial diseases are deadly without treatment and can cause widespread infections.

Antibiotics are substances that harm or kill bacteria. Erythromycin and penicillin are examples of commonly used antibiotics. Discovered in the 1920s, these substances are produced naturally by a variety of organisms, such as bacteria themselves and fungi. The production and use of antibiotics has dramatically reduced the number of deaths and illnesses from bacterial disease.

What Are the Variables?

Variables are anything that might affect the results of an experiment. Here are the main variables in this experiment:

- the size of the paper disks
- the growth substance
- the temperature of the bacteria's environment
- the substance placed on the bacteria
- the type of bacteria

In other words, the variables in this experiment are everything that might affect the zone of inhibition. If you change more than one variable at a time, you will not be able to tell which variable impacted bacterial growth.

In the modern day, people are facing the growing public-health problem of antibiotic resistance. This is when disease-causing bacteria have become resistant to an antibiotic, thereby lessening the effectiveness of the drug. Resistance can occur when a single bacterium acquires the genetic ability to resist, or block, the antibiotic. This one bacterium will rapidly reproduce and produce an antibiotic-resistant population. An overexposure to an antibiotic is one way bacteria can acquire resistance. The antibiotic will kill the weak bacteria and allow the stronger, resistant ones to survive. Patients who are prescribed antibiotics but do not take the full dosage can also contribute to resistance. If all the bacteria are not killed, the strong, resistant bacteria that live can pass on resistance to the next generation.

EXPERIMENT 1

Bacterial Growth: How do certain substances inhibit or promote bacterial growth?

Purpose/Hypothesis There are many kinds of bacteria, but a great many of the bacteria that you encounter daily share similar growth requirements.

In this experiment you will investigate substances that affect the growth of common household bacteria. You will collect a sample of bacteria from one of numerous possible sources. You can use your imagination on where to collect the bacteria. Because bacteria need moisture to live, possible sources include the base of a faucet, on someone's hands, inside someone's cheek, or on a bathroom doorknob. You will then streak the bacteria on a growth substance. Bacteria grow well on a substance called agar. Nutrient agar is a jellylike substance that contains food for the bacteria. You can order prepared nutrient agar in a petri dish.

You will use paper disks to place the substances on a section of the bacteria. You can use the suggested liquids or select different ones. Saturate each paper disk with the item to be tested, and place the disk on the bacteria. After giving the bacteria time to grow, you will measure the diameter of the clear area around the paper disk where the bacteria did not grow. This area is called the zone of inhibition. If there is a large zone of inhibition, the substance inhibits bacteria growth. If there is no clear zone of inhibition, the substance does not inhibit bacterial growth. If there is a larger amount of bacteria around and under the disk than when you started, the substance promotes growth.

In this experiment, you will be using more than one type of bacteria. Different types of bacteria often live together. When you collect your sample, you will probably gather more than one type. The experiment will still be valid because bacteria that grow together naturally usually do so because they respond the same way to their environment—something that promotes growth for one of them will be good for all of them, and something that inhibits growth for one will be bad for all.

Before you begin, make an educated guess about the outcome of this experiment based on your knowledge of bacteria. This educated guess, or prediction, is your hypothesis. A hypothesis should explain these things:

- the topic of the experiment
- the variable you will change
- the variable you will measure
- what you expect to happen

A hypothesis should be brief, specific, and measurable. It must be something you can test through further investigation. Your experiment will prove or disprove whether your hypothesis is correct. Here is one possible hypothesis for this experiment: "The acidic and cleaning substances will inhibit bacterial growth; the protein and sugary substances will promote bacterial growth."

In this case, the variable you will change is the substance you place on the bacteria. The variable you will measure is the distance from the disk to the bacterial growth.

Conducting a control experiment will help you isolate each variable and measure the changes in the dependent variable. Only one variable will change between the control and the experimental bacterial growth. The control experiment will have no substance on the paper disk. At the end of the experiment, you will compare the growth of the control bacteria with the experimental bacteria.

How to Experiment Safely

When working with bacteria, you should consider the bacteria capable of causing disease and follow the appropriate safety procedures. Handle the cultures carefully. If there is a spill, wipe up the material using a disinfectant-soaked paper towel, then throw the towel away immediately. Throw away or sterilize all items that touch the bacteria.

Always wash your hands after using live materials. Thoroughly wipe your working area with a disinfectant cleansing agent after you have finished with the setup. Keep your plate closed and store it in a safe area that will not be disturbed. Keep younger children away from the experiment area.

Be careful when working with the hot water.

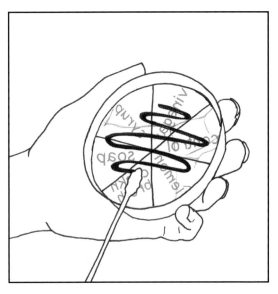

Step 5: Spread the bacteria over the entire plate. GALE GROUP.

Step 11: Lift the petri lid just high enough to place the paper disk into its marked section.
GALE GROUP.

Level of Difficulty Medium to Difficult.

Materials Needed

- rubbing alcohol
- small cup
- tweezers
- paper hole puncher
- white nonglossy paper
- cotton swab
- nutrient agar plates* (available from a biological supply company)
- bacteria source
- test substances: chicken broth (can be made from bouillon), coffee, lemon juice, syrup, vinegar, liquid soap
- distilled water
- 5 small cups or plates
- marking pen
- filter paper
- ruler, with millimeters
- magnifying glass (optional)
- microscope (optional)

Depending on how many bacteria experiments you plan to conduct, you may consider less expensive options than that of purchasing ready-made nutrient agar plates. You can order the nutrient agar and plates separately and pour the agar into the plates yourself. You can also order nutrient agar that needs to be made. This process may take some practice so allow yourself extra time. There are also recipes for agar using common household items. Gelatin is also an alternative for nutrient agar. Look on the Internet for these recipes or ask your science teacher. Allow extra time for this process, as you may have to experiment with what recipe best promotes bacterial growth.

Approximate Budget3 $25.

Timetable One hour setup and followup; two days waiting.

Step-by-Step Instructions

1. Turn the covered petri dish upside down. Use the marker to divide the dish into six even sections, like a pie. On each section write the name of one of the five substances. Write "Control" on the sixth section.

2. Write the date on the side of the dish.

3. Dip a cotton swab in distilled water.

4. Run the swab over the source of bacteria.

5. Spread the bacteria over the entire plate. Hold the swab flat or at a slight angle so as not to puncture the agar.

6. Cover the plate and throw the swab away.

7. Use a hole puncher to make at least five paper disks.

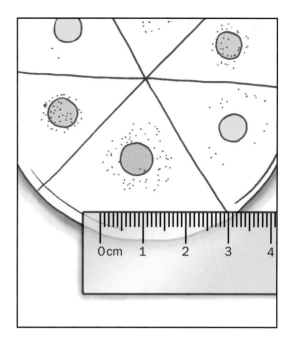

Step 19: Measure the diameter of the zone of inhibition, in millimeters, from the left edge of the clear area to the right edge. GALE GROUP.

8. Sterilize the tweezers: Pour rubbing alcohol into a small cup to cover the bottom. Hold or place the end of the tweezers into the alcohol and wait at least one minute. Rinse in water and shake any excess off the tweezers.

9. Pour several drops of each of the substances you are to test into its own cup or small plate.

10. Pick up a paper disk with the tweezers and dip it into one of the liquids. The disk should be wet but not dripping.

11. Lift the petri lid just high enough to place the paper disk into the middle of its marked section.

12. Hold the tweezers under running water for at least five seconds to clean.

13. Continue wetting each paper disk in the liquid, and placing the disk in its allotted section. Rinse the tweezers in hot water between each paper disk.

14. With clean tweezers, put a plain paper disk in the Control section.

15. Invert or turn the plate upside down. (Condensation may collect on the top lid. Turning the plates upside down prevents the condensation from falling on the bacteria and allows a clear view of growth.)

16. Store the plate in a warm, nonbright area for 24 hours.

Troubleshooter's Guide

Below are some problems that may arise during this experiment, some possible causes, and some ways to remedy the problems.

Problem: Bacteria grew in some areas of the plate but not in others.

Possible cause: You may not have streaked the entire plate with the bacteria. Repeat the experiment, spreading the bacteria around so that the entire plate is covered with the microorganism.

Problem: There was no growth.

Possible cause: You may have stored the plate in an environment that harmed the bacteria or caused it not to grow, such as if it was too cold. Repeat the experiment, storing the plate in a warm environment.

Possible cause: You may not have picked up enough bacteria on the swab. Make sure the cotton swab is wet and repeat the experiment, using the same or a different source for the bacteria.

Problem: My results were not as expected.

Possible cause: You may not have rinsed off the tweezers thoroughly after touching each paper disk, mixing together some of the substances on a disk. Repeat the experiment, making sure to rinse the tweezers in the hot water after each disk is complete.

17. Check the plate for growth. If there is little to no growth, wait another 24 hours.
18. Observe each section for zones of inhibition, the clear area around the disk in which bacteria have not grown.
19. Measure the diameter of the zone of inhibition, in millimeters, from the left edge of the clear area to the right edge. Repeat this step for all 6 substances.
20. Record the measurements in a data chart. Note also if there is no zone of inhibition, or if there is increased growth compared to that of the Control.
21. When you have completed the summary, throw away the agar plate.

Summary of Results Create a graph illustrating the data chart. Make sure you label the graph carefully. Can you tell if the bacteria grew more in certain substances than in others? What substances inhibited bacterial growth the greatest amount? Were there any substances that promoted bacterial growth?

Compare each substance to the control experiment. Examine the differences between the growth in the Control section and growth in any substances that were not inhibited by the substance. Analyze the main ingredient in each of your substances that may have inhibited or promoted growth,

Change the Variables You can vary this experiment in several ways:

- Change the substance on the paper disks
- Use one substance and change the concentration of that substance
- Alter the growing temperature of the bacteria
- Isolate one type of bacteria before you begin the experiment (the easiest way is to purchase a single type of bacteria from a biological supply company; you could also streak a bacteria mix onto an agar

plate to thin out the population until a bacteria of one color and shape grow).

- Grow the bacteria under different lighting conditions

EXPERIMENT 2

Bacterial Resistance: Can bacteria gain resistance to a substance after exposure?

Purpose/Hypothesis Antibiotic resistance is a growing health problem around the world. In this experiment, you will explore bacterial resistance by experimenting with bacteria and antibacterial soap.

Ever since the mid 1990s, soap manufacturers have put antibacterial agents in their products, such as body washes, toothpaste, and hand soaps. The number of antibacterial soaps has increased over the years. In modern day, the majority of soaps carry some antibacterial agent. Researchers have theorized that bacteria may develop a resistance to antibacterial agents over time. If the bacteria develop a resistance to the agent, the agent will no longer be effective in slowing down their growth or killing them.

In this experiment, you will collect a sample of bacteria and spread it on a growth substance. Bacteria grow well on a substance called agar. Nutrient agar is a jellylike substance that contains food for the bacteria. You can order prepared nutrient agar in a petri dish. On top of the nutrient agar you will spread a low concentration of antibacterial soap. The bacteria that survive this concentration of soap will be introduced to a higher concentration of soap. You will continue this process for five growth cycles. After the last plate of bacteria has grown, you can compare the surviving bacteria with the bacteria that have had no exposure to antibacterial soap. You will measure the bacterial growth by counting the number of colonies.

The concentrations of soap provided in this experiments are guidelines. The type of soap you use and the bacteria you collect will influence how bacteria respond to the different concentrations. If you want to determine the concentration that would best suit your materials, read the Trouble-shooter's Guide before you begin.

What Are the Variables?

Variables are anything that might affect the results of an experiment. Here are the main variables in this experiment:

- the concentration of soap
- the type of bacteria
- the type of soap
- the environmental conditions of each plate

In other words, the variables in this experiment are everything that might affect the zone of inhibition. If you change more than one variable at a time, you will not be able to tell which variable impacted bacterial growth.

How to Experiment Safely

When working with bacteria, you should consider the bacteria capable of causing disease and follow the appropriate safety procedures. Handle the cultures carefully. If there is a spill, wipe up the material using a disinfectant-soaked paper towel, then throw the towel away immediately. Throw away or sterilize all items that touch the bacteria.

Always wash your hands after using live materials. Thoroughly wipe your working area with a disinfectant cleansing agent after you have finished with the setup. Keep your plate closed and store it in a safe area that will not be disturbed. Keep younger children away from the experiment area.

In this experiment, you will be using more than one type of bacteria. Different types of bacteria live together. When you gather a swab of bacteria you have gathered a number of different populations. To draw conclusions about a single type of bacteria, you can order one from a biological supply house.

Before you begin, make an educated guess about the outcome of this experiment based on your knowledge of bacteria and resistance. This educated guess, or prediction, is your hypothesis. A hypothesis should explain these things:

- the topic of the experiment
- the variable you will change
- the variable you will measure
- what you expect to happen

A hypothesis should be brief, specific, and measurable. It must be something you can test through further investigation. Your experiment will prove or disprove whether your hypothesis is correct. Here is one possible hypothesis for this experiment: "Bacteria that are exposed to an increasingly greater concentration of soap will survive a concentration that will kill unexposed bacteria."

In this case, the variable you will change is the concentration of the soap. The variable you will measure is the number of bacteria colonies that grow.

Conducting a control experiment will help you isolate each variable and measure the changes in the dependent variable. Only one variable will change between the control and the experimental bacterial growth. Each phase of this experiment will have a control. The control bacteria will grow on nutrient agar with no soap. At each phase of the experiment, you should compare the growth of the control bacteria with the experimental bacteria.

Level of Difficulty Difficult.

Materials Needed

- cotton swabs
- 6 (at least) nutrient agar plates* (available from a biological supply company)
- antibacterial liquid soap
- measuring cups

- measuring spoons
- 5 containers with covers
- stirring spoons
- marking pen
- magnifying glass (optional)
- microscope (optional)

*Depending on how many bacteria experiments you plan on conducting, you may consider less expensive options than that of purchasing ready-made nutrient agar plates. You can order the nutrient agar and plates separately and pour the agar into the plates yourself. You can also order nutrient agar that needs to be made. This process may take some practice so allow yourself extra time. There are also recipes for agar using common household items. Gelatin is also an alternative for nutrient agar. Look on the Internet for these recipes or ask your science teacher. Allow extra time for this process, as you may have to experiment with what recipe best promotes bacterial growth.

Approximate Budget $20.

Timetable One hour and 30 minutes working time; six days waiting time.

Step-by-Step Instructions

1. Turn the covered petri dish upside down and use a pen to divide the plate in half. Mark the left half ".0001%" and the right half "Control." Write the date on the side of the dish.
2. Make up the concentrations by first mixing a 1% concentration of soap water. Stir 1 teaspoon (5 milliliters) of liquid soap with 2 cups and 4 teaspoons (500 milliliters) of water. Mix thoroughly, cover, and label "1%."
3. To make a .1% concentration: Measure 1 teaspoon of the 1% solution and add to a clean container. Mix in 9 teaspoons of water. Mix thoroughly, cover, and label "1%."
4. To make a .01percent concentration: Measure 1 teaspoon of the .1% solution and add to another clean container. Mix in 9 teaspoons of water. Mix thoroughly, cover, and label ".01%."

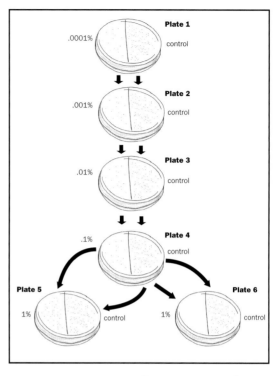

Experiment 2 setup. Plate progression: Bacteria exposed to soap move to increasingly higher concentrations; the control bacteria are never exposed to soap. GALE GROUP.

5. To make a .001% concentration: Measure 1 teaspoon of the .01% solution and add to another clean container. Mix in 9 teaspoons of water. Mix thoroughly, cover, and label ".001%."

6. To make a .0001% concentration: Measure 1 teaspoon of the .001% solution and add to another clean container. Mix in 9 teaspoons of water. Mix thoroughly, cover, and label ".0001%."

7. Use a fresh cotton swab to spread the .0001% solution over the agar that is marked ".0001%." Keep the swab flat or at a slight angle so as not to puncture the agar.

8. Dip a cotton swab in distilled water.

9. Run the swab over a source of bacteria and spread the bacteria over the agar in the soap half of the dish.

10. Get a new cotton swab. Use the same source of bacteria and spread the bacteria over the Control half of the dish.

11. Place the lid on Plate 1 and turn it upside down. Store it in a warm temperature for 24 hours. (If there is little to no growth on both the Control and soap sides, let sit another 24 hours.)

12. Repeat Step 1 with Plate 2, marking the left half ".001%."

13. With a fresh cotton swab, collect bacteria from the soap water side of Plate 1 and spread it on the half of the agar marked ".001%" in Plate 2.

14. Use a fresh cotton swab to collect bacteria from the Control side of Plate 1 and spread it on the half of the agar marked Control in Plate 2. Throw Plate 1 away. Place the lid on Plate 2 and turn it upside down. Store in a warm temperature for 24 hours.

15. Repeat this process for the .01% (Plate 3) and .1% (Plate 4), waiting 24 hours or longer between new plates.

16. Have ready Plate 5 and Plate 6. After dividing the plates, mark the left-hand side of both plates "1%."

17. Use a cotton swab to collect bacteria from the .1% side of Plate 4 and spread it on the 1% half of Plate 5.

18. With a new swab, collect some of the Control bacteria from Plate 4 and spread it on the Control on Plate 5, the Control for Plate 6, and the 1% on Plate 6. This bacteria has had no exposure to any soap.

19. Place lids on Plates 5 and 6 and turn them upside down. Store in a warm temperature for 24 hours.

20. Count the colonies on the 1% solution on both Plate 5 and Plate 6.

Summary of Results Examine your data. How do the bacterial growths on Plates 5 and 6 compare with each other? Was your hypothesis correct? Write a description of the bacteria on both plates. If you have a magnifying glass or microscope you could take a closeup look at the bacteria. What was the main difference between the bacteria spread on both plates? Write a summary of the experiment that explains each step in the process and the reason for it.

Change the Variables There are several variables you can change in this experiment to provide new data:

- Change the brand or type of soap, to a nonantibacterial soap, for instance, or to an antibacterial soap that has a different main ingredient
- Use a cleansing agent instead of soap
- Alter the growing temperature of the bacteria
- Use one type of bacteria by isolating one type before you begin the experiment (the easiest way is to purchase a single type of bacteria from a biological supply company; you could also streak a bacteria mix onto an agar plate to thin out the population until a bacteria of one color and shape grow)
- Use a mixture of different bacteria by collecting it from another source

Troubleshooter's Guide

Below are some problems that may arise during this experiment, some possible causes, and some ways to remedy the problems.

Problem: There was no difference in the amount of growth between the bacteria on Plates 5 and 6.

Possible cause: The soap that you used may need a higher concentration than 1% to inhibit bacterial growth. Spread varying concentrations of the soap on nutrient agar plates and grow bacteria on each concentration. When you have determined the concentration that kills most of the bacteria, use that figure as the end concentration that will go on Plates 5 and 6. Dilute that concentration one thousand fold and repeat the experiment, increasing the concentration by tenfold each growth period.

Problem: At one point there was no growth on a plate.

Possible cause: You may have stored the plate in an environment that harmed the bacteria or caused it not to grow, such as if it was too cold. Continue the experiment at the last plate with growth, storing the plate in a warm environment.

Modify the Experiment This experiment requires numerous steps and careful measuring. For a simpler variation that also explores antibacterial soaps and bacteria you can compare how antibacterial and non-antibacterial soaps affect bacteria. Make a hypothesis on whether antibacterial soap will get rid of the amount of bacteria more, less, or the same as the non-antibacterial counterpart.

You will need an antibiotic and non-antibiotic soap that are the same brand and type (such as liquid or a bar), cotton swabs, and three nutrient agar plates (or other growth medium). You can use your fingers for a source of bacteria so find a time right before your hands are ready to be washed. Gently rub a cotton swab down the side of one finger and spread the swab over the agar in a plate labeled "Control." Wash one of your fingers with bacterial soap, rinse and allow your finger to dry. Make sure you don't rub your finger against your clothes or other item where bacteria may live. Rub a swab along your finger and spread this swab over the agar in a plate labeled "Antibacterial." Wash a third finger with non-antibacterial, plain soap. Rinse, dry, swab, and spread the swab to a "Plain Soap" agar plate. Cover and place all three plates in a warm area.

After several days examine the three plates for bacteria. How does the control compare to the soap plates? If there is no growth on the control, your fingers may have been too clean! Do the two plates from the different soaps contain about the same amount of bacteria? Was your hypothesis correct? Consider when using antibacterial soap might or might not be a good idea. You may want to allow the plates to sit for several more days to observe bacteria growth.

Design Your Own Experiment

How to Select a Topic Relating to this Concept There are thousands of species of bacteria living and growing around you, in you, and on you. For a project, you could examine the differences among different types of bacteria. You could also examine bacteria's growth requirements, or how bacteria have impacted life on Earth.

Check the Further Readings section and talk with your biology teacher to learn more about bacteria. You could also try to get access to a microscope so that you can look at the bacteria in more detail.

Steps in the Scientific Method To conduct an original experiment, you need to plan carefully and think things through. Otherwise, you might not be sure what question you are answering, what you are or should be measuring, or what your findings prove or disprove.

Here are the steps in designing an experiment:

- State the purpose of—and the underlying question behind—the experiment you propose to do.

- Recognize the variables involved and select one that will help you answer the question at hand.

- State your hypothesis, an educated guess about the answer to your question.

- Decide how to change the variable you selected.

- Decide how to measure your results.

Recording Data and Summarizing the Results In any experiment you conduct, you should look for ways to clearly convey your data. You can do this by including charts and graphs for the experiments. They should be clearly labeled and easy to read. You may also want to include photographs and drawings of your experimental setup and results, which will help others visualize the steps in the experiment. You might decide to conduct an experiment that lasts several months. In this case, include pictures or drawings of the results taken at regular intervals.

A decomposing house plant is a common example of bacteria at work. Many bacteria live in soil and decompose dead plants, returning needed nutrients back into the environment.
© KELLY A. QUIN.

If you are preparing an exhibit, you may want to display your results, such as any experimental setup you designed. If you have completed a nonexperimental project, explain clearly what your research question was and illustrate your findings.

Related Projects Bacteria are in and around people every day, opening the door to many projects that are interesting and inexpensive. You could experiment with different growth mediums, making your own or adding variables to one medium. You could explore bacteria's role in the life cycle, conducting a project with plants and bacteria. You could look at how different plants use bacteria. Other bacteria roles you could look at are in the soil and natural water sources. People and animals also house thousands of different bacteria. You could try to isolate some types of bacteria and determine their role and growing requirements.

You can also examine people's use of bacteria. Foods make use of these microorganisms' natural role. You could also examine how bacteria cause foods to spoil. Bacteria are the key to making cheeses. Yogurt and buttermilk are made from the bacteria in milk. You could experiment with using bacteria to grow yogurt. In biotechnology, people use bacteria to produce medicines, improve cleaning products, and make proteins. You could conduct a research project on how extremophiles and other more common types of bacteria are used.

For More Information

American Museum of Natural History. "The Microbe Size-O-Meter." *Meet the Microbes!* http://www.amnh.org/nationalcenter/infection/01_mic/01d_size01. html (accessed on March 2, 2008). A look at the sizes of bacteria relative to familiar objects.

American Society of Microbiologists. *Meet the Microbes.* http://www. microbeworld.org/microbes (accessed on March 2, 2008). Clear information on bacteria and other microorganisms, and the people who study them.

"The Germ Theory of Disease." *Timeline Science.* http://www. timelinescience.org/resource/students/pencilin/pencilin.htm (accessed on March 2, 2008). A brief history of the many people and events that led to understand microorganisms and disease.

"Microbiology." *Cells alive!* http://www.cellsalive.com/toc_micro.htm (accessed on March 2, 2008). Interactive animations, articles, and real-time bacteria growing.

U.S. Food and Drug Administration. "The Bad Bug Book: Foodborne Pathogenic Microorganisms and Natural Toxins Handbook." *Center for Food Safety & Applied Nutrition.* http://vm.cfsan.fda.gov/~mow/intro.html (accessed on March 2, 2008). Detailed information on microbes that can contaminate food and cause diseases.

8

Biomes

If you have ever hiked in a forest or driven through a desert, what you saw was a biome. Biomes are large geographical areas with specific climates and soils, as well as distinct plant and animal communities that are all interdependent.

Most biomes are on land. Our oceans make up a single biome. Besides temperate forest and desert, the major land biomes include tundra, taiga (pronounced TIE-gah), temperate deciduous (pronounced deh-SID-you-us) forest, tropical rainforest, and grassland. To understand how biomes work, let us look at some of them.

Into the woods Maybe you have hiked in a taiga biome, the biome that receives the most snow. Unlike its neighboring biome, the tundra, which is treeless and characterized by low-lying plants, the taiga is sometimes called the boreal (pronounced BORE-e-al) coniferous (pronounced CONE-if-er-us) forest and is probably the largest of all the land biomes. The taiga biome extends across the northern parts of North America, Asia, and Europe. It is dominated by coniferous, or cone-bearing, trees such as pine, spruce, larch, and fir. These trees resist cold, which is a good thing, because temperatures have been recorded as low as–90°F (–67°C) and reach an average of only 59°F (15°C). The tree roots do not penetrate deeply and tend to interconnect with other tree roots around them. Each tree is basically held down by its neighbors on all sides.

Trees in the taiga biome survive in soil that is frozen for most of the year. Soil moisture comes from melted snow and summer rains, but during the winter, the cold temperatures make water absorption difficult because the ground is frozen. So these trees have built-in adapters to help them survive. For example, spruce and fir trees have long, thin, wax-covered needles. The waxy surface acts as an insulator, helping them retain water and heat. Snow slides off more easily, avoiding branch breakage. These needles conduct photosynthesis so efficiently that they can make food even during winter, when the Sun's rays are weaker.

Pine, spruce, and fir trees form part of the taiga biome. PHOTO RESEARCHERS INC.

Trees are not the only inhabitants of this biome. About 50 species of insects, including mites, live here. Moose, snowshoe hares, deer, and elk make their home in the taiga as well as wolves, porcupines, lynxes, and martens, who roam the taiga during the summer. Seeds from the cones of the trees are food for red squirrels and for birds such as crossbills and siskins.

Life in the desert—with air conditioning

If you drive through a desert, do you see much life from your car window? Do not be fooled. There is more living here than just cactus plants. Desert biomes are on every major continent and cover more than a fifth of Earth's surface. While these biomes receive less than 10 inches (25 centimeters) of rainfall a year, with temperatures that range from 75°F (23°C) to 91°F (32°C), desert plants and animals thrive here. Deserts can usually be found in the centers of continents and in the rain shadows of mountains.

Lizards, snakes, and other animals pop up at sundown when the soil is cool, then wriggle back into their habitats when the temperature becomes too chilly. They can reappear again at dawn, remaining until the temperature gets too hot. Some of the rodents and other animals that burrow under the soil actually enjoy a kind of underground air-conditioning. They form elaborate tunnels where the Sun's heat cannot penetrate. And moisture from the animals' exhaled breath cools the air and makes their burrows a

Low-growing bushes in Monument Valley are part of this biome's vegetation. PHOTO RESEARCHERS INC.

comfortable 85°F (29°C). Kangaroo rats in the American Southwest and the gerbils of North African and Asiatic deserts choose foods that reduce the amount of water needed for digestion. These rodents can actually absorb water from their urine before excreting wastes.

Many desert plants are xerophytes (pronounced ZERO-fights), plants that require little water to survive. There are also ephemerals (pronounced eh-FEM-er-als), plants that can suspend their life processes for years when the soil becomes too dry. When major rainstorms occur, they burst into life. Succulents are another type of plant. They retain water in thick fleshy tissues. Birds use the giant saguaro (pronounced sah-GWA-ro; from the Spanish word for the Pima Native American name of this plant) cactus, a succulent plant that grows 50 feet (15 m) high, as nesting and resting areas in place of trees.

The saguaro cactus is a good example of the interdependence that takes place in a biome. Red-tailed hawks use the branches to nest. Hollowed-out trunk and arm spaces are a home for elf owls and gila woodpeckers. The cactus fruits are eaten by rodents, birds, and bats.

Why save the rainforests? Many people are concerned about saving rainforests because these biomes contain a large number of unique plants. Several acres of rainforest in Borneo may contain 700 different species of trees. More than 50,000 plant species make their home in the rainforests of the Amazon Basin in South America. Up to 80 different species of plant life might grow on one tree. Tropical rainforests are found only in regions north of the

Heat and humidity helped form this lush Costa Rican rainforest.
PHOTO RESEARCHERS INC.

WORDS TO KNOW

Biomes: Large geographical areas with specific climates and soils, as well as distinct plant and animal communities that are interdependent.

Boreal: Northern.

Coniferous: Refers to trees, such as pines and firs, that bear cones and have needle-like leaves that are not shed all at once.

Deciduous: Plants that lose their leaves during some season of the year, and then grow them back during another season.

Desert: A biome with a hot-to-cool climate and dry weather.

Desertification: Transformation of arid or semiarid productive land into desert.

Ecosystem: An ecological community, including plants, animals and microorganisms, considered together with their enviroment.

Ephemerals: Plants that lie dormant in dry soil for years until major rainstorms occur.

Fungus (fungi): Various single-celled or multicellular organisms, including mushrooms, molds, yeasts, and mildews, that do not contain chlorophyll.

Hypothesis: An idea in the form of a statement that can be tested by observation and/or experiment.

Succulent: Plants that live in dry environments and have water storage tissue.

Taiga: A large land biome mostly dominated by coniferous trees.

Temperate: Mild or moderate weather conditions.

Tundra: A treeless, frozen biome with low-lying plants.

Variable: Something that can affect the results of an experiment.

Xerophytes: Plants that require little water to survive.

equator on the Tropic of Cancer and south of the equator in the Tropic of Capricorn. Destroying the rainforests reduces the diversity of life on Earth.

If you have ever been in a steamy greenhouse, then you can imagine what a rainforest is like. Warm temperatures average 75°F (23°C) and humidity peaks at a dripping 90% for days at a time. This climate encourages an explosion of plant life that supports many different animals. Some scientists estimate that half the living species on Earth live in the rainforests.

Constructing your own mini-biome will help you understand some of the major factors that influence these important areas of life and can cause them to survive or fail.

Materials for Project 1. GALE GROUP.

PROJECT 1

Building a Temperate Forest Biome

Purpose/Hypothesis Biomes are strongly influenced by the climate and soil type in a particular region. These same factors determine the success of a mini-biome model. In this project, you will attempt to build, grow, and maintain a temperate forest biome. This particular biome is characterized by a temperature range of 32 to 68°F (0 to 20°C). It has an annual precipitation of 20 to 95 inches (50 to 240 cm) and a fairly deep soil layer. The purpose of this project is to try to maintain the correct climate, soil, and vegetation in the temperate forest biome.

Level of Difficulty Moderate. (This project requires continuous tending and attention to maintain a proper climate.)

Materials Needed

- 10-gallon fish tank (plastic, if possible, for safety)
- indoor/outdoor thermometer
- watering container
- gravel
- sand
- topsoil
- incandescent light fixture with a 40-watt bulb (optional)
- plants and/or seeds (choose oak, maple, sassafras, hickory, tulip trees, sweet gum, dogwood)

Note: Choose all deciduous trees. Seeds may be hard to grow unless they have been chilled. If you use trees, they should be very small saplings.

Approximate Budget $25. (Try to use an old fish tank if possible.)

Timetable One hour to set up the project and at least six months to maintain the trees and observe changes.

Maple and oak leaves, examples of deciduous trees. GALE GROUP.

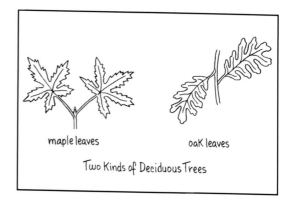

maple leaves   oak leaves

Two Kinds of Deciduous Trees

Troubleshooter's Guide

When you are building a natural environment, many forces of nature can affect the experiment. These include fungus, insects, and too much or too little water. Here are some common problems and a few tips to maintain the best environment.

- Mushrooms, a kind of fungus, may grow. Water less, but never allow the soil to dry completely.

- Pests such as insects and spiders may make this biome their home. If they are eating the plants, remove the pests. If not, keep them. They are performing their natural role in the ecosystem. Their presence is a sign of a healthy biome.

- Drastic temperature changes overnight can kill the plants. Do your best to maintain an acceptable climate in the fish tank. You may have to move it inside or place it in a shady spot outside, protected from too much rain.

Steps 1 to 5: Set-up for fish tank with plants and overhead light.

GALE GROUP.

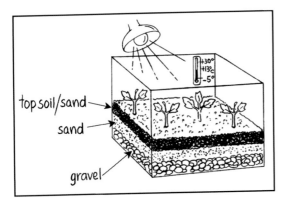

Step-by-Step Instructions

1. l. Place a 1-inch (2.5-centimeter) layer of gravel on the bottom of the fish tank.
2. Place a 1-inch (2.5- centimeter) layer of sand over the gravel.
3. Mix 2 parts of topsoil to 1 part of sand. Place a 2- to 3-inch (5- to 7.5- centimeter) layer of the sand/topsoil mixture over the sand layer.
4. Plant four to six trees. Be sure to cover all the roots. If seeds are being used, place them 1 inch (2.5 cm) down in the soil and allow one month for them to sprout.
5. Place the thermometer inside the terrarium against the back wall.
6. Water gently until approximately 0.25 inch (0.6 centimeter) of water has accumulated in the gravel layer.
7. Place the fish tank outside or in a sunny place indoors. You must maintain the temperature of the fish tank in the range of 32 to 60°F (0 to 15°C). If you need to provide artificial light, place the incandescent fixture above the fish tank and provide five to 10 hours of light per day.
8. Check the project daily, and maintain 0.25 inch (0.6 centimeter) of water in the gravel.
9. Record the growth of the plants and the temperature range.

Summary of Results Graph the data you have collected over the six-month period. The overall growth of the plants will demonstrate the health of the biome environment.

PROJECT 2

Building a Desert Biome

Purpose/Hypothesis In this project, you will build, grow, and maintain a desert biome. The desert biome is characterized mainly by its lack of

Experiment Central, 2nd edition

water, which causes harsh growing conditions. Maintaining the right climate, soil, and vegetation is the goal. This particular biome is characterized by a temperature range of 23 to 60°F (6 to 30°C).

Level of Difficulty Moderate to difficult because of the length of time needed for the project.

Materials Needed

- 10-gallon fish tank
- indoor/outdoor thermometer
- watering container
- gravel
- sand
- topsoil
- incandescent light with 60-watt bulb
- succulent plants, such as jade plant, strawberry cactus, barrel cactus, etc.

Note: Most plants are easily found in local nursery stores selling houseplants.

Approximate Budget $25. (Try to get an old fish tank to use.)

Timetable One hour to set up the project and at least six months to maintain the plants and observe changes.

Step-by-Step Instructions

1. Place a 1-inch (2.5-centimeter) layer of gravel in the bottom of the fish tank.
2. Mix 1 to 2 cups of topsoil with 6 to 10 cups of sand. Place this mixture over the gravel layer.
3. Place 2 inches (5 centimeter) of sand over the sand/topsoil layer.
4. Plant the cactus and succulents in the fish tank and cover the roots completely.
5. Place the thermometer inside the fish tank, against the back wall.

How to Experiment Safely

Ask for assistance when moving the fish tank. Do not leave the light fixture on for more than 10 hours at a time, as it will get too hot.

Strawberry and barrel cactuses.
GALE GROUP.

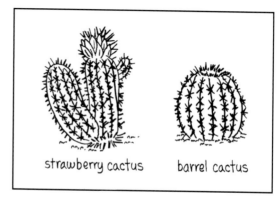

strawberry cactus   barrel cactus

Troubleshooter's Guide

In this model, climate conditions are designed to be extreme. The plants have special adaptations to adjust. If insects become a problem, remove them.

6. Water sparingly. Pour 2 cups of water on the sand to start. Water the fish tank with 1 cup of water every week after that.
7. Place the light fixture above the fish tank and leave it on for eight to 10 hours a day.
8. Check the fish tank daily. Record any differences in the plants' growth and in the temperature range.

Summary of Results Graph the data you collected during the project, as illustrated in the Desert Biome Growth Chart. You will notice very little change, as the plants have a very slow growth cycle.

Modify the Experiment For a more in depth understanding of desert biomes, you can further investigate how organisms have adapted to life in the desert. In Project 2 you constructed a desert biome, concentrating on the physical features of a desert. Now you can measure one way in which desert plants have adapted to their environment.

Cacti have many adaptations that help them collect and store water. Do you think if cacti were given the same amount of water as a leafy, temperate forest plant it would release the same amount of water? Begin the experiment in the morning. Collect one of the leafy plants you used in the temperate biome project and one cacti from the desert biome. Both should be healthy,

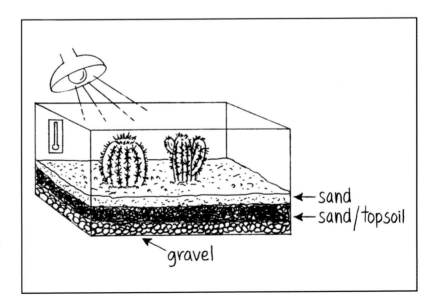

Steps 1 to 5: Set-up for fish tank with cactus, light, thermometer, and sand and gravel layers.
GALE GROUP.

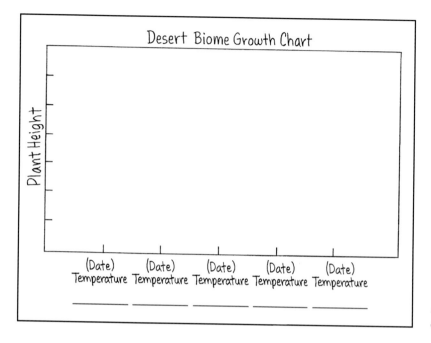

Desert Biome Growth Chart

Plant Height

(Date) Temperature (Date) Temperature (Date) Temperature (Date) Temperature (Date) Temperature

Desert Biome Growth Chart.
GALE GROUP.

growing in a pot. Gently place a small baggie over the top of the cactus and tie with a twisty-tie or string. Tie a small baggie over the leaf of the temperate plant. Pour one-quarter cup of water in each pot. If the plants are large, you may want to use more water. The exact amount does not matter, as long as it is the same for both plants. Place both plants in the sun or under a plant light.

At the end of the day, examine the bags. Are there droplets of water in one bag and not the other? Take off the bags and replace them the next morning (the plants need oxygen to live). Did you see the same thing at the end of the second day? Examine the structure of the cactus compared to the temperate plant. Where do you think it is storing water?

Design Your Own Experiment

How to Select a Topic Relating to this Concept The fish tank projects are models of what takes place in a biome. Many plants and animals have specific adaptations that are suited to that biome or region. What happens when you change the climate of a biome? How does the introduction of a plant from a different biome affect the other plants? There are many experiments you could design to investigate the interactions of plants and animals with their biomes.

Check the Further Readings section and talk with your science teacher or school or community media specialist to start gathering information on biome questions that interest you.

Steps in the Scientific Method To do an original experiment, you need to plan carefully and think things through. Otherwise, you might not be sure what question you are answering, what you are or should be measuring, or what your findings prove or disprove.

Here are the steps in designing an experiment:

- State the purpose of—and the underlying question behind—the experiment you propose to do.
- Recognize the variables involved, and select one that will help you answer the question at hand.
- State a testable hypothesis, an educated guess about the answer to your question.
- Decide how to change the variable you selected.
- Decide how to measure your results.

Recording Data and Summarizing the Results It is important to document as much information as possible about your experiment. Part of your presentation should be visual, using charts and graphs. Remember, whether or not your experiment is successful, your conclusions and experiences can benefit others.

Related Projects More specific projects can be performed to get more detailed information about biomes. For instance, scientists are finding that many rainforests are getting drier. Also, a phenomenon called desertification has been occurring, turning naturally dry land into desert. Try an experiment in desertification, reducing water to see what happens.

For More Information

Morrison, Marion. *The Amazing Rain Forest and Its People.* New York: Thompson Learning, 1993. Provides a good summary of this ecological community and how interdependency affects this biome.

Rainis, Kenneth. *Environmental Science Projects for Young Scientists.* New York: Franklin Watts, 1994. Describes biome and related projects for young people.

Sayre, April Pulley. *Taiga.* New York: Twenty-First Century Books, 1994. Explores the taiga biome, its animals, plant life, the people who live there, and their impact.

University of California Museum of Paleontology. "The world's biomes." http://www.ucmp.berkeley.edu/exhibits/biomes/index.php (accessed on January 18, 2008).

Bones and Muscles

Whenever you run, sit, walk, or even stand, your bones and muscles are working together in the activity. Bones are similar to the framework of a building; they provide the shape and protection. Our bones also produce our much-needed supply of daily blood cells—about 200 billion a day! They are the holding places for minerals and other key substances the body needs.

Many muscles are attached to bones and they pull the bones for movement. Other muscles provide much-needed functions for daily life. Even when you are just sitting still, your muscles are at work. They are allowing you to breath, swallow, smile, and even move your eyes. And it is a muscle that powers your entire body—the heart muscle. Working nonstop through a person's life, this vital muscle beats an average of seventy times per minute.

Bones, bones, bones An adult body has about 206 bones. The number varies from person to person because of differences in the number of small bones. Some bones are responsible for movement, including bones in the hands, feet, and limbs. Other bones primarily give protection to the internal structures, such as the skull protecting the brain and the ribs shielding the heart, lungs, and liver.

When looking at animal bones or at a skeleton, bones may appear to be static and dead, but in the body they are actually full of activity. Bones grow and change along with the person. They are made of living and nonliving materials: About 70% of an adult's bones are composed of minerals. The remaining part is bone tissue, a group of similar cells with a common function. Bone tissue is constantly building new bone. In fact, about every seven years your bone tissue makes essentially a whole new skeleton.

Wherever two bones meet there is a joint. In some places, such as the bones in the skull, the joints are locked together and do not move. Most joints are movable, though, and are coated with a fluid that acts as a lubricant. Ligaments are a tough connective tissue that links bones together at the joints. Ligaments prevent the bones at the joints from becoming

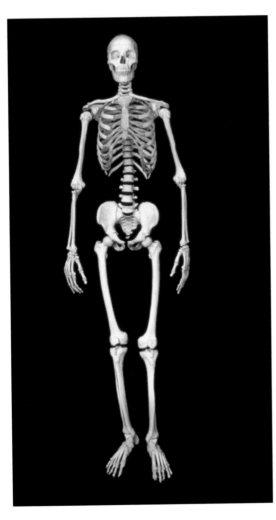

Full frontal view of a human skeleton. PHOTO RESEARCHERS INC.

dislocated. Cartilage is another connective tissue found at the end of the bones and in the joints. This is a smooth and flexible tissue that lets one bone slide smoothly over another.

Hard and spongy Almost every bone in the body is made of the same materials: The outside of the bone is the hard layer that is strong. It is made of living cells and is called compact or hard bone. Holes and channels run through the compact bone, carrying blood vessels and nerves to its inner parts. Inside this layer is cancellous bone or spongy bone. Cancellous bone has cells with large spaces in between them like a honeycomb. The spaces in this network are filled with a jellylike red-and-yellow bone marrow. Red bone marrow, found mainly at the ends of bones, makes most of our body's blood cells. Red bone marrow also produces white blood cells, which help fight infection, and platelets, which help blood clot. Yellow bone marrow stores fat and releases it when it is needed somewhere in the body.

Bones contain large amounts of a protein called collagen as well as minerals, including calcium and phosphorous. Collagen gives bones their elasticity. Calcium is what gives bones their strength. Extra minerals are stored in the bone, and the bones release them when they are needed by other parts of the body. The amount of minerals that a person eats affects how many minerals the bones contain and store.

As a person gets older, the amount of new bone created slows down and bones break down at a faster rate than they are being made. Women especially may lose the stored calcium in their bodies that helps keep their bones strong and healthy. This causes the bones to become weak, which can lead to breaks. The disease osteoporosis occurs most often among older people. In osteoporosis bone tissue becomes brittle and thin. Bones break easily, and the spine can begin to collapse. Building up adequate stores of calcium in the bones as a young adult is one important way people can prevent or delay the development of this disease.

Muscular strength Bones are moved by muscles attached to them. These muscles are fastened to bones by a thin, tough tissue called tendons, which also link muscles to other muscles.

Muscles come in all shapes and sizes. The human body has about 650 muscles, which make up about 40% of a person's body weight. Muscles are classified as voluntary or involuntary. Voluntary muscles are those you can control at will, such as moving your arm. Involuntary muscles act automatically, such as your stomach muscles digesting food. Some muscles fit into both categories, such as the muscle used in blinking your eyes.

Muscles are made of stacks of long, thin cells called muscle fibers. Each muscle fiber is a single cell and contains at least one nucleus. The nucleus (plural: nuclei) is an enclosed structure that contains the cell's genetic material and controls its growth and reproduction. There are three types of muscle fibers: skeletal, smooth, and cardiac. Skeletal muscle fibers are attached to bone and are voluntary muscles. They are the most abundant and largest of the three, with some fibers running more than a foot long. Each skeletal muscle fiber has several nuclei. Smooth muscle fibers are involuntary, as in the stomach and intestines. They are smaller than the skeletal muscles and are narrow at the ends, with one nucleus in each cell. Cardiac muscles are found only in the heart. These muscles have fibers that are tightly packed together and have branches. A cardiac muscle cell usually has a single nucleus.

When muscles go into action they work in terms of contractions and relaxations. Muscles can only pull bones because they can only contract, or get shorter. They cannot push bones back into their original position. Because of this, muscles work in pairs. When one muscle contracts it can bend a limb; then when that muscle is finished contracting, its partner muscle contracts to extend or straighten the limb. Whenever you bend your arm, for example, the bicep muscle in the front of the upper arm contracts. When the arm

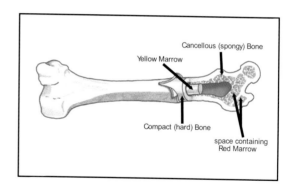

Parts of the human bone. GALE GROUP.

The three types of muscle fibers. GALE GROUP.

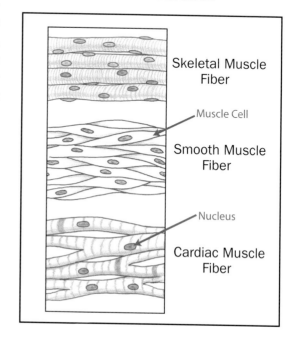

A humped back is a sign of osteoporosis. Elderly women especially are prone to developing this disease. © LESTER V. BERGMAN/CORBIS.

straightens, the bicep relaxes and the tricep muscle at the back of the upper arm contracts.

All the energy that muscles use is created when muscle cells process the carbohydrates, fats, and proteins in foods. Healthy muscles burn nutrients efficiently. The amount a person exercises and his or her general health will make muscles work better and become less fatigued. Muscle fatigue occurs when the muscle stops contracting. When muscle cells run out of oxygen, they reach a point where the muscles have a reduced ability to contract. When a person builds his or her muscles, the muscle fibers grow. This increases the blood flow in the fibers, increasing their ability to contract.

EXPERIMENT 1

Bone Loss: How does the loss of calcium affect bone strength?

Purpose/Hypothesis Your bones are lightweight and incredibly strong. Bones get their strength from a hard outer shell that contains the mineral calcium carbonate. The calcium keeps the bone stiff and rigid. A strong acid can chemically react with the bones and remove much of the calcium carbonate.

Muscles work in pairs because they can only contract. Here, one contracts to bend the arm; its partner muscle contracts to straighten it. GALE GROUP.

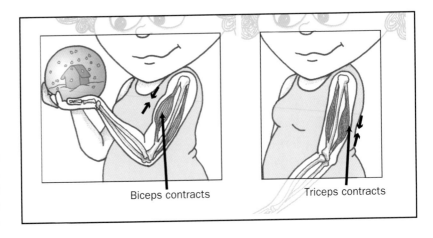

Biceps contracts   Triceps contracts

WORDS TO KNOW

Bone joint: A place in the body where two or more bones are connected.

Bone marrow: The spongy center of many bones in which blood cells are manufactured.

Bone tissue: A group of similar cells in the bone with a common function.

Cancellous bone: Also called spongy bone, the inner layer of a bone that has cells with large spaces in between them filled with marrow.

Cartilage: The connective tissue that covers and protects the bones.

Collagen: A protein in bone that gives the bone elasticity.

Compact bone: The outer, hard layer of the bone.

Contract: To shorten, pull together.

Control experiment: A setup that is identical to the experiment, but is not affected by the variable that acts on the experimental group.

Hypothesis: An idea in the form of a statement that can be tested by observation and/or experiment.

Ligaments: Tough, fibrous tissue connecting bones.

Muscle fibers: Stacks of long, thin cells that make up muscle; there are three types of muscle fiber: skeletal, cardiac, and smooth.

Nucleus, cell: Enclosed structure within a cell that contains the cell's genetic material and controls its growth and reproduction. (Plural: nuclei.)

Tendon: Tough, fibrous connective tissue that attaches muscle to bone.

Variable: Something that can affect the results of an experiment.

In this experiment you will determine how the loss of calcium carbonate affects the strength of bones. You will use vinegar as the acid. The vinegar will react with three bones for varying lengths of time. The longer the vinegar reacts with the bone, the more calcium the vinegar will remove from the bone. How much you can bend the bone will allow you determine the bone's strength.

Before you begin, make an educated guess about the outcome of this experiment based on your knowledge of bones and the mineral calcium. This educated guess, or prediction, is your hypothesis. A hypothesis should explain these things:

- the topic of the experiment
- the variable you will change
- the variable you will measure
- what you expect to happen

What Are the Variables?

Variables are anything that might affect the results of an experiment. Here are the main variables in this experiment:

- the type of bone you use
- the thickness of the bone
- the cleanliness of the bone
- the solution the bone is soaked in
- residue in the jars
- the environment of the bones when they are not soaking

In other words, the variables in this experiment are everything that might affect the vinegar reacting with the bone. If you change more than one variable at the same time, you will not be able to tell which variable had the most effect on bone strength.

A hypothesis should be brief, specific, and measurable. It must be something you can test through further investigation. Your experiment will prove or disprove whether your hypothesis is correct. Here is one possible hypothesis for this experiment: "The more calcium a bone loses, the weaker the bone will be and the more it will bend."

In this case, the variable you will change is the amount of time the bones react with the vinegar or acid. The variable you will measure is the bone's strength or how much the bone bends.

Conducting a control experiment will help you isolate each variable and measure the changes in the dependent variable. Only one variable will change between the control and the experimental bones, and that is the solution that immerses the bones. For the control, you will soak a bone in plain water, which does not react with the bone. At the end of the experiment you will compare the water-soaked bone with each of the vinegar-soaked bones.

For your experiment you will select four bones of the same type that are of equal thickness and general appearance. You will soak three of the bones in vinegar and one of the bones in water. Every four days you will remove each of the vinegar-soaked bones and test its strength. To compare the bones again at the end of the experiment, you will wrap each of the bones after the allotted period of time. If you leave them in the open air, the bone will react with the carbon dioxide in the air and harden again.

Level of Difficulty Easy/Moderate.

Materials Needed

- 4 similar chicken bones (drumsticks from chicken wings work well)
- vinegar, white
- 4 glass jars with lids, large enough to hold a bone
- marking pen
- masking tape
- plastic wrap

Approximate Budget $5.

Timetable 20 minutes initial setup time; another 30 minutes spread out over the next 12 days.

Step-by-Step Instructions

1. Clean the four bones thoroughly, scrubbing them with water.

2. Place a piece of masking tape on each jar and label the first jar "Control," the second jar "4 Days," the third "8 Days," and the last "12 Days."

3. In the control jar, cover the bone with water. In the other three jars, cover the bones with vinegar. Set the jars aside.

4. After four days, open the "4 Day" jar and rinse off the bone with water. Test the strength of the bone by trying to bend it. While the bone is still wet, wrap it in plastic wrap thoroughly. Rinse the jar clean and place the wrapped bone back in the jar, screw on the lid and set it aside.

5. Repeat Step 4 after another four days for the bone in the "8 Day" jar. Repeat again four days later for the "12 Day" jar, except do not place the bone in plastic wrap.

How to Experiment Safely

Vinegar is an acid. Be careful about getting any of the vinegar in your eyes. Do not eat any of the vinegar-soaked bones. Throw them out after the experiment is complete.

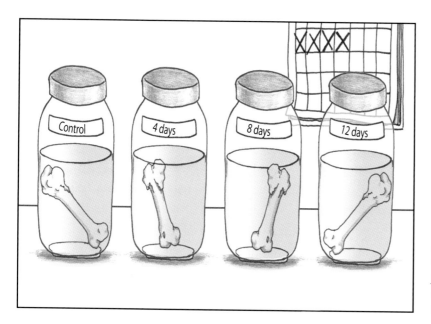

Steps 2 and 3: Label each jar. Cover the bone in the control jar with water; cover the bones in the other jars with vinegar.
GALE GROUP.

Troubleshooter's Guide

Below is a problem that may arise during this experiment, a possible cause, and a way to remedy the problem.

Problem: The bones all have the same strength, even after 12 days.

Possible cause: The bones you used may be too thick. Try repeating the experiment, increasing the amount of soaking time by doubling the days. You could also repeat the experiment using bones that are thinner.

6. Unwrap the other bones and examine how far each bone bends. Rinse the control bone with water and compare the strength of the three bones to the control.

7. Create a graph of the results, using an estimate of the degree the bones bend for the y-axis, and the number of days of calcium loss on the x-axis.

Summary of Results Examine your graph of the data. How did the control bone compare to the bone with the greatest calcium loss? What do the bones feel like? Do they feel different from each other? Think about how the loss of calcium in bones would affect a person. What can this experiment teach you about osteoporosis in older people?

Change the Variables You can vary this experiment by changing the thickness or type of bone you use. Do you get the same results with a turkey bone as a chicken bone? You could also try leaving the bones out in the air for several days after they have finished soaking in vinegar and compare the results. You could also try comparing the same type bone from a young animal and an old animal. You may have to talk with your local butcher for help in selecting the bones.

EXPERIMENT 2

Muscles: How does the strength of muscles affect fatigue over time?

Purpose/Hypothesis Skeleton muscles are the muscles attached to bones that are at work during physical activity. A muscle contracts when it is flexed or at work. The number of contractions a muscle can make is affected by fatigue.

In this experiment you will examine if a muscle can increase the number of contractions with muscle use, thereby reducing muscle fatigue. You will measure your muscle contractions through squats. The quadriceps muscles in the front of the upper legs are one of the main muscles used in a squat. A squat also uses the gluteus, hamstrings, and calf muscles.

A friend or family member will time the length of time you conduct the activity before you are fatigued. This partner will also count the number of squats you carry out and note them in a chart that you should not look at until you have completed the entire experiment. Not allowing you to know the number of muscle contractions you have completed will make the experiment more objective by not giving you a number to "beat." Try to think of something else during the experiment so you do not count the squats for yourself.

You will repeat the experiment every other day, until you have completed 10 trials.

Before you begin, make an educated guess about the outcome of this experiment based on your knowledge of muscle strength and fatigue. This educated guess, or prediction, is your hypothesis. A hypothesis should explain these things:

- the topic of the experiment
- the variable you will change
- the variable you will measure
- what you expect to happen

A hypothesis should be brief, specific, and measurable. It must be something you can test through further investigation. Your experiment will prove or disprove whether your hypothesis is correct. Here is one possible hypothesis for this experiment: "The stronger muscles will become less fatigued and will gain strength over time."

In this case, the variable you will change is the strength of the muscles. The variable you will measure is the number of times your muscles can contract. To equate all the other variables, conduct the experiment at roughly the same time of day. At the end of the experiment you will examine how your muscles have changed over time.

Level of Difficulty Easy

Materials Needed

- partner
- watch with second hand

What Are the Variables?

Variables are anything that might affect the results of an experiment. Here are the main variables in this experiment:

- the time of day
- your nutritional level before you conduct the trial

In other words, the variables in this experiment are everything that might affect how many times you can complete a squat. If you change more than one variable at the same time, you will not be able to tell which variable had the most effect on fatigue.

How to Experiment Safely

Working a muscle too hard can cause soreness and damage to your muscle. Stop the activity if you feel dizzy or experience physical discomfort. Keep your feet firmly on the floor at all times and breathe regularly. If you have knee problems, do not do this experiment. Check with a parent or physical education teacher for a replacement activity.

Approximate Budget $0.

Timetable Approximately five minutes per trial for a period of 10 trials.

Step-by-Step Instructions

1. Have your partner begin timing when you start your first squat. Your partner will count the number of squats you do at each trial. Try to think of something else during the experiment so you do not count the squats for yourself.

2. To conduct the squat, get into a comfortable upright stance, with your feet shoulder-width apart and your toes pointed straight ahead. Don't point your toes inward, because this will put a lot of strain on your knees.

3. Extend your arms. Squat down until your knees are over your toes. Pretend you are sitting in a chair.

4. Make sure to keep your heels planted firmly on the floor.

5. Return in an upright position and repeat at a regular pace.

6. When your muscles become fatigued then stop. Have your partner note the number of squats and the amount of time. Do not look at the chart.

7. Repeat this process every other day for a period of 10 trials.

Step 3: Squat until your knees are above your toes; stop when you get fatigued. GALE GROUP.

Summary of Results Graph the results of your data from your first trial to the last trial, making the x-axis the number of squats and the y-axis the trial number. Does the number of muscles' contractions change over time? Construct a second graph that marks the length of time of each trial on the x-axis with the trial number on the y-axis. How does the length of time you were able to contract your muscles change over time? Write a brief summary of the experiment that relates your results to muscle strength and movement.

Modify the Experiment You can alter this experiment by simplifying the activity and focusing on how nutrition contributes to muscle fatigue. The body converts nutrients (carbohydrates, fats, and proteins) into energy. Carbohydrates are the nutrient most quickly turned into energy for muscles. If you match muscle fatigue to nutrient intake, you can gather data about how nutrients may affect muscles. You will need to test several people (you can be one of them). First, make a hypothesis about how nutrient intake will affect muscle fatigue.

For the physical activity, look for a hard rubber ball that fits in your hand. You will also need a clock with a minute hand. You will measure how many times you can squeeze the ball in a 30 second time period. Make a note of the number in a chart.

Conduct the test two to four times throughout the day, both before you have eaten and after. You could conduct the activity in the morning, both before you eat breakfast and 30 minutes after breakfast. Test several people, also before and after they eat. If possible, test people outside of your family. Make sure you always use about the same time period both before and after eating. For example, if you count the number of times you squeeze the ball after you have not eaten for four hours and then 30 minutes after eating, test other people using those same times. You also may want to note what nutrients you and your test subjects ate. Write down the results in a chart. When you finish, look for any patterns in the chart. Was your hypothesis correct? Aside from nutrients, consider what other factors might contribute to muscle fatigue.

> ## Troubleshooter's Guide
>
> Below is a problem that may arise during this experiment, a possible cause, and a way to remedy the problem.
>
> **Problem:** There is no change in muscle fatigue over the trials.
>
> **Possible cause:** You may be squatting further down over the trials, which uses more muscle. Repeat the experiment making sure to stop your squat each time when your knees are over your toes.

Design Your Own Experiment

How to Select a Topic Relating to this Concept To select a related project, you can explore the different ways that you use your bones and muscles throughout the day. An experiment with bones could include comparing bones from different species. An experiment with muscles could work to identify the characteristics of each of the three muscle fibers. Check the Further Readings section and talk with your science, health, or physical education teacher to learn more about bones and muscles.

Regular exercise allows muscles to burn nutrients more efficiently and increases their ability to contract. © KARL WEATHERLY/CORBIS.

Steps in the Scientific Method To do an original experiment, you need to plan carefully and think things through. Otherwise, you might not be sure what question you are answering, what you are or should be measuring, or what your findings prove or disprove.

Here are the steps in designing an experiment:

- State the purpose of—and the underlying question behind—the experiment you propose to do.
- Recognize the variables involved and select one that will help you answer the question at hand.
- State your hypothesis, an educated guess about the answer to your question.
- Decide how to change the variable you selected.
- Decide how to measure your results.

Recording Data and Summarizing the Results Your data should include charts and graphs such as the one you did for these experiments. They should be clearly labeled and easy to read. You may also want to include photographs and drawings of your experimental setup and results, which will help others visualize the steps in the experiment.

If you are preparing an exhibit, you may want to display your results, such as any experimental setup you designed. If you have completed a nonexperimental project, explain clearly what your research question was and illustrate your findings.

Related Projects You can design your own experiments on bones and muscles. Think of some other reasons why people might experience bone decalcification. Investigate a method for testing the impact of other minerals in a bone. You could explore how the bones in different species compare to each other. Do species that are physically similar have similar bone structures?

For a muscle experiment, you could examine the characteristics of each of the three types of muscle fibers by purchasing the three different muscles from a butcher. Examine muscle fatigue further by investigating if fatigue is greater at certain times of the day. You could investigate if there are particular activities that women find fatiguing and men do not. Are there different muscles in the bones of women and men?

For More Information

KidsHealth. "The Big Story on Bones." *My Body.* http://www.kidshealth.org/kid/body/bones_noSW.html (accessed February 25, 2008). Basic information and diagrams about bones and muscles.

MyHealthScore.com. *Human Anatomy Online.* http://www.innerbody.com/htm/body.html (accessed February 25, 2008). An interactive look at the skeleton and muscular systems, with descriptions and animations.

Simon, Seymour. *Bones: Your Skeleton System.* New York: Morrow Junior Books, 1998. Clear introduction to the skeleton system using photographs.

Simon, Seymour. *Muscles: Your Muscular System.* New York: Morrow Junior Books, 1998. Clear introduction to the muscular system using photographs.

White, Katherine. *The Muscular System.* New York: Rosen Publishing, 2001. Basic information about the muscular system.

10

Caves

Caves, also called caverns, are natural hollow areas inside the ground that are large enough for a person to fit inside. There are millions of caves on Earth. Some caves, are only a few yards (meters) deep. Others stretch hundreds of miles underground, splitting into numerous rooms and passageways. There are caves underwater, on the sides of mountains, and beneath flat land. Interiors of caves often contain unique landscapes and life forms that are spectacular sights.

Along with their awesome beauty, caves have provided people with important clues to ancient life and geology. The scientific study of caves is called speleology (pronounced spee-lee-AH-lu-gy), from the Greek words for cave, *spelaion,* and knowledge, *logos.* Scientists who study these caves are known as speleologists and they are only beginning to unearth the treasure of information that caves contain. Speleologists have found unique animals, new plant life, and clues to Earth's history.

Forming the holes Caves take hundreds of thousands of years to form. There are caves in the process of forming right now, and already-formed caves that are undergoing continuous change. The majority of caves are made out of the rock limestone. Limestone is a rock formed millions of years ago out of the hardened remains of layers of sea animals.

The formation of a limestone cave begins with water. When rain falls it collects a small amount of the gas carbon dioxide from the air. As the water trickles into the soil, it passes through tiny pockets of air in the soil. The soil is where it picks up most of the carbon dioxide. Carbon dioxide that mixes with water causes the water to change into an acid, called carbonic acid. Carbonic acid water slowly eats away at the soft limestone. It seeps into small cracks, causing the cracks to widen and allowing more water to flow through. Gradually, the water causes the rock to dissolve. The dissolved area grows into a hole, then a larger hole, and still larger. Eventually, over a few million years, the water carves an underground room where there was

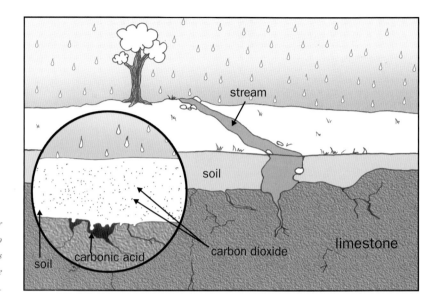

Cave formation begins: Water mixes with carbon dioxide to form carbonic acid, which seeps into small cracks in the limestone. GALE GROUP.

once only rock. In time, that room increases in size and can become many rooms with passageways between them.

A newly formed cave is filled with water. This water can stay in the cave for hundreds or thousands of years. Water drains out of the cave only when some type of geological shift occurs. The cave may be lifted above the water by a

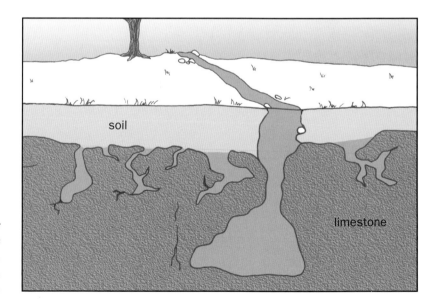

Cave formation continues: The dissolved rock grows in an increasingly larger hole, eventually forming a cave. GALE GROUP.

gradual uplifting of the ground. Or a nearby stream of water can flow through the cave, slicing a deep swath through the cave and causing the water level to drop. Caves often contain remnants of the water in streams or ponds. When the cave is lifted above the water, water flows out of the hole and the cave fills with air.

There are several other types of caves also. Sea caves form along rocky shores from the constant pounding of ocean waves. The waves wear away the base of the rocky cliff where the rock is soft or has cracks in it. Seawater carries the rock away and, over time, a cave forms. Lava caves are made after a volcano erupts and the molten, hot lava flows down the side of the volcano. The outer layer of the lava cools and hardens; hot lava continues to flow underneath. When this hot lava drains away it can leave a cave behind.

More recently, scientists have discovered that caves can also form from a type of bacteria that live deep beneath Earth. These bacteria use oil for food and release the gas hydrogen sulfide. Hydrogen sulfide reacts with oxygen to produce sulfuric acid, which can dissolve limestone. The Carlsbad Caverns in New Mexico is an example of a limestone cave carved out of sulfuric acid. These caverns contain 83 caves and include the nation's deepest limestone cave at 1,567 feet (478 meters), and one of the world's largest chambers.

Sea caves form along rocky shores from the constant pounding of ocean waves.
FIELD MARK PUBLICATIONS.

Natural extensions The slow drainage of carbonic acid water can cause the formation of dramatic cave features created after the underground chamber is formed. These features come in many shapes and several different colors. Two types of attributes common in limestone caves are icicle-like extensions that sprout up from the floor or hang down from its ceiling. Stalactites are cave features that hang from the ceiling; stalagmites grow upward from the floor.

The formation of these two types of features begins with water droplets. After most of the water has drained from a cave, water continues to flow through layers of the limestone rocks. All the water droplets contain a small amount of dissolved limestone, which carries the mineral calcite. A stalactite begins when a drop of this water hangs from the ceiling. The

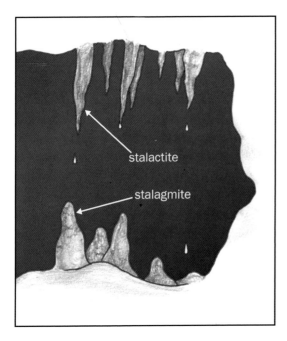

stalactite

stalagmite

Stalactites and stalagmites, common in limestone caves, form gradually over time from the buildup of calcite. GALE GROUP.

water evaporates or drips to the ground and the calcite in the water remains. One droplet builds upon another, the calcite deposits increase and a stalactite grows. Stalactites can reach down hundreds of meters, but watching one grow is a lengthy process. On average, a stalactite grows only about half an inch every hundred years.

The upward-growing stalagmites form when water droplets drip from the ceiling or a stalactite above. When the water droplet hits the floor it spatters the calcite deposits outward, but close together. The calcite builds up over time to create finger-like shapes with rounded tops. Stalagmites can grow to both amazing widths and heights, some growing more than 45 feet (13 meters) wide and 30 feet (9 meters) tall.

Stalactites and stalagmites are often white or nearly white because the most common form of calcite is white. Iron and other minerals or materials mixing with the calcite create rich-colored stalactites and stalagmites, including red, yellow, orange, and black.

Life in the dark lane A cave's darkness may deter many life forms from making a home inside, but caves are crawling with organisms that like what a cave offers. Scientists have separated cave animals into three distinct types.

Animals that can only survive in the deep interior of caves' pitch-blackness are called troglobites, from the Greek word meaning cave life. Types of troglobites include species of shrimp, insects, and spiders. Many of these animals feature small eyes or blindness, no pigment, and a well-developed sense of touch and smell. Other animals are part-time cave dwellers. Called trogloxenes, meaning cave guest, these animals stay in the cave for sleep, warmth, protection, and to raise their young. Bats are an example of this type of animal. The nocturnal bats doze away the sunny hours in the darkness of a cave. Bats live in colonies and feed at night, catching insects such as moths, beetles, and mosquitoes. Bat colonies are among the largest grouping of mammals in the world. The Bracken Cave in Texas houses twenty million Mexican free-tail bats that eat more than 250,000 pounds of insects every night. Bears, crickets, and pack rats are other examples of trogloxenes.

The last type, troglophiles, meaning cave lovers, are animals that live most of their lives in caves but also have the ability to live outside. They like the dampness of the cave and may venture outside to forage for food.

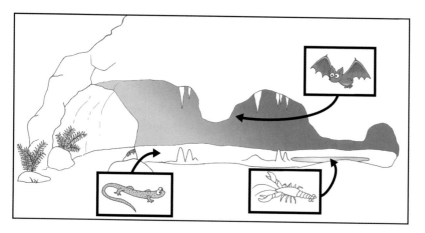

Cave life includes three general categories of animals that live in different areas of the cave. GALE GROUP.

Troglophiles include species of salamanders, frogs, beetles, millipedes, snails, and mites.

Because green plants need light to live, plants only grow near the entrance where light penetrates. Mosses and ferns are the plants commonly found near the cave opening; algae grows on the rocks. Caves are also teeming with fungi and bacteria that keep the chain of cave life flowing. Droppings from animals, such as bats, can provide the major food source for other cave life, yet few animals can feed on these. Bacteria and fungi decompose these materials into simple foods and nutrients. Small animals, such as insects, also munch on fungi and bacteria for their food supply. These insects then become food, in turn, for larger predators.

Fruit bats hang from the walls of a cave in Bali, Indonesia. © ROBERT GILL/CORBIS.

WORDS TO KNOW

Carbonic acid: A weak acid that forms from the mixture of water and carbon dioxide.

Cave: Also called cavern, a hollow or natural passage under or into the ground large enough for a person to enter.

Control experiment: A setup that is identical to the experiment, but is not affected by the variable that acts on the experimental group.

Hypothesis: An idea in the form of a statement that can be tested by observation and/or experiment.

Lava cave: A cave formed from the flow of lava streaming over solid matter.

Sea cave: A cave in sea cliffs, formed most commonly by waves eroding the rock.

Speleologist: One who studies caves.

Speleology: Scientific study of caves and their plant and animal life.

Spelunkers: Also called cavers, people who explore caves for a hobby.

Stalactite: Cylindrical or icicle-shaped mineral deposit projecting downward from the roof of a cave. (Pronounced sta-LACK-tite.)

Stalagmite: Cylindrical or icicle-shaped mineral deposit projecting upward from the floor of a cave. (Pronounced sta-LAG-mite.)

Troglobite: An animal that lives in a cave and is unable to live outside of one.

Troglophile: An animal that lives the majority of its life cycle in a cave but is also able to live outside of the cave.

Trogloxene: An animal that spends only part of its life cycle in a cave and returns periodically to the cave.

Variable: Something that can affect the results of an experiment.

Some like it dark Speleologists are not the only people who like to study caves. People who explore caves for a hobby are called cavers or spelunkers. Spelunking can be a somewhat dangerous hobby. There are narrow passages, steep cliffs, and long distances—all in the dark. With caves that stretch steeply downward, spelunkers need to have many of the skills and equipment of mountain climbers. The darkness of a cave and its vastness also take some skill to navigate.

EXPERIMENT 1

Cave Formation: How does the acidity of a substance affect the formation of a cave?

Purpose/Hypothesis The majority of caves are formed when limestone is dissolved by carbonic acid. In this experiment you will determine why acidic substances form caves by comparing how acidic and nonacidic solutions react with different geologic materials. You will use chalk, seashells, and rocks as the geologic materials. Chalk and seashells are both types of limestone.

Carbonic acid, a mixture of carbon dioxide and water, is the same compound found in soda. Carbonic acid is a weak acid. It is carbonic acid that makes soda fizz. A liquid can also be a base or it can be neutral. Pure water is an example of a neutral. A mixture of baking soda in water is an example of a base.

After determining the acidity of the liquids, you will place drops of the liquids on each material and note the results.

Before you begin, make an educated guess about the outcome of this experiment based on your knowledge of limestone and carbonic acid. This educated guess, or prediction, is your hypothesis. A hypothesis should explain these things:

- the topic of the experiment

- the variable you will change

- the variable you will measure

- what you expect to happen

A hypothesis should be brief, specific, and measurable. It must be something you can test through further investigation. Your experiment will prove or disprove whether your hypothesis is correct. Here is one possible hypothesis for this experiment: "Only the limestone materials will have a reaction with the acidic liquids."

In this case, the variable you will change is the acidity of the solution. The variable you will measure is the reaction of the liquid on the geologic substance.

Conducting a control experiment will help you isolate each variable and measure the changes in the dependent variable. Only one variable will change between the control and the experimental setup, and that is the solution you drop on the solid material. For the control in this experiment you will use plain water.

Level of Difficulty Easy to Moderate.

What Are the Variables?

Variables are anything that might affect the results of an experiment. Here are the main variables in this experiment:

- the solid material

- the liquid

- the liquid's acidity

- the amount of liquid poured

In other words, the variables in this experiment are everything that might affect the limestone's reaction with the liquid. If you change more than one variable at the same time, you will not be able to tell which variable had the most effect on dissolving the limestone.

How to Experiment Safely

There are no safety hazards in this experiment.

Materials Needed

- acid/base indicator strips
- baking soda
- clear soda pop
- distilled water
- dropper or spoon
- six clear or plastic cups
- spoon
- measuring spoon
- dropper
- three pieces pure white chalk
- three small rocks/pebbles
- three seashells or seashell pieces

Approximate Budget $5.

Timetable 30 minutes.

Step-by-Step Instructions

1. Create a data chart, listing the liquids across the top columns and the different substances in the rows.
2. Prepare a basic solution: Mix 1 teaspoon (5 milliliters) of baking soda with one cup of water. Stir thoroughly and label the cup "Baking soda."
3. Pour water in another cup and label as "Water"; pour soda in yet another cup and label as "Soda."
4. With an acid/base indicator strip, first test the water, then the baking-soda solution, and, finally, the soda for acidity. Use a new strip for each test and dip the strip briefly in each liquid. An acid will turn the paper red, a base will turn the paper blue, and a neutral substance will not change the color of the strip. Note on your chart whether each liquid is an acid, base, or neutral.
5. Take three new, empty cups: Place one piece of chalk in one; one pebble in a second; and one seashell piece in the third.

Some of the materials needed for Experiment 1. GALE GROUP.

6. Use a dropper to drip 3 to 4 drops of the soda on the limestone chalk. Note in your chart a description of the sound and appearance. Does the limestone absorb the soda? Does the soda give any indication that it is dissolving the chalk?

7. Drip the same amount of soda over a piece of the seashell and the pebble. Describe the reaction of each on the seashell and the pebble.

8. Repeat Steps 6 and 7, replacing the soda with the baking-soda solution, and then with the water. (You may use the same cups to test all three liquids.) Note the reactions in the chart.

Troubleshooter's Guide

Below is a problem that may arise during this experiment, a possible cause, and a way to remedy the problem.

Problem: There was no reaction with any of the substances.

Possible cause: You may have used soda that was flat, meaning that all the carbonic dioxide has escaped and there is no carbonic acid. Repeat the experiment, making sure to use a fresh, fizzy can of soda.

Summary of Results Examine the reactions of each liquid on the solid material. How did the acidity level of the liquid affect the reaction? Was your hypothesis correct? Hypothesize what would occur to each material if you soaked it in the liquids for several weeks. What would happen to each substance if you dropped a stronger acid on it? Write a brief summary of the experiment and your analysis.

Change the Variables There are several ways you can modify the experiment by changing the variables. You can change the type of geologic substance, using different types of rocks or granite, for example. You can vary the acidity level of the liquid, such as by using vinegar (an acid) or soap (a base). There are charts available where you can look up the strengths of the acids and bases. Many cleaning products also contain strong acidic substances: Use these carefully and with adult supervision. You can also alter the experiment by lengthening the amount of time the liquid sits on the substance.

EXPERIMENT 2

Cave Icicles: How does the mineral content of water affect the formation of stalactites and stalagmites?

Purpose/Hypothesis The formation of stalactites and stalagmites in a cave is a slow process that depends on the mineral content of the water and the

What Are the Variables?

Variables are anything that might affect the results of an experiment. Here are the main variables in this experiment:

- the saturation level of solution
- the environment allowed to grow
- the string
- the mineral

In other words, variables in this experiment are everything that might affect the formation of the stalactites. If you change more than one variable, you will not be able to tell which variable impacted their formation.

evaporation rate. In this experiment, you will form your own mini-cave icicles using two different types of minerals.

Most caves are formed in limestone. Limestone is a form of the mineral calcite, which is made up largely of calcium carbonate. In this experiment, you will use two compounds made from similar minerals: baking soda and Epsom salt. Baking soda is sodium bicarbonate, a mineral that is a form of carbonate; Epsom salt is magnesium sulfate, another type of mineral, but not a carbonate.

In order for the minerals to join together to make a stalactite or stalagmite, you have to make a water solution brimming with the minerals. Hot water can dissolve more minerals than cold water. When as much of a substance as possible is dissolved in hot water and the water is allowed to cool, that solution is called supersaturated. The molecules in a supersaturated solution are so crammed together that they readily stick to each other. When you dip a length of yarn in this solution, the solution will creep up the yarn. As the air evaporates some of the water, the solid material will remain on the string. Just as stalactites and stalagmites form in a cave, the minerals will build up over time.

Before you begin, make an educated guess about the outcome of this experiment based on your knowledge of the formation of stalactites and stalagmites. This educated guess, or prediction, is your hypothesis. A hypothesis should explain these things:

- the topic of the experiment
- the variable you will change
- the variable you will measure
- what you expect to happen

A hypothesis should be brief, specific, and measurable. It must be something you can test through further investigation. Your experiment will prove or disprove whether your hypothesis is correct. Here is one possible hypothesis for this experiment: "The cave formations will accumulate better when they are made out of baking soda, the same carbonate mineral that is in a cave."

In this case, the variable you will change is the type of mineral in each solution. The variable you will measure is the formation of the stalactites and (perhaps) stalagmites.

Level of Difficulty Moderate.

Materials Needed

- four clear glasses or small glass jars (same size)
- hot water
- baking soda
- Epsom salt
- two spoons
- dark construction paper, 8.5 x 11 inches (22 x 28 centimeters)
- four small washers (or paper clips)
- scissors
- bowl
- thick woolen yarn, about 2 feet (0.6 meters)
- masking tape
- marking pen

Approximate Budget $5.

Timetable 45 minutes for setup and followup; 5 to 10 minutes per day for about 8 to 12 days to observe and record the results.

Step-by-Step Instructions

1. Pour 2 cups of very hot water into a bowl and dissolve as much baking soda as you can to make a saturated solution. Stir after every addition. When the solution is saturated, small bits of baking soda will fall to the bottom and will not dissolve no matter how hard you stir.

2. Pour half the water in one cup and half in another cup.

3. Cut the construction paper in half. Place the two glasses close to either end of the dark paper.

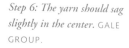

Step 6: The yarn should sag slightly in the center. GALE GROUP.

Troubleshooter's Guide

Below is a problem that may arise during this experiment, some possible causes, and some ways to remedy the problem.

Problem: No crystals grew in one or more of the solutions.

Possible cause: The solution may not have been saturated when the water was hot. You may not have stirred enough to dissolve the solids. Pour the solution back in the saucepan. Reheat the solution, adding more of the substance and stirring well after each addition until you see bits of the substance fall to the bottom.

Possible cause: The water may not have been hot enough. It does not need to be at the boiling point, but it does need to be hot. Pour the solution back in the saucepan. Reheat the solution, adding more of the substance and stirring well after each addition until it is saturated.

4. Stretch the yarn between the glasses and cut a piece that is about double that length. The yarn should be long enough to go inside each glass and hang loosely.

5. Tie a washer or paper clip to each end of the yarn.

6. Carefully lower the weighted ends of the yarn into the two glasses. The yarn should sag slightly in the center.

7. Label the two glasses "sodium bicarbonate."

8. Repeat Steps 1 through 7, replacing the baking soda with Epsom salt. Label the second set of glasses "magnesium sulfate."

9. Allow the glasses to sit undisturbed for at least 8 to 12 days. (A warm, sunny area works well.)

10. Illustrate what happens each day.

Summary of Results Look at your progression of pictures over the time of the experiment. What has formed on the string? Has anything begun to form on the construction paper? Compare the pictures of the two types of minerals? Write up a summary of the experiment, explaining the process of the mineral formations.

Change the Variables There are several ways you can vary this experiment. You can use a different type of mineral to form the solution, such as sodium carbonate (washing soda) or sodium chloride (salt). You can also alter the environment that the minerals form in, such as a humid or a dry environment.

Modify the Project For an advanced project, you could combine all the concepts you learned about caves to produce a model of a cave. This project will take about two weeks, as you will probably want to grow several stalactites or stalagmites. You can look at the color of different minerals in caves and add dye to the solutions to produce red, yellow or other color cave formations.

Once you have grown stalactites or stalagmites, you can form a cave with clay or another hard, moldable material. You can tape the mineral formations onto the cave floor or ceilings. You can also use the minerals from Experiment 2 to make other cave formation, such as popcorn. Popcorn is a small mineral cluster that often grows on cave walls. Think about where the water will flow in relation to the growth of the cave formations? Consider if you want water at the bottom of your cave. You could also add some plant life at the cave opening. Write down the explanations behind the features and formations of your cave.

A Native American cave dwelling at Canyonlands National Park, Utah. © PBNJ PRODUCTIONS/CORBIS.

Design Your Own Experiment

How to Select a Topic Relating to this Concept Cave formations are often intriguing to view and study. These structures are continuing to provide new information to spelunkers, speleologists, and other explorers. For a related project, you could investigate the history, geology, life, and formation of caves. You could also find out if there are any caves in your area that are open to visitors.

Check the Further Readings section and talk with your science teacher to learn more about caves. If you decide to visit a cave, make sure you are accompanied by an adult knowledgeable about caving.

Steps in the Scientific Method To conduct an original experiment, you need to plan carefully and think things through. Otherwise, you might not be sure what question you are answering, what you are or should be measuring, or what your findings prove or disprove.

Here are the steps in designing an experiment:

- State the purpose of—and the underlying question behind—the experiment you propose to do
- Recognize the variables involved and select one that will help you answer the question at hand
- State your hypothesis, an educated guess about the answer to your question
- Decide how to change the variable you selected
- Decide how to measure your results

Recording Data and Summarizing the Results Your data should include charts and graphs such as the one you did for these experiments. They should be clearly labeled and easy to read. You may also want to include photographs and drawings of your experimental setup and results, which will help other people visualize the steps in the experiment.

If you are preparing an exhibit, you may want to display your results, such as any experimental setup you designed. If you have completed a nonexperimental project, explain clearly what your research question was and illustrate your findings.

Related Projects There are multiple projects related to caves that you can undertake. You can study the animal and plant life in a cave through research and visits to museums or other facilities that may house some cave creatures. If there is a cave in your area that is open to the public, you could visit the cave and use a magnifying glass to examine the plant and animal life. Make sure you do not collect or touch any of the plant or animal life so as not to disturb their habitat. This project could also include an examination of how each type of animal and plant has adapted to the cave environment. If you decide to conduct a cave exploration, make sure an adult who is knowledgeable in caving accompanies you.

You can also investigate the formation of different types of caves, such as caves that form from volcanoes or out of ice. You could conduct a research project on the information that caves have provided in many fields of study. Another research project could be to examine how cultures throughout history have used caves in their daily life and rituals.

For More Information

Good Earth Graphics. "The Virtual Cave." http://www.goodearth graphics.com/virtcave (accessed on February 3, 2008). Images of different types of caves from around the world.

Groleau, Rick "How Caves Form." *NOVA.* http://www.pbs.org/wgbh/nova/caves/form.html# (accessed on February 3, 2008). Animated depiction of the formation of caves with clear explanations.

Hadingham, Evan. "Subterranean Surprises." *Smithsonian Magazine,* October 2002, pp. 68–74. This article can also be found online at http://www.smithsonianmag.com/science-nature/subterranean.html (accessed February 3, 2008). Detailed article on information scientists are learning about caves.

Taylor, Michael Ray and Ronal C. Kerbo. *Caves: Exploring Hidden Realms.* Washington, DC: National Geographic, 2001.

The National Speleological Society. http://www.caves.org/ (accessed on February 3, 2008). Homepage for the National Speleological Society describing their purpose and activities.

11

Cells

What do slimy earthworms, majestic lions, and giant redwood trees have in common with humans? We all have cells, tiny units of life that grow and duplicate, gather fuel and building materials, and make energy. Cells are present in all living things. Some living things, such as bacteria and some plants, consist of only one cell where all the functions of life take place. They are known as unicellular. The average human has 50 to 100 trillion cells. Living things with a great many cells that are joined together are called multicellular.

Looks like a monk's cell to me All humans begin life as a single cell. It weighs no more than a millionth of an ounce. The naked eye cannot see anything that tiny. So no one could have known cells existed until the compound microscope was invented in the late sixteenth century. Between 1590 and 1609, Dutchmen Hans Janssen, his son Zacharias, and Hans Lippershey designed several compound microscopes. In a compound microscope, two or more lenses are arranged to produce a greatly enlarged image.

In 1660, a Dutch drape maker named Anton van Leeuwenhoek (1632–1723) used a microscope to peer at his textiles. He began studying the invisible worlds of nature. Leeuwenhoek designed 250 different microscopes to further his studies. Around that time, Robert Hooke (1635–1703), an English scientist, slid a piece of cork under a microscope. The mass he saw seemed to be made of chambers, like monks' cells in a monastery. He called these chambers "cells."

Developing the cell theory Hooke's cells were from a cork tree's dead and dry bark. The fact that cells are units of life was not understood until the nineteenth century. Between 1838 and

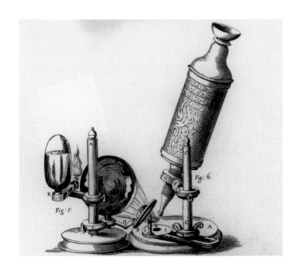

Based on his observations from his microscope, Robert Hooke wrote the book Micrographi *in 1665, which was the first to describe the structure of plant and animal cells.* LIAISON AGENCY.

141

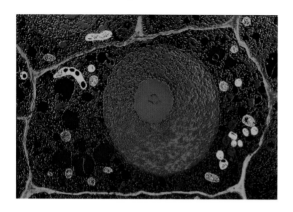

In this slide of a plant, can you find the nucleus and cytoplasm?
PHOTO RESEARCHERS INC.

Genetic researchers in silhouette against magnified DNA strands. PHOTO RESEARCHERS, INC.

1839 Theodor Schwann and Matthias Schleiden, both German zoologists, independently said that all living things have one or more cells, that all cells are similar, and that in order to exist, these cells carry out the same functions. These facts are now called the cell theory. The study of cells is called cytology. Rudolf Virchow, a German pathologist, took the cell theory further in 1855 and suggested that all cells are formed by the division of pre-existing cells. Without the cell theory we would never know how organisms grow and develop. We could not treat diseases or pains in our joints, for instance, without knowing what cells do and how they function.

What's in there? Cells are not lifeless blobs. Chemical changes within each cell accomplish many functions, including digestion and breathing. There are two basic types of cells, plant cells and animal cells. Almost all cells share similar features, such as a cell membrane, which surrounds the cell. The cell membrane is a thin wall that lets gases, such as oxygen, and fluids, such as nutrients, pass through. Cytoplasm (pronounced CY-tow-pla-sim) is the gray, jellylike substance inside the cell membrane. It consists mostly of water but also has many other substances important for cells to function.

Think of a cell as a factory with each division performing specific jobs. Organelles (pronounced OR-gan-ells) in the cytoplasm represent those divisions. For instance, Golgi bodies are organelles that act as the cleaning crew. Golgi absorb waste, package it up, and send it out for disposal. Vacuoles (pronounced VAC-u-ols) are organelles that act as the storage crew. They store food, waste, and chemicals. While there are similarities in cells, there are differences between plant and animal cells. The cytoplasm of plants, for example, contains chloroplasts, which gives the plant the ability to make its own food.

It's what makes your hair curly The nucleus, another organelle, is the cell's library. It lies in the center of the cell and contains DNA. DNA, an abbreviation for deoxyribonucleic acid, are molecules that store information. They tell each cell how to develop into a nerve cell, a blood cell, and so on. What makes you unique, as well as what makes you similar to other people, was

WORDS TO KNOW

Cells: The basic unit for living organisms; cells are structured to perform highly specialized functions.

Cell membrane: A thin-layered tissue that surrounds a cell.

Cell theory: All living things have one or more similar cells that carry out the same functions for the living process.

Chloroplasts: Small structures in plant cells that contain chlorophyll and in which the process of photosynthesis takes place.

Cytology: The branch of biology concerned with the study of cells.

Cytoplasm: The semifluid substance inside a cell that surrounds the nucleus and the other membrane-enclosed organelles.

Dicot: Plants with a pair of embryonic seeds that appear at germination.

DNA: Large, complex molecules found in nuclei of cells that carry genetic information for an organism's development.

Embryonic: The earliest stages of development.

Germination: The beginning of growth of a seed.

Golgi body: An organelles that sorts, modifies, and packages molecules.

Hypothesis: An idea in the form of a statement that can be tested by observation and/or experiment.

Monocot: Plants with a single embryonic leaf at germination.

Multicellular: Living things with many cells joined together.

Organelles: Membrane-bounded cellular "organs" performing a specific set of functions within a cell.

Pnematocysts: Stinging cells.

Protozoan: Minute, one-celled animals.

Unicellular: Living things that have one cell. Protozoans are unicellular, for example.

Vacuoles: A part of plant cells where food, waste, and chemicals are stored.

Variable: Something that can affect the results of an experiment.

---

programmed into your DNA. Each cell contains many strands of DNA. If you put them all together, they would stretch thousands of miles.

Cells are like little companies. They contain tiny workers with functions that help the living organism survive. A company's main goal is to make a profit. A cell's main goal is sustaining life. Cells also reproduce themselves by dividing. Cell division is a process where a cell divides into two cells. Yeast cells undergo a process of cell division called budding. The parent cell forms a bud on the outside of the cell wall. This bud continues to grow until it reaches the size of the parent cell and then it separates from the parent cell and

How to Experiment Safely

Use caution when collecting cells with toothpicks. When carrying the compound microscope, use two hands. After collecting pond water, wash your hands. Be careful not to stain your clothes or furniture when using the iodine.

the process starts again. Conducting projects with a microscope will enable you to see the way in which cells function and reproduce as a life force.

PROJECT 1

Investigating Cells: What are the differences between a multicellular organism and a unicellular organism?

Purpose/Hypothesis In this project, you will collect, prepare, mount, and compare cells from a multicellular organism and a single-celled protozoan. This will allow you to observe the differences between these two basic forms of organisms.

Level of Difficulty Moderate/difficult, because it requires the use of a compound microscope. (If you are unfamiliar with its use, please ask a teacher or other adult for assistance.)

Materials Needed

- compound microscope (try to borrow one from a school or friend)
- slides and cover slips, glass or plastic (Note: If your slides are plastic, use plastic cover slips.)
- stain (iodine from drugstore is good; avoid any solution with alcohol, as it will kill any organisms)
- toothpicks (flat-end toothpicks work best)
- eye dropper
- small jar filled with pond water, the dirtier the better

Approximate Budget $10 for stain, slides, cover slips, and eye dropper.

Timetable About 1 hour.

Step-by-Step Instructions

1. Use the flat end of a toothpick to gently scrape the inside of your cheek. Don't press too hard! Scrape gently five to 10 times.

Step 4: Cell culture slide, with cover slip tipping over the cell culture. GALE GROUP.

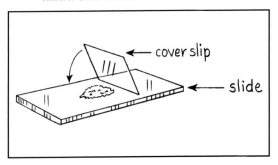

cover slip

slide

2. Smear the cells from the end of the tooth-pick onto a clean slide.
3. Place one drop of stain onto the slide, covering the cells.
4. Gently place the cover slip over the cell culture. (Hint: Gently rest one side on the slide and slowly lower the cover slip until it rests flat.)
5. Examine the slide under the microscope, using low power.
6. Draw what you see and label any parts you recognize.
7. Place two drops of pond water on the center of the slide.
8. Place a drop of stain on the pond water drops.
9. Place the cover slip over the slide using the same technique as with the cheek cells.
10. Examine the slide under the microscope, using low power.
11. Draw what you see and label the parts.

Troubleshooter's Guide

Here is a problem that may arise, a possible cause, and a way to remedy the problem.

Problem: Nothing appears on the slide.

Possible cause: You are probably out of focus. Place a small piece of paper on the slide and focus until it is clear. Use the fine focus knob.

Summary of Results Compare your diagrams and data of the cheek cells and protozoans from the pond water. Determine which cells had a more complex structure. Record a list of the differences between cheek cells and protozoan cells. Note differences such as movement, shape, presence of a cell membrane, and the presence of other cell stuctures. Summarize your observations with sketches and in writing.

PROJECT 2

Plant Cells: What are the cell differences between monocot and dicot plants?

Purpose/Hypothesis In this experiment, you will collect, prepare, and mount cells from two multicellular plants. The multicellular plants you will be working with are monocot, that is, plants with a single embryonic leaf at germina-tion, and dicot, plants with a pair of embryonic leaves at germination.

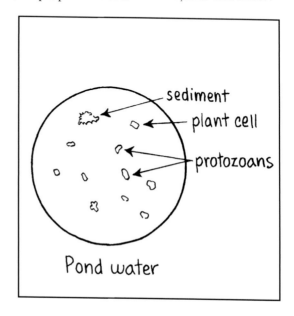

Step 7: Pond water cheek cells on low power. GALE GROUP.

How to Experiment Safely

When carrying the compound microscope, use two hands. Ask an adult to use the razor blade.

Level of Difficulty Moderate/difficult, because it requires the use of a compound microscope. (If you are unfamiliar with its use, please ask a teacher or other adult for assistance.)

Materials Needed

- compound microscope (try to borrow one from a school or friend)
- slides and cover slips, glass or plastic (Note: If you are using plastic slides, use plastic cover slips.)
- single-edge razor blade
- thread spool
- plant stems—tulip and daisy preferred (Go to a local florist and ask for a clipping of the stem.)

Approximate Budget $6 for the slides and cover slips.

Timetable About 1 hour.

Step-by-Step Instructions

1. Push the tulip stem through the hole in the thread spool until it pokes out the opposite end.

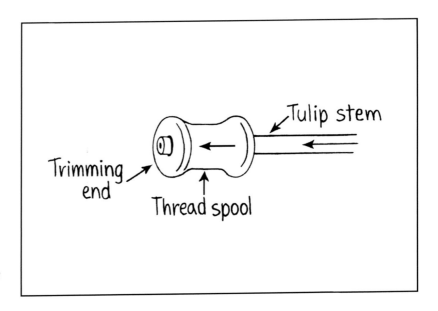

Step 1: Tulip stem in the thread spool. GALE GROUP.

2. Have an adult use the razor to trim the tulip stem, flush to the thread spool. Discard the trimmed piece.

3. Push the tulip stem through the thread spool so about .03 inch (1.0 millimeter) of stem is exposed.

4. Carefully using the razor, trim the .03 inch (1 millimeter) of tulip stem flush to the thread spool. Save the trimmed stem.

5. Place the stem slice on the slide and cover with the cover slip.

6. Place the slide on the microscope and examine under low power. Record your observations using drawings and descriptions.

7. Repeat steps 1 through 6 for the daisy stem.

8. Record and compare your observations.

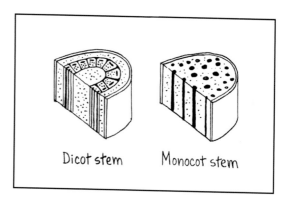

Basic differences between monocot and dicot stems: Dicot stem cells are more orderly; monocot stem cells are more random. GALE GROUP.

Summary of Results Compare your diagrams of the tulip and daisy stems. Which stem had cell patterns that were more orderly? Which stem had more random patterns? A tulip is a monocot, and a daisy is a dicot. Can you tell the difference between monocot and dicot plants by examining their stems?

PROJECT 3

Yeast Cells: How do they reproduce?

Purpose/Hypothesis In this experiment, you will prepare a yeast solution and mount these cells on slides to be viewed under the microscope. Yeast need water, food, and warmth to thrive. The food source you will use is sugar. Once the yeast are in a comfortable environment with food, you can observe the reproduction of the cells.

Step 4: Slice of tulip stem trimmed off spool by razor. GALE GROUP.

Level of Difficulty Moderate/Difficult, because it requires the use of a compound microscope. (If you are unfamiliar with its use, please ask a teacher or other adult for assistance.)

Materials Needed

- compound microscope (try to use one from your school, local community college, or university)

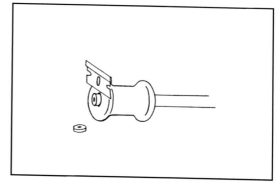

Troubleshooter's Guide

Here is a problem that may arise, a possible cause, and a way to remedy the problem.

Problem: You cannot see anything.

Possible cause: The stem is too thick. Try cutting the plant stem thinner so the light passes through it.

How to Experiment Safely

When lifting or carrying the compound microscope, use two hands. If you have not used a compound microscope before, you may need an adult to help you set up.

- slides and cover slips, glass or plastic (Note: If you are using plastic slides, use plastic cover slips.)
- yeast, available in grocery stores
- shallow, glass dish
- sugar
- warm water
- eye dropper

Approximate Budget $6

Timetable About 1 hour.

Step-by-Step Instructions

1. Prepare the yeast as recommended on the back of the package, using the warm water and sugar to activate the yeast.
2. Using the eye dropper, place one drop of water onto the slide.
3. When the yeast mixture begins to froth, place a dab of the frothy yeast onto the drop of water on the slide. Cover with cover slip.
4. Place the slide under the microscope and observe the cells. You will need a magnification of 650 to see the cells.
5. Look for cells that have another smaller cell attached to it. This is the beginning of the cell separation known as budding. If you look at the cells long enough (about 20 minutes), you should see the beginning of cell reproduction.
6. Record your observations using drawings and descriptions.

Step 1: Warm water and sugar, combined with the yeast, creates a frothy mixture.
ILLUSTRATION BY TEMAH NELSON.

Summary of Results What did you see? Were you able to see the yeast cells budding? If possible, continue to observe the yeast every five minutes. Diagram your observations.

Design Your Own Experiment

How to Select a Topic Relating to this Concept

If you choose a topic in biology, you can

generally involve the topic of cells. For example, you may be interested in jellyfish and sea anemones. These two creatures share a type of stinging cell called a pnematocyst, which paralyzes and kills their prey. The small differences in cell structure give rise to different behaviors and structure of animals and plants.

Check the Further Readings section and talk with your science teacher or school or community media specialist to start gathering information on cell questions that interest you.

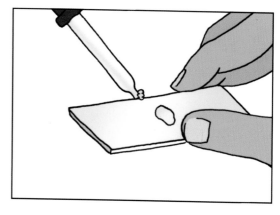

Step 2: A small amount of yeast is placed on the slide. ILLUSTRATION BY TEMAH NELSON.

Steps in the Scientific Method To do an original experiment, you need to plan carefully and think things through. Otherwise, you might not be sure what question you are answering, what you are or should be measuring, or what your findings prove or disprove.

Here are the steps in designing an experiment:

- State the purpose of—and the underlying question behind—the experiment you propose to do.
- Recognize the variables involved, and select one that will help you answer the question at hand.
- State a testable hypothesis, an educated guess about the answer to your question.
- Decide how to change the variable you selected.
- Decide how to measure your results.

Step 4: Budding can be observed after about 20 minutes. ILLUSTRATION BY TEMAH NELSON.

Recording Data and Summarizing the Results Your experiment can be useful to others studying the same topic. When designing your experiment, develop a simple method to record your data. This method should be simple and clear enough so that others who want to do the experiment can follow it. Your final results should be summarized and put into simple graphs, tables, and charts to display the outcome of your experiment.

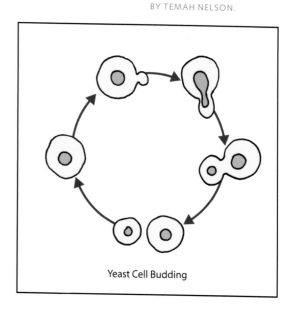

Yeast Cell Budding

Related Projects Creating a project about cells offers endless possibilities. You can create a slide

Troubleshooter's Guide

Here is a problem that may arise, a possible cause, and a way to remedy the problem.

Problem: You cannot see anything.

Possible cause: You do not have the correct level of magnification. Make sure the microscope is set with a high enough magnification power in order to observe the cells.

Problem: The yeast cells are too close together to observe budding.

Possible cause: You may have too much of the yeast mixture on your slide. Take another slide, add a droplet of water and place a smaller amount of the yeast mixture onto the slide.

Problem: The yeast cells are not budding.

Possible cause: The yeast may not have been alive Purchase a fresh container of yeast. Try again, making sure that the water is not too hot or it may kill the yeast.

collection of cells from many different plants (stem, seed, leaf, needle, root, etc.). You can create a model of a cell labeling the parts and functions. Making a model from colored plastic clay is inexpensive and informative.

For More Information

Andrew Rader Studios. "Cell Structures." *Rader's Biology4kids.com.* http://www.biology4kids.com/files/cell_main.html (accessed on January 19, 2008). Information on cell structures and functions.

Bender, Lionel. *Atoms and Cells.* Glouster, ME: Glouster Press, 1990 Provides background and functions of atoms and cells.

Cells Alive! http://cellsalive.com Interactive graphics and pictures of cells in motion.

Young, John K. *Cells: Amazing Forms and Functions.* New York: Franklin Watts, 1990. Good, understandable overview of these units of life for young people.

12

Chemical Energy

Chemical energy is the energy stored within the bonds of atoms. A bond is the force that holds two atoms together. Different substances have bonds held together by different amounts of energy. When those bonds are released, a chemical reaction takes place, and a new substance is created. Chemical reactions that break these bonds and form new ones sometimes release the excess energy as heat and sometimes absorb heat energy from whatever is around them.

Thus, heat energy can be produced or absorbed during a chemical reaction. Reactions that release heat energy are called exothermic. Reactions that take in heat energy from the surrounding environment are called endothermic. Whether heat energy is given off or absorbed during a chemical reaction depends on the bonds that hold the atoms together.

In a chemical reaction, the original substances are called reactants. The new substances that are formed are called products. When the bonding structure of the products requires less energy than the bonding structure of the reactants, the excess energy may be released as heat. When the bonding structure of the products requires more energy than the structure of the reactants, it gets that energy by removing heat from its surroundings.

For example, when iron rusts, the iron atoms are combining with oxygen molecules in the air to form iron oxide. The chemical reaction of rusting breaks the bonds in the oxygen molecules, releasing heat energy. The bonds between the oxygen atoms and the iron atoms do not require as much heat energy as the bonds within the oxygen molecules, so a small amount of energy is released, making the reaction exothermic. The amount of heat released is quite small, and the reaction is normally quite slow, so rusting iron does not feel hot to us. Yet, the energy released can be measured with a thermometer. In the first experiment, you will observe the change in temperature resulting from rusting.

The chemical reaction that occurs when iron rusts actually gives off small amounts of heat energy. PHOTO RESEARCHERS INC.

Some exothermic reactions are quite common. One is combustion, the burning of organic substances during which oxygen is used to form carbon dioxide and water vapor. The substances formed (ashes, for example) hold less heat energy than the substances burned held. The excess energy is released as heat. The reactions between some chemicals, such as aluminum oxide and iron oxide, can produce great amounts of heat. This reaction is used to produce very high temperatures for industrial purposes.

Endothermic reactions are more rare in nature, but scientists have found ways to create them. For example, an endothermic reaction occurs when you use a chemical cold pack. These packs contain a chemical in powder form that reacts with water. Squeezing the pack breaks down the wall separating the powder from the water. The reaction that occurs absorbs more energy than it releases, making the pack feel cold to you. In the second experiment, you will compare four chemical reactions and determine whether each one is exothermic or endothermic.

This hot pack releases an exothermic reaction. PHOTO RESEARCHERS INC.

EXPERIMENT 1

Rusting: Is the chemical reaction exothermic, endothermic, or neither?

Purpose/Hypothesis In this experiment, you will measure the heat energy released or absorbed by the chemical reaction of rusting, the transformation of iron and atmospheric oxygen into iron oxide. Before you begin, make an educated guess about the outcome of this experiment based on your knowledge of rusting. This educated guess, or prediction, is your hypothesis. A hypothesis should explain these things:

- the topic of the experiment
- the variable you will change
- the variable you will measure
- what you expect to happen

WORDS TO KNOW

Atom: The smallest unit of an element, made up of protons and neutrons in a central nucleus surrounded by moving electrons.

Bond: The force that holds two atoms together.

Chemical energy: Energy stored in chemical bonds.

Chemical reaction: Any chemical change in which at least one new substance is formed.

Combustion: Any chemical reaction in which heat, and usually light, is produced. It is commonly the burning of organic substances during which oxygen from the air is used to form carbon dioxide and water vapor.

Control experiment: A set-up that is identical to the experiment but is not affected by the variable that will be changed during the experiment.

Endothermic: A chemical reaction that takes in heat energy.

Exothermic: A chemical reaction that gives off heat energy.

Heat: A form of energy produced by the motion of molecules that make up a substance.

Hypothesis: An idea in the form of a statement that can be tested by observation and/or experiment.

Molecule: The smallest particle of a substance that retains all the properties of the substance and is composed of one or more atoms.

Product: A compound that is formed as a result of a chemical reaction.

Reactant: A compound present at the beginning of a chemical reaction.

Variable: Something that can affect the results of an experiment.

A hypothesis should be brief, specific, and measurable. It must be something you can test through observation. Your experiment will prove or disprove whether your hypothesis is correct. Here is one possible hypothesis for this experiment: "A rise in air temperature will show that rusting is an exothermic reaction."

In this case, the variable you will change is the number of rusting pads in each cup, and the variable you will measure is any change in air temperature. You expect the temperature to go up in the cups with rusting pads and the temperature to go up the most in the cup with the most pads.

As a control experiment, you will leave one cup empty and monitor any change in temperature there. If the temperature is higher in the cup with

How to Experiment Safely

Wear protective gloves when handling the steel wool and vinegar.

What Are the Variables?

Variables are anything that might affect the results of an experiment. Here are the main variables in this experiment:

- the type of reactants used (iron in the pads and atmospheric oxygen)
- the temperature of the environment in which the samples are tested
- the number of rusting pads in each cup

In other words, the variables in this experiment are everything that might affect the temperature in the cup. If you change more than one variable, you will not be able to tell which variable had the most effect on the temperature.

more pads and does not change in the empty cup, your hypothesis will be supported.

Level of Difficulty Moderate.

Materials Needed

- 4 large Styrofoam cups
- aluminum foil
- 7 steel wool pads (not pads treated with detergent or soap)
- vinegar
- 4 digital laboratory thermometers
- rubber or surgical gloves
- paper towels
- large bowl

Approximate Budget $10. (If four thermometers are unavailable, the four parts of this experiment can be performed separately with one thermometer.)

Timetable About 45 minutes.

Step-by-Step Instructions

1. Line the inside of each of the four cups with aluminum foil.
2. Place the seven steel wool pads in the large bowl and soak them thoroughly in vinegar (to remove any coating and encourage rusting). Blot them dry with paper towels.
3. Place one pad in the first cup, two pads in the second cup, and four pads in the third cup. The fourth cup will be empty—your control.
4. Push the bulb of one thermometer gently into the steel wool in the first cup. Do not push the bulb down to or near the bottom of the cup. Cover the opening of the cup with aluminum foil. The stem on the thermometer must be visible.
5. Repeat Step 4 for the second, third, and fourth (control) cups.
6. Place all four cups where no other heat sources will affect their temperature.
7. Prepare a chart similar to the one illustrated so you can record your observations.

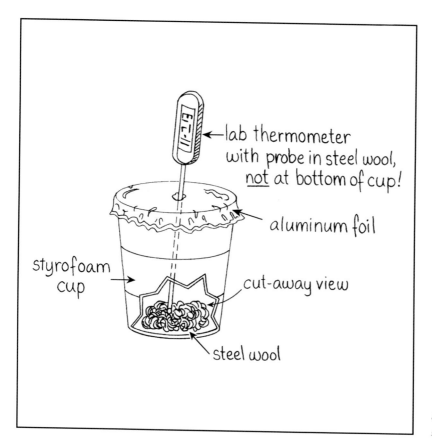

Step 4: Illustration of rusting set-up. GALE GROUP.

8. Observe and record any change in temperature in any of the four cups every 10 minutes. The rusting process will begin immediately, but the resulting change in temperature will be gradual and

	10 min.	20 min.	30 min.	40 min.
Cup 1				
2				
3				
4				

Step 7: Temperature recording chart. GALE GROUP.

Troubleshooter's Guide

Few problems should arise if the steps in this experiment are followed closely. However, when doing experiments involving the mixing of substances, be aware that a number of variables—such as temperature and impurity of substances—can affect your results. Here is a problem that may arise, a possible cause, and a way to remedy the problem.

Problem: You observed little or no temperature change in the cups.

Possible cause: The steel wool is not rusting. Try soaking it in vinegar again for several minutes to remove any protective layers and then repeat the experiment.

small. Make sure that external factors are not affecting the temperature, such as sunlight or heat from a lamp.

Summary of Results Examine your results and determine whether your hypothesis is correct. Did the temperature rise higher when more wool pads were in the cup? Did it rise in the empty cup? If the reactions resulted in an increase in temperature, then rusting is indeed exothermic. Make sure that your chart shows clearly the result of the tests on each sample.

Change the Variables You can vary this experiment. Here are some possibilities:

- Other metals will oxidize, though at much slower rates. See if you can measure the temperature change resulting from the oxidation of copper (loops of copper wire may be best).

- Compare the heat energy released by different kinds of oxidation. What about the oxidation you can see occurring on the cut surface of an apple? Find a way to determine if that reaction is exothermic. Always check first with your teacher before altering the materials used in your experiments.

EXPERIMENT 2

Exothermic or Endothermic: Determining whether various chemical reactions are exothermic or endothermic

Purpose/Hypothesis In this experiment, you will measure the heat energy released or absorbed as four different chemicals (see the materials list) are mixed with water. You expect that the temperature of the solution will go up if the reaction is exothermic and go down if the reaction is endothermic. Before you begin, make an educated guess about the outcome of each reaction based on your knowledge of the chemicals and reactions involved. This educated guess, or prediction, is your hypothesis. A hypothesis should explain these things:

- the topic of the experiment
- the variable you will change
- the variable you will measure
- what you expect to happen

A hypothesis should be brief, specific, and measurable. It must be something you can test through observation. Your experiment will prove or disprove whether your hypothesis is correct. Here is one possible hypothesis for one of the reactions in this experiment: "Mixing water with calcium chloride will produce an exothermic reaction."

In this case, the variable you will change is the chemical being reacted with water, and the variable you will measure is the resulting temperature of the solution. In the case of calcium chloride, you expect the temperature to go up.

As a control experiment, you will measure the temperature in a beaker of distilled water with no chemical in it. If the temperature changes in the beakers with chemicals as predicted and remains steady in the control beaker, you will know your hypothesis is supported.

Level of Difficulty Moderate; an adult's supervision is required.

Materials Needed

- 5 glass beakers
- 1 graduated cylinder
- 1 glass stirring rod
- 1 small spoon or spatula
- 1 digital laboratory thermometer
- 1 pint (500 milliliters) distilled water
- 1 tablespoon (14 grams) calcium chloride
- 1 tablespoon (14 grams) sodium hydrocarbonate
- 1 tablespoon (14 grams) ammonium nitrate

What Are the Variables?

Variables are anything that might affect the results of an experiment. Here are the main variables in this experiment:

- the type of reactants used
- the purity of the reactants
- the temperature of the environment in which the samples are tested

In other words, the variables in this experiment are everything that might affect the temperature of the solutions. If you change more than one variable, you will not be able to tell which variable had the most effect on the temperature.

Wear gloves and safety glasses or goggles at all times while performing this experiment. GALE GROUP.

How to Experiment Safely

This experiment involves dangerous and toxic substances. No part of this experiment should be performed without adult supervision. You must be especially careful handling the sulfuric acid, which is highly corrosive. **Wear gloves and safety glasses or goggles at all times!** When you are finished with the experiment, the chemicals used must be disposed of properly and with supervision. Ask your teacher for help in handling, neutralizing, and disposing of the sulfuric acid.

- 2 teaspoons (10 milliliters) concentrated sulfuric acid
- safety glasses or goggles
- rubber or surgical gloves

Approximate Budget $25. (This experiment should be performed only with the appropriate lab equipment and materials. Ask your teacher about ordering the chemicals.)

Timetable One hour.

Step-by-Step Instructions

1. Place the five beakers on a clean, stable surface and use the graduated cylinder to

Exothermic vs. Endothermic					
	30 sec.	1 min.	1½ min.	2 min.	2½ min.
water only (control)					
water and calcium chloride					
water and sodium hydrocarbonate					
water and ammonium nitrate					
water and sulfuric acid					

Step 2: Exothermic vs. endothermic recording chart.
GALE GROUP.

measure and pour 3½ tablespoons (about 50 milliliters) of distilled water into each one.

2. Prepare a chart on which you will record your observations. Your chart should look something like the illustration.

3. Place the thermometer in the first beaker and record the temperature on your chart. This sample, which contains only the distilled water, will be your control.

4. Using the spoon or small spatula, add about half the sample of calcium chloride to the second beaker. Stir it gently until it is mixed with the distilled water.

5. Place the thermometer in the beaker and note the temperature once each 30 seconds for five minutes. Record the temperatures on the chart. When you are done, be sure to rinse the thermometer with room-temperature distilled water.

6. Repeat Steps 4 and 5 for the sodium hydrocarbonate and the ammonium nitrate. Remember to rinse the thermometer, stirring rod, spatula, or spoon in distilled water after each test.

7. In the last beaker, slowly and gently add all of the sulfuric acid to the water. Be careful not to spill or splash the acid. Place the thermometer in the beaker and note the temperature once each 30 seconds for five minutes. Record the temperature changes on your chart. When you are done, be sure to rinse the thermometer.

Summary of Results Examine your results and determine whether each of your hypotheses is correct. If any reactions resulted in an increase in temperature, those reactions are exothermic. If any reactions resulted in

Steps 3 to 7: Exothermic vs. endothermic set-up beakers.
GALE GROUP.

Troubleshooter's Guide

When doing experiments involving the mixing of substances, be aware that a number of variables—such as temperature and impurity of substances—can affect your results. When mixing substances, you must keep the mixing containers and utensils clean. Even tiny impurities in a mixture can drastically alter your results.

Here is a problem that may arise, a possible cause, and a way to remedy the problem.

Problem: You observed little or no temperature change in the beakers.

Possible cause: You are not placing enough of the solid reactants in the water. Try increasing the amount of solid reactant.

a decrease in temperature, they are endothermic. Make sure that your chart shows clearly the result of the tests on each set of reactants. It may be helpful to those viewing your results to see a diagram outlining the procedure you followed.

Change the Variables You can vary this experiment by trying reactions involving different household materials or chemical compounds. Do not mix them with anything other than water. Always check first with your teacher before altering the materials used in your experiments.

Design Your Own Experiment

How to Select a Topic Relating to this Concept Other kinds of experiments can reveal interesting facts about endothermic and exothermic reactions. Our bodies produce exothermic reactions when we turn food into energy. Can you measure the amount of food energy available in a sample by burning it and measuring the resulting temperature change in a sample of water? Review the description of how cold packs work. Can you think of a way to design a homemade cold pack?

Check the Further Readings section and talk with your science teacher or school or community media specialist to start gathering information on chemical reaction questions that interest you.

Steps in the Scientific Method To do an original experiment, you need to plan carefully and think things through. Otherwise, you might not be sure what question you are answering, what you are or should be measuring, or what your findings prove or disprove.

Here are the steps in designing an experiment:

- State the purpose of—and the underlying question behind—the experiment you propose to do.
- Recognize the variables involved, and select one that will help you answer the question at hand.
- State a testable hypothesis, an educated guess about the answer to your question.

- Decide how to change the variable you selected.
- Decide how to measure your results.

Recording Data and Summarizing the Results In the experiments included here and in any experiments you develop, strive to display your data in accurate and interesting ways. Remember that those who view your results may not have seen the experiment performed, so you must present the information you have gath-

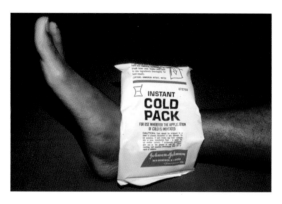

Some cold packs use a chemical reaction that starts when you squeeze the pack. The pack cools off in an endothermic reaction. PHOTO RESEARCHERS INC.

ered as clearly as possible. Including photographs or illustrations of the steps in the experiment is a good way to show a viewer how you got from your hypothesis to your conclusion.

Related Projects Chemical energy is a basic and crucial part of life processes as well as technological processes. Projects that determine the energy produced by different fuels and compare the by-products of those fuels can help to demonstrate the necessity for developing alternative energy sources. Examining different reactions and determining their endothermic or exothermic rate can help us understand where so much of the energy we use goes.

For More Information

BBC. "Mixtures." *Schools. Science: Chemistry.* http://www.bbc.co.uk/schools/ ks3bitesize/science/chemistry/index.shtml (accessed on February 18, 2008). Basic information on the chemistry of mixtures.

California Energy Commission. "What is Energy?" *Energy Story.* http:// www.energyquest.ca.gov/story/chapter01.html (accessed on February 28, 2008). Explanation of the different types of energy.

Gillett, Kate, ed. *The Knowledge Factory.* Brookfield, CT: Copper Beech Books, 1996. Provides some fun and enlightening observations on questions relevant to this topic, along with good ideas for projects and demonstrations.

13

Chemical Properties

How many ways can you describe a substance? Two common ways are by listing its physical properties and its chemical properties. A physical property is a characteristic of a substance that you can detect with your senses, such as its color, shape, size, smell, taste, texture, temperature, density, or volume. For example, a lemon is yellow, oval-shaped, and smaller than a grapefruit. It has a sharp smell and a rough texture.

A physical change changes a physical property but does not change the identity or molecular makeup of the substance. One example of a physical change is salt crystals dissolving in water, which changes their shape. When the water evaporates, you can see the salt crystals again, unchanged by being dissolved in the water. Tearing paper into small pieces is also a physical change. The bits of paper look different, but they are still composed of the same molecules as when they were joined together.

A chemical property is the ability of a substance to react with other substances or to decompose. For example, a chemical property of iron is that it reacts with oxygen and rusts. A chemical property of a substance allows it to undergo a chemical change. A chemical change is the change of one or more substances into another substance. A chemical change is also called a chemical reaction.

During some chemical reactions, two or more substances are combined to form one new substance. An example is oxygen combining with iron to form rust. This is called a synthesis reaction. During other chemical reactions, one substance is broken down into two or more new substances. An example of this is hydrogen peroxide, which is used to treat small cuts. It breaks down into oxygen and water in the presence of light, which is why hydrogen peroxide is stored in dark bottles. This is called a decomposition reaction. A chemical reaction can be very quick, such as paper burning, or very slow, such as food digesting in your stomach.

Ice melting is an example of a physical change. FIELDMARK PUBLICATIONS.

Burning is a chemical change or reaction, producing new substances. Some substances are more flammable than others. AP IMAGES.

What are some examples of chemical properties? Chemical properties include flammability (the ability to catch on fire), toxicity (the ability to be poisonous), oxidation (the ability to react with oxygen, which causes apple slices to turn brown and iron to rust), radioactivity (spontaneously emitting energy in the form of particles or waves by the disintegration of their atomic nuclei), and sensitivity to light (which causes newspaper to turn yellow).

Being acidic or basic is another kind of chemical property. An acid is a substance that can react with, or corrode, other substances. A base is a substance that feels slippery when dissolved in water. When an acid and a base are combined, they react chemically with each other to produce new substances: a salt and water.

Many foods contain acids, including tomatoes, lemons, oranges, and carbonated soft drinks. For most people, eating the small amounts of acid in these foods does not cause a problem. In fact, the hydrochloric acid in our stomachs helps produce the chemical reaction called digestion. However, the acid in tomatoes reacts so strongly with aluminum that foods containing tomato sauce should not be stored in aluminum foil. The acid in tomatoes can actually burn holes in the foil.

Acids can also damage the environment. Burning coal produces nitric and sulfuric acids that combine with the water vapor in the air to create acid rain. Acid rain burns trees and plants. It can cause lakes and rivers to become so acidic that fish and plants can no longer survive there.

Many cleaning products are bases, including soaps, drain cleaners, and ammonia. Basic substances, too, can damage the skin and eyes. For example, some people who breathe ammonia fumes get nosebleeds as the fumes react with the sensitive tissues in their noses.

What happens during a chemical reaction? In a chemical reaction, the substances you begin with are called reactants. The new substances that are formed are called products.

The explosion of fireworks produces heat, light, and sound energy in an exothermic reaction. PHOTO RESEARCHERS INC.

For example, when the acetic acid in vinegar and baking soda (reactants) are combined, the products are bubbles of carbon dioxide gas, water, and sodium acetate.

The chemical properties of the reactants determine what happens during the reaction—and how quickly it happens. For example, one chemical property of magnesium is that it reacts strongly with hydrochloric acid to produce bubbles of hydrogen gas. Not all metals have this property. Dipping a strip of copper into hydrochloric acid produces no hydrogen bubbles. Dipping zinc into the acid results in some bubbles, but fewer than for the magnesium.

In the same way, iron reacts strongly with oxygen to produce rust. However, other metals, such as silver and gold, do not react with oxygen (do not have this chemical property) and so do not rust when exposed to the air.

Many chemical reactions produce energy. For example, when something burns, it produces heat energy. Thus, smoke is one sign of a chemical reaction. Other signs of chemical reactions include foaming, a smell, a sound, and a change in color. A chemical reaction that releases heat or light energy is called an exothermic reaction. Examples include fireworks explosions, luminescent "light sticks," and the digestive process in your body.

Some chemical reactions absorb heat or light energy and are called endothermic reactions. One example is the way green plants absorb sunlight and change it into the chemical energy in sugar and in oxygen.

WORDS TO KNOW

Acid: Substance that when dissolved in water is capable of reacting with a base to form salts and release hydrogen ions.

Base: Substance that when dissolved in water is capable of reacting with an acid to form salts and release hydrogen ions.

Chemical change: The change of one or more substances into other substances.

Chemical property: A characteristic of a substance that allows it to undergo a chemical change. Chemical properties include flammability and sensitivity to light.

Chemical reaction: Any chemical change in which at least one new substance is formed.

Control experiment: A set-up that is identical to the experiment but is not affected by the variable that affects the experimental group.

Decompose: To break down into two or more simpler substances.

Decomposition reaction: A chemical reaction in which one substance is broken down into two or more substances.

Endothermic reaction: A chemical reaction that absorbs heat or light energy, such as photosynthesis, the production of food by plant cells.

Exothermic reaction: A chemical reaction that releases heat or light energy, such as the burning of fuel.

Hypothesis: An idea phrased in the form of a statement that can be tested by observation and/or experiment.

Luminescent: Producing light through a chemical process.

Physical change: A change in which the substance keeps its molecular identity, such as a piece of chalk that has been ground up.

Physical property: A characteristic that you can detect with your senses, such as color and shape.

Product: A compound that is formed as a result of a chemical reaction.

Reactant: A compound present at the beginning of a chemical reaction.

Synthesis reaction: A chemical reaction in which two or more substances combine to form a new substance.

Variable: Something that can change the results of an experiment.

In the two experiments that follow, you will have an opportunity to produce chemical reactions by using the chemical properties of certain substances. In one experiment, you will combine white glue and borax (a mineral that acts as a laundry booster) to create an entirely new substance. In the second experiment, you will combine water, iodine, and oil to see what kind of chemical reaction occurs. The more you understand about chemical reactions, the better you will understand the workings of the world around—and inside—you.

EXPERIMENT 1

Slime: What happens when white glue and borax mix?

Purpose/Hypothesis In this experiment, you will mix two substances to see if a chemical reaction occurs. The chemical name of one of the substances, white glue, is polyvinylacetate. You will mix the polyvinylacetate with borax, a laundry booster (sodium borate). Borax is a natural mineral, found in the ground. It's made of boron, sodium, oxygen, and water. It is used to strengthen the cleaning power of laundry detergents.

To begin the experiment, make an educated guess about what will happen when you combine these two substances. Will there be a chemical reaction? Will it produce a new substance? If so, what might the substance look like? This guess, or prediction, is your hypothesis. A hypothesis should explain these things:

- the topic of the experiment
- the variable you will change
- the variable you will measure
- what you expect to happen

A hypothesis should be brief, specific, and measurable. It must be something you can test through observation. Your experiment will prove or disprove whether your hypothesis is correct. Here is one possible hypothesis for this experiment: "Mixing polyvinylacetate with borax will create a chemical reaction and produce a new substance."

In this experiment, the variable you will change is the mixing of the two substances, and the variable you will measure (or examine) is the product of this mixture. As a control experiment, you will observe a sample of polyvinylacetate that is not mixed with borax to see if a chemical reaction occurs. If only the mixture with the borax in it produces a new substance, your hypothesis will be supported.

Level of Difficulty Easy/moderate.

Materials Needed

- white glue
- water

What Are the Variables?

Variables are anything that might affect the results of an experiment. Here are the variables in this experiment:

- the amounts of the substances used in the actual experiment and the control experiment
- the length of time the mixtures are shaken

If you change more than one variable between the actual experiment and the control experiment, you will not be able to determine which variable affected the results.

- food coloring
- 3 jars with lids
- borax
- labels
- spoons
- measuring spoons
- sealable plastic bag
- goggles

Approximate Budget Up to $5.

Timetable 10 minutes to set up; 1 hour to observe.

Step-by-Step Instructions

1. Measure 3 tablespoons (44 milliliters) of water and the same amount of white glue into one jar.
2. Add several drops of food coloring to the jar.
3. Close the jar and shake the mixture vigorously until the glue dissolves in the water. Label the jar "experiment."
4. Repeat Steps 1 to 3, using another jar, and label this jar "control."
5. In the third jar, put 3 tablespoons (44 milliliters) of water. Slowly pour in 2 tablespoons (30 milliliters) of borax. Allow the mixture to settle for a minute.
6. Carefully pour the excess water from the third jar down a sink drain.
7. Use a spoon to scrape the wet borax mixture into the experiment jar.
8. With the lids closed, shake both the experiment and control jars for at least two minutes.
9. Record your observations of the experiment jar and the control jar in a table similar to the one illustrated. Wait half an hour and record them again. After another half an hour, record your final observations.

Step 7: Use a spoon to scrape the wet borax mixture into the experiment jar. GALE GROUP.

Table 1: Observations of Change

	Experiment jar	Control jar
Beginning of experiment		
After ½ hour		
After 1 hour		

Step 9: Recording table for Experiment 1. GALE GROUP.

10. Open the experimental jar and remove the product you have created. Observe and experiment with its new physical properties.

11. Store your "slime" in the sealable plastic bag to keep it from spoiling.

Summary of Results Study your observations and decide whether your hypothesis was correct. Did the combination of white glue and borax produce a chemical reaction? How do you know? Did the same reaction occur in the control jar without the borax?

What happened here? In a liquid form, the molecules in polyvinylacetate are separate, allowing the glue to flow. When you added the borax, a chemical reaction caused the molecules in the white glue to wrap around each other, forming a soft ball. The combination of the two substances produced an entirely new substance that looks and feels like slime.

Write a paragraph summarizing your findings and explaining whether they support your hypothesis.

Step 10: Observe and experiment with the "slime" you have created. GALE GROUP.

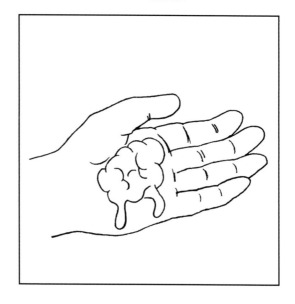

What Are the Variables?

Variables are anything that might affect the results of an experiment. Here are the main variables in this experiment:

- the amount of iodine added to the water in the experiment
- the temperature of the ingredients (they will remain at room temperature to control this variable)
- the kind of oil used (other kinds of oil may react differently)

If you change more than one variable, you will not be able to tell which variable had the most effect on the chemical reaction.

Step 3: Add about five drops of iodine to the experiment jar.
GALE GROUP.

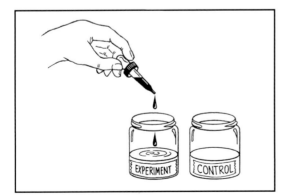

Change the Variables You can vary this experiment by changing the amount of borax you mix with the white glue solution. Your products will range from sticky slime, to a bouncy ball, to a very hard ball.

You might also experiment with other types of glue, such as gel glue and washable glue, to see if they form the same kind of product when mixed with borax.

EXPERIMENT 2

Chemical Reactions: What happens when mineral oil, water, and iodine mix?

Purpose/Hypothesis In this experiment, you will mix water with iodine and then add mineral oil to see whether a chemical reaction occurs. Remember the possible signs of a chemical reaction: the production or absorption of heat or light energy, smoke, bubbles of gas, a smell, a sound, and a change in color.

You know that water and oil do not mix. Instead, they remain as separate layers. You probably also know that a combination of water and oil does not produce any sign of a chemical reaction. If such a reaction is to occur, it must be caused by the iodine. Make an educated guess about the outcome of this experiment. This guess, or prediction, is your hypothesis. A hypothesis should explain these things:

- the topic of the experiment
- the variable you will change
- the variable you will measure
- what you expect to happen

A hypothesis should be brief, specific, and measurable. It must be something you can test through observation. Your experiment will prove or disprove whether your hypothesis is correct. Here is one possible hypothesis for this experiment: "Iodine will cause a chemical reaction when mixed with mineral oil and water."

In this case, the variable you will change is the presence of iodine. The variable you will measure or observe is evidence of a chemical reaction. As your control experiment, you will combine mineral oil and water, without adding iodine, and watch for signs of a chemical reaction. If a change occurs only in the mixture with the iodine, your hypothesis will be supported.

How to Experiment Safely

Wear goggles to protect your eyes from possible splashes of iodine. Avoid getting iodine or mineral oil on your clothing or furniture, as it will stain.

Level of Difficulty Easy/moderate.

Materials Needed Note: All ingredients should be at room temperature.

- 2 jars with lids, such as peanut butter jars
- labels
- water
- a container of iodine with a dropper
- mineral oil
- measuring cups
- goggles

Approximate Budget $5 for iodine and mineral oil; other materials should be available in the average household.

Table 2: Evidence of a Chemical Change	Experiment jar	Control jar
After adding iodine		———————
After adding mineral oil		
After vigorous shaking		

Step 4: Recording table for Experiment 2. GALE GROUP.

Troubleshooter's Guide

Below is a problem that may arise during this experiment, a possible cause, and a way to remedy the problem.

Problem: The mixture with iodine did not change color.

Possible cause: You did not shake it long enough. Shake it some more and observe what happens.

Timetable 30 minutes.

Step-by-Step Instructions

1. Label one jar "experiment" and one jar "control."

2. Pour $\frac{1}{4}$ cup (60 milliliters) of water into each jar.

3. Add about five drops of iodine to the experiment jar.

4. Record your observations on a table similar to the one illustrated.

5. Pour $\frac{1}{4}$ cup (60 milliliters) of mineral oil into each jar. Record your observations in the table.

6. Shake both jars, one in each hand, for two minutes. Again, record any changes you observe.

Summary of Results Study the observations on your table and decide whether your hypothesis was correct. Did a chemical reaction take place in the mixture containing iodine? How can you tell? Did a chemical reaction occur in the mixture without the iodine? Write a paragraph summarizing your findings and explaining whether they support your hypothesis.

Step 6: Shake both jars, one in each hand, for two minutes. GALE GROUP.

When you shook the mixture containing iodine, the iodine moved from the water into the oil, causing a color change, which is evidence of a chemical reaction. If you shake the experiment jar long enough, all the iodine will move into the oil, and the water will become clear again. The iodine causes the chemical reaction, so the mixture without iodine did not change.

Change the Variables Here are some ways you can vary this experiment:

- Use other kinds of oil, such as safflower or peanut oil, to see if the same color change results.

- Use very hot or icy-cold water to see how a change in temperature affects this chemical reaction.

PROJECT 3

Chemical Patination: Producing chemical reactions on metal

A patina is a change in an object's surface layer, which can occur from natural weathering or a controlled reaction. Outdoor copper and bronze are examples of natural greens and browns that are possible. Patinas form from a chemical reaction called oxidation. Chemical patination is often used for decorative effect to produce metals that are black, blues, and greens.

The color a chemical patination produces depends upon the type of metal and the chemistry of the solutions applied to the metal. It also depends upon the way the treatment is applied, such as the length of time and temperature. In the project, you will experiment with chemical patination on copper to observe how different solutions react with the metal. In two of the tests, the metal will react with the vapor of the solution while also reacting with oxygen. For the third test, you will wipe the solution onto the metal.

Level of Difficulty Moderate, because of the time involved.

Materials Needed

- white vinegar
- ammonia
- salt
- lemon juice
- measuring cup
- small bowl
- 3 sheets of thin copper, several inches long, available from craft or art stores
- 3 lidded plastic containers that the copper sheet fits into
- sandpaper
- washers, brass nuts, or other metal objects that fit inside the plastic containers

> ## How to Experiment Safely
>
> Work in a well-ventilated area because ammonia can have an odor that may cause irritation. Wash your hands after the experiment and dispose of the contents carefully. Never mix ammonia with a substance without first asking a knowledgeable adult.

Step 3: Place a metal object, such as a several washers or a brass nut, on the bottom of the container. The copper sheet will sit on the object.
ILLUSTRATION BY TEMAH NELSON.

Step 4: Pour vinegar slightly below the top of the object.
ILLUSTRATION BY TEMAH NELSON.

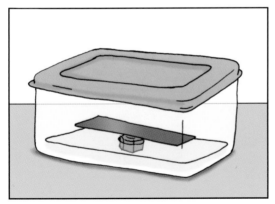

- aluminum foil
- cloth

Approximate Budget $12.

Timetable 30 minutes to set up; at least eight hours to three days to observe changes.

Step-by-Step Instructions

1. If the copper sheets are not clean, wash with soap and allow them to dry.
2. Lightly sand the copper sheets and wipe well.

Test 1

3. Place a metal object, such as a several washers or a brass nut, on the bottom of the container. The copper sheet will sit on the object. You will want the sheet resting slightly above the solution. See illustration.
4. Pour vinegar slightly below the top of the object.
5. Place the copper sheet on the washers (or other object) and loosely cover (do not seal the cover). Leave overnight or for at least eight hours.

Test 2

6. Place a metal object, such as a several washers or a brass nut, on the bottom of the container. Again, you will want the sheet resting slightly above the solution.
7. Pour ammonia slightly below the top of the object.
8. Place the copper sheet on the washers (or other object) and loosely cover. Leave overnight or for at least eight hours.

Test 3

9. In a small bowl, combine one-quarter cup lemon juice, one-quarter cup table salt, one-quarter cup household ammonia, and one-half cup vinegar.

10. Set the third copper sheet on a piece of aluminum foil. Use the cloth to wipe the solution onto the sheet.

11. Wait approximately two hours or until the copper is dry. Apply another coat and allow to dry. You will need to apply the solution at least six times.

Summary of Results Record how each of the copper sheets appear. Describe the colors and deepness of each chemical patination. Where did the patination occur on the metal? Try scraping the color off with your fingernail. If you want to try and reproduce or produce more of one color, make sure you check with an adult if you are when making up your solutions.

Design Your Own Experiment

How to Select a Topic Relating to this Concept The world—and your own life—depend on chemical properties and the chemical reactions that result from them. Consider what you would like to know about these properties and reactions. For example, what chemical reactions occur inside your body? Which ones are essential in manufacturing? What chemical reactions help shape the landscape?

Check the Further Readings section and talk with your science teacher or school or community media specialist to start gathering information on questions that interest you. As you consider possible experiments, be sure to discuss them with your science teacher or another knowledgeable adult before trying them. Combining certain materials can be dangerous.

Steps in the Scientific Method To do an original experiment, you need to plan carefully and think things through. Otherwise, you might not be sure which question you are answering,

Troubleshooter's Guide

Here is a common problem that you may experience during this project and tips to remedy the problems.

Problem: The copper does not change color in the first two trials.

Possible causes:

1. The copper may not be getting enough oxygen. Make sure the copper solution is not sealed completely, and the metal is not immersed in the solution. Try the trial again.

2. There may not be enough vapor for the chemical patination to occur. The lid might be too loose. Place the lid so it fits neatly over the container, but do not seal, and try the test again.

Record how each of the copper sheets appear. ILLUSTRATION BY TEMAH NELSON.

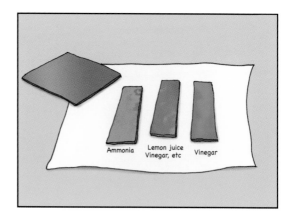

what you are or should be measuring, or what your findings prove or disprove.

Here are the steps in designing an experiment:

- State the purpose of—and the underlying question behind—the experiment you propose to do.
- Recognize the variables involved, and select one that will help you answer the question at hand.
- State a testable hypothesis, an educated guess about the answer to your question.
- Decide how to change the variable you selected.
- Decide how to measure your results.

Recording Data and Summarizing the Results In your "slime" and iodine experiments, your raw data might include tables, drawings, and photographs of the changes you observed. If you display your experiment, make clear the question you are trying to answer, the variable you changed, the variable you measured, the results, and your conclusions. Explain what materials you used, how long each step took, and other basic information.

Related Projects You can undertake a variety of projects related to chemical reactions. For example, a number of chemical reactions occur in the kitchen as food cooks on the stove or bakes in the oven. Breads and cakes rise because of a chemical reaction. Some medicines for an upset stomach depend on chemical reactions to cause fizz in a glass of water. You can even make pennies turn green because of a chemical reaction!

For More Information

Gardner, Robert. *Science Projects about Chemistry*. Hillside, NJ: Enslow Publishers, 1994. Focuses on experiments in causing and analyzing chemical reactions.

Mebane, Robert, and Thomas Rybolt. *Adventures with Atoms and Molecules*. Hillside, NJ: Enslow Publishers, 1991. Clearly describes 30 doable experiments in chemistry and chemical reactions.

VanCleave, Janice. *A+ Projects in Chemistry*. New York: Wiley and Sons, 1993. Outlines experiments that show chemical reactions relating to the weather, biochemistry, electricity, and other topics.

14

Chemosenses

People depend on taste and smell to recognize a delicious meal, but these senses also play a key part in helping keep us alive. Both senses can warn us of trouble and both are linked to what we eat. Pleasant tastes and smells ensure that a person or animal continues to eat and acquire energy from foods. Unpleasant tastes and smells are one way to ensure a person does not eat poisons or other materials that can cause harm.

People get information about the world around them through their senses of hearing, touch, sight, taste, and smell. Each of these five senses is tuned to a specific sensation. You are always using at least one of your senses. The senses send messages to the brain, which processes the information. Taste and smell belong to the chemical-sensing system group, known as chemosenses, which means that the sense is stimulated by specific chemicals. These chemicals trigger a nerve signal to the brain that then "reads" the signal.

How taste works When people say something tastes good, they are usually referring to the flavor of the food or drink. Flavor is a combination of taste, smell, texture, and other characteristics of the food itself, such as temperature. The sense of taste is complex because it is so intricately linked with flavor and weaves in many of the other senses, especially the sense of smell. There are five basic tastes: sweet, sour, salty, bitter, and umami (pronounced oo-MAM-ee). Umami was described in the early 1900s, but only in the late 1990s did food researchers officially recognize it as a distinct taste. Umami is the taste that occurs when foods with the protein glutamate are eaten. Glutamate is found in meat, fish, and the flavor-enhancing chemical monosodium glutamate, or MSG.

Humans get the sensation of taste through their taste cells, which lie within the taste bud. The average person has about 10,000 taste buds. People regenerate new taste buds every three to ten days. As people grow

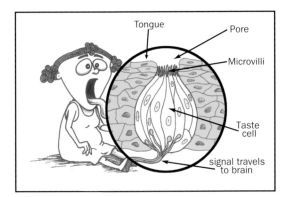

Taste buds are onion-shaped structures located primarily on a person's tongue. GALE GROUP.

older their taste buds regenerate at a slower rate, causing their sense of taste to lessen. An elderly person may have only 5,000 taste buds.

Taste buds are onion-shaped structures located primarily on a person's tongue. The majority of buds on the tongue are scattered on the papillae (pronounced pah-PILL-ee), the small projections that give your tongue its rough appearance. Taste buds are also located on the throat, roof of the mouth, and pharynx, but the buds on your tongue provide most of your taste experience. Each taste bud is made up of about 50 to 150 taste cells. Every cell has a fingerlike extension called a microvilli that connects with an opening at the top of the taste bud, called the taste pore.

For food to have taste, its chemicals need to reach your taste cells. The instant you take a bite of food, saliva or spit in the mouth starts breaking down the food's chemical components. These components, or molecules, travel through the pores in the papillae to bind to specific taste cells. The chemicals cause a change in the taste cell, sending a signal via nerves to the brain, which processes the signals.

In order for food to have taste, its chemical components need to reach the taste cells in your mouth. COPYRIGHT © KELLY A. QUIN.

The chemical reaction in the taste cells varies depending on the taste group involved. For example, salty foods trigger a change in taste cells when enough sodium (the main component of salt) molecules enter the cells through the microvilli. Each taste cell has the ability to recognize different taste groups, yet taste cells specialize in processing one particular group. Researchers have found that taste buds with common taste perceptions may be bunched together on the papillae. Many of the taste buds more sensitive to bitterness, for example, are located on the back of the tongue. This can cause an automatic gag-reflex to help prevent poisoning if something too bitter is ingested.

Smells at work: Lime or lemon? It is the olfactory sense, or sense of smell, that plays a key role in determining your perception of how tasty something is, or its flavor. Flavor is so strongly linked to the olfactory sense that researchers estimate 70–75% of what humans perceive as taste actually comes from the sense of smell.

Special olfactory cells, located inside the uppermost part of the nose, recognize specific odors. These odors, or chemical molecules, enter the nose and rise upward until they reach the olfactory epithelium, a postage-stamp-size area that contains olfactory receptor cells. Olfactory receptor cells are nerve cells, and each cell lasts about four to five weeks before it is replaced with a new one. These cells have hairlike projections called cilia that are sensitive to odor molecules. A specific odor molecule dissolves in the mucus of the nose. Mucus is a slippery substance that protects and moistens. The odor molecule binds to specific receptors on the cilia, which trigger a chemical signal in the receptor cell. The cell then sends its signal to the olfactory bulb of the brain, and then on to other areas of the brain that recognize it as a specific odor. There can be hundreds of receptors that take part in recognizing one smell.

Olfactory cells can recognize thousands of different odors. The chemical molecules reach the cells through the air you breathe and the food you eat. When you put food in your mouth, chemicals are released while you are chewing. Molecules from the food travel through the passage between your nose and mouth to the olfactory epithelium.

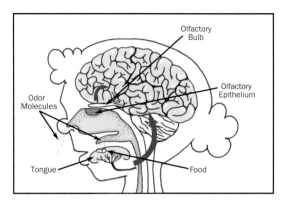

How tastes and smells are recognized. Food and odor molecules attach to olfactory cells that send signals to the brain. GALE GROUP.

The olfactory epithelium. Odor molecules bind to specific receptors on the cilia, which triggers a chemical signal in the receptor cell. The cell then sends its signal to the olfactory bulb of the brain, and then on to other areas of the brain that recognize it as a specific odor. GALE GROUP.

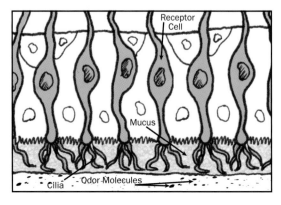

If a person's nose is congested, mucus in the nasal passages can block the odor molecules from reaching the olfactory cells; thus, the brain receives no signal telling it what the object smells like. COPYRIGHT © KELLY A. QUIN.

If a person's nose is congested, mucus in the nasal passages can block the odor molecules from reaching the olfactory cells. This will block surrounding smells, and food will lose much of its flavor.

All senses are not created equal Because the chemosenses are complex mechanisms, there are several reasons why people have varying preferences for smells and tastes. A person's genetics (physiological makeup), upbringing, and familiarity with specific smells and foods can influence his or her likes and dislikes. Odor molecules transmit their signals to areas of the brain that are involved with emotional behavior and memory. When a person smells something, it often brings back memories associated with the object, and those memories can help shape a person's perception of that smell.

Genetics is also a factor in tasting ability. In the early 1930s researchers discovered an inherited trait that determined people's sensitivity to a bitter taste. They classified people as "tasters" or "nontasters" based on whether they were able to detect a specific chemical, which tastes bitter to some people and tasteless to others. Later research found that some people are especially sensitive to this bitter taste. These people are born with more than the average number of taste buds and, as a result, perceive tastes more intensely than the average person. For these supertasters bitter tastes more bitter, sweet tastes sweeter, and salt tastes saltier. Researchers theorize that about 25% of the people in the United States are supertasters, 25% are nontasters, and the remaining 50% are regular tasters.

In the two experiments that follow, you will use the scientific method to examine if genetics affects the sense of taste and how closely linked these two senses are.

EXPERIMENT 1

Supertasters: Is there a correlation between the number of taste buds and taste perception?

Purpose/Hypothesis In this experiment, you will test varying concentrations of three tastes on people to predict whether they fall into the category of nontaster, taster, or supertaster. Then you will test your hypothesis by

WORDS TO KNOW

Chemosense: A sense stimulated by specific chemicals that cause the sensory cell to transmit a signal to the brain.

Cilia: Hairlike structures on olfactory receptor cells that sense odor molecules.

Control experiment: A setup that is identical to the experiment, but is not affected by the variable that acts on the experimental group.

Hypothesis: An idea in the form of a statement that can be tested by observation and/or experiment.

Microvilli: The extension of each taste cell that pokes through the taste pore and first senses the chemicals.

Mucus: A thick, slippery substance that serves as a protective lubricant coating in passages of the body that communicate with the air.

Olfactory: Relating to the sense of smell.

Olfactory bulb: The part of the brain that processes olfactory (smell) information.

Olfactory epithelium: The patch of mucous membrane at the top of the nasal cavity that contains the olfactory (smell) nerve cells.

Olfactory receptor cells: Nerve cells in the olfactory epithelium that detect odors and transmit the information to the brain.

Papillae: The raised bumps on the tongue that contain the taste buds.

Saliva: Watery mixture with chemicals that lubricates chewed food.

Supertaster: A person who is extremely sensitive to specific tastes due to a greater number of taste buds.

Taste buds: Groups of taste cells located on the papillae that recognize the different tastes.

Taste pore: The opening at the top of the taste bud from which chemicals reach the taste cells.

Variable: Something that can affect the results of an experiment.

---

counting the number of papillae of each person to estimate the number of taste buds each person has. If a person has more than twenty-five in a punch-hole-size area, then he/she is classified as a supertaster, five or less is considered a nontaster, and anywhere in between is an average taster.

Before you begin, make an educated guess about the outcome of this experiment based on your knowledge of the sense of taste. This educated guess, or prediction, is your hypothesis. A hypothesis should explain these things:

- the topic of the experiment
- the variable you will change
- the variable you will measure
- what you expect to happen

What Are the Variables?

Variables are anything that might affect the results of an experiment. Here are the main variables in this experiment:

- The participants in the experiment
- The cleanliness of the person's palette before the experiment
- The size of the paper hole
- The concentration of the taste
- The substance people are tasting

In other words, the variables in this experiment are everything that might affect the relationship between a person's sensitivity to taste and the number of his or her taste buds. If you change more than one variable at the same time, you will not be able to tell which variable had the most effect on taste.

A hypothesis should be brief, specific, and measurable. It must be something you can test through further investigation. Your experiment will prove or disprove your hypothesis. Here is one possible hypothesis for this experiment: "People who are more sensitive to tastes will have a greater number of taste buds."

Variables are anything you can change in an experiment. In this case, the variable you will change will be the concentration of the solutions. The variable you will measure will be the number of taste buds.

Setting up a control experiment will help you isolate each variable and measure the changes in the dependent variable. Only one variable will change between the control and the experimental setup, and that is the concentration of the solution. For the control in this experiment you will use a cup of plain water (tasteless). For your experiment, you will determine sensitivity to three tastes: bitter, salty, and sweet.

You will first make a 10% solution for each substance, then dilute the solutions. Sugar and salt are solids and you will make a 10% weight/weight (gram/gram) solution. For liquids you will make a 10% volume/volume (milliliter/milliliter) solution. One gram of water equals 1 ml of water.

You will rate people's sensitivity to varying concentrations of grapefruit juice (bitter), sugary water, and salty water. Then you will use blue dye to color each person's tongue's papillae. Because you are relying on human subjectivity, the more people you test, the more accurate your results.

Level of Difficulty Easy to Moderate.

Materials Needed

- grapefruit juice
- sugar
- salt
- water
- measuring spoons
- gram scale

- 3 to 4 helpers
- 16 small disposable paper cups
- light-colored pen
- blue food coloring
- cotton swabs
- piece of paper
- hole punch (standard 1/4-inch size)
- mirror
- magnifying glass

Approximate Budget $5.

Timetable 1 hour.

Step-by-Step Instructions

1. Measure out 10 tablespoons (150 milliliters of water) and pour into a cup. Add 4 teaspoons (15 grams) of sugar for a total volume of 150 ml and stir until all the sugar is dissolved. Write on the cup: "10% sugar." Repeat this process for the salt, labeling the cup: "10% salt."

2. Measure out 9 tablespoons (135 ml) water and pour into a cup. Add 1 tablespoon (15 ml) grapefruit juice for a total volume of 150 ml and stir thoroughly. Label the cup: "10% grapefruit."

3. Dilute each solution by 10%. From the sugar solution measure out 1 tablespoon (15 ml) and pour into a clean cup. Add 9 tablespoons (135 ml) of water and stir until all sugar is dissolved. Label the cup: "1% sugar."

4. To make a 0.1% solution: From the 1% sugar solution measure out 1 tablespoon (15 ml) and pour into a clean cup. Add 9 tablespoons (135 ml) of water and stir until all sugar is dissolved. Label the cup: "0.1% sugar."

5. To make a 0.01% solution: From the 0.1% sugar solution measure out 1 tablespoon (15 ml) and pour into a clean cup. Add 9 tablespoons (135 ml) of water and stir until all sugar is dissolved. Label the cup: "0.01% sugar."

6. To make a 0.001% solution: From the 0.01% sugar solution measure out 1 tablespoon (15 ml) and pour into a clean cup. Add 9 tablespoons (135 ml) of water and stir until all sugar is dissolved. Label the cup: "0.001% sugar."

7. Repeat this process for the salt solution and the grapefruit juice.

	Sweet	Bitter	Salty	# of Papillae
10%				
1%				
.1%				
.01%				
.001%				
water				

Step 9: Data chart for Experiment 1. GALE GROUP.

8. Place plain water in a cup for the control solution.

9. Create a chart that lists the concentrations and the control on the left, and the three tastes across the top.

10. Have the taster rinse out his or her mouth with water and make sure the mouth is relatively dry before beginning.

11. Start with one taste. Switch the five cups around, including the cup of water, not allowing the taster to see the labels. Have the taster dip a clean cotton swab into the solution, smear it over his/her tongue, and wait a few moments. Ask the taster if he/she can identify a taste. If the taster can identify a taste, make a checkmark sign in the box; if not, make a "x" in the box.

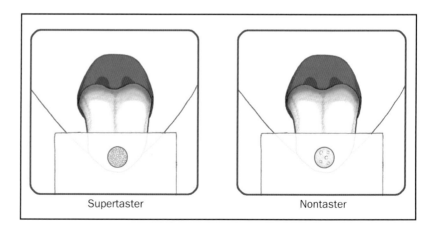

Supertaster   Nontaster

Step 17: Look at each tongue and count the round structures, the papillae, that are visible in the paper hole. GALE GROUP.

12. Have the taster rinse out his/her mouth with water and repeat the process for all the dilutions, including the control. Once the taster has completed one taste, repeat the process with another taste.

13. When one taster has finished sampling the three sets of tastes, repeat the process with another helper. Have a helper mix the samples so that you can also sample the dilutions yourself.

14. Punch a hole in a piece of paper for each taster.

15. Dip a cotton swab in the blue food coloring and have the tasters wipe the blue swab on the tip of their tongues.

16. Place the paper hole on the blue area of each tongue.

17. Using a magnifying glass, look at each tongue and count the round structures, the papillae, that are visible in the paper hole. Look in the mirror to count your own papillae. Write down the results for each taster.

Troubleshooter's Guide

Below are some problems that may occur during this experiment, some possible causes, and some ways to remedy the problems.

Problem: A person's responses were inconsistent, sometimes saying he or she could taste the higher concentration and lower concentrated solution, but not the in-between solutions.

Possible causes: The person may have been mixing up tastes. Try repeating the test with that person, making sure the taster cleans his/her mouth with water carefully every time.

Problem: There was no correlation between number of taste buds and perceived taste.

Possible causes: Human error. Examine the taster's reaction to the control solution to ensure that he/she is not mistakenly identifying tastes where there is none. If the taste of water has a checkmark then try repeating the experiment with that person, or with someone else. The more people you test, the less chance human error will have a statistical impact on your results.

Summary of Results Compare the results of each person's data chart with the number of his or her taste buds. Did your results support your hypothesis? Did the people who were more sensitive to tastes have a greater number of taste buds? Could the people in the nontaster category only taste the higher concentrations, and the supertasters taste the lower concentrations? Share your results and discuss if the tasters with the greater number of taste buds have a higher sensitivity to tastes in general. If there are any supertasters, do they have a strong dislike for broccoli, cabbage, and cauliflower (bitter tastes) and for strong sweet tastes such as frosting?

Change the Variables Try repeating the experiment (with new helpers) using different concentrations of the solutions, both higher and lower, to get an increased number of data points. You can also change the type of bitter solution you use (for example, a beverage with caffeine in it or tonic water).

What Are the Variables?

Variables are anything that might affect the results of an experiment. Here are the main variables in this experiment:

- The participants in the experiment
- The cleanliness of the person's palate before the experiment
- The substance people are tasting

In other words, the variables in this experiment are everything that might affect the relationship between a person's ability to recognize foods by their smell and taste. If you change more than one variable at the same time, you will not be able to tell which variable had the most effect on identifying the foods.

Another variable you can change is to replace one of the tastes with the sour taste (lemon juice). Always check with an adult before you or anyone else tastes any of the solutions to make sure there are no dietary restrictions.

EXPERIMENT 2

Smell and Taste: How does smell affect the sense of taste?

Purpose/Hypothesis Humans can perceive only five tastes, but can recognize thousands of smells. In this experiment you will test how closely the two chemosenses, the sense of smell and taste, are related. Blocking each sense independently, you will test and identify foods to determine which of the two senses sends the clearer message to the brain on what you are eating. You will use foods that have similar textures so that the feel of the food in your mouth is not a factor.

Before you begin, make an educated guess about the outcome of this experiment based on your knowledge of the sense of taste. This educated guess, or prediction, is your hypothesis. A hypothesis should explain these things:

- the topic of the experiment
- the variable you will change
- the variable you will measure
- what you expect to happen

A hypothesis should be brief, specific, and measurable. It must be something you can test through further investigation. Your experiment will prove or disprove your hypothesis. Here is one possible hypothesis for this experiment: "Humans need both the sense of smell and taste working together to identify foods."

Variables are anything you can change in an experiment. In this case, the variable you will change will be which sense or senses you use. The variable you will measure will be the identification of the food. You will test each sense separately, then together.

Level of Difficulty Easy.

Materials Needed

- onion
- raw potato
- roll of flavored candy
- chocolate ice cream
- strawberry ice cream
- knife
- four spoons
- helper

Approximate Budget $5.

Timetable About 20 minutes.

Step-by-Step Instructions

1. Carefully cut off a small piece of the onion and potato and then cut each into even smaller pieces. Place each on a separate spoon.
2. Ready spoonfuls of the chocolate ice cream and strawberry ice cream.
3. Set out two different-flavored hard candies; (e.g., one green and one red).
4. Make a chart listing the foods across the top and writing "Smell," "Taste," and "Both" down the page on the left.
5. Close your eyes and hold your nose tightly. Have your helper hand you the spoons one by one, in groups of two: onion and potato, chocolate and strawberry ice creams, and red and green hard candies. Taste each one and say what you think it is—don't peek.
6. Have your helper write down what you guessed.
7. Keeping your eyes closed, have your partner refill the spoons and again hand you the spoons in the same groups of two as before. This time, only smell what is on the spoon and say what it is.
8. Have your helper write down what you guessed.

How to Experiment Safely

Check with an adult before you or your helpers taste any of the foods to make sure none of you has any allergies to the foods, or other dietary restrictions. Use fresh utensils if more than one person conducts this experiment. Always use caution when working with any sharp objects, such as the knife.

Step 5: Block your sense of smell while tasting the food. GALE GROUP.

Troubleshooter's Guide

Below is a problem that may occur during this experiment, some possible causes, and some ways to remedy the problem.

Problem: Results were not as hypothesized.

Possible causes: Make sure you do not have a cold or are congested during this experiment. Always make sure the utensils are clean. Make sure you dice the potato and onion into small enough pieces so that they have the same feel on the tongue.

9. Repeat the procedure, keeping your eyes closed, this time using both your sense of taste and smell. Have your helper write down what you guessed.

Summary of Results Examine your results and determine whether your original hypothesis was correct. Which sense identified the correct flavor more often? Did one sense tell your brain the specific food you were eating? Did you need both senses working together to identify the flavors? Summarize the results of your experiment.

Change the Variables You can vary this experiment several ways. For example, why is it that you are keeping your eyes covered during this experiment? The sense of vision plays a significant role in identifying foods. People have expectations that certain colors will relate to specific flavors, such as a green jellybean tasting like lime, even when the flavor is different than expected. Try putting different-flavored fruit juices in dark cups and testing how much of an impact your sense of vision has on your taste perception.

You can also try holding only half your nose, to see how much of an impact half of your olfactory receptors have on your taste perception.

Modify the Experiment This experiment uses single food tastings to examine how the sense of smell and taste are used to recognize food. You can modify this experiment by conducting multiple food tastings to examine sensory adaptation. Sensory adaptation is when the sensitivity of the receptors decreases after repeated exposure to the same taste, smell, or other experience.

For you to explore how sensory adaptation affects your senses, you will need a glass of strong salt water and sugar water, along with plain water. You will also need a helper. Ask your helper to take a small sip of the sugar water and write down the taste. It should taste extremely sweet. Now ask your helper to gargle with the sugar water for at least 30 seconds. After spitting out the water, have your helper take another small sip of the sugar water and ask how it tastes? Repeat the gargling and sip. Again, ask the helper to identify the taste. Is there a difference in how strong it tastes?

Repeat the steps, except have your helper drink several large sips of plain water after gargling. Rinsing the mouth with water should refresh the receptors. When your helper now takes a sip of the sugar water, can he or she better recognize the taste? Does is have the strength as the first sip? Repeat this entire process with the salt water. Compare the taste experiences with and without drinking pure water. Try the experiment on yourself. You can explore whether you need more or less time to sensitize your receptors to the taste.

Design Your Own Experiment

How to Select a Topic Relating to this Concept If you are interested in the senses of taste and smell, there are many other possible experiments and projects. Because taste has a genetic component, you can try repeating Experiment 1 for groups of families. Compare family members' reactions to different tastes and their number of taste buds to each other. Then compare that data to a different family. Are members of one family more likely to all be either tasters, nontasters, or supertasters?

If you are interested in the sense of smell, you can examine the sensitivity of the olfactory sense by collecting and testing different concentrations of scents. Is there a genetic component to the sense of smell? How is the sense of smell different in other species from that of humans? What are some possible explanations for this?

Check the Further Readings section and talk with your science teacher or librarian to start gathering information on any questions that interest you.

Steps in the Scientific Method To do an original experiment, you need to plan carefully and think things through. Otherwise, you might not be sure what question you are answering, what you are or should be measuring, or what your findings prove or disprove.

Here are the steps in designing an experiment:

- State the purpose of—and the underlying question behind—the experiment you propose to do.
- Recognize the variables involved and select one that will help you answer the question at hand.
- State your hypothesis, an educated guess about the answer to your question.
- Decide how to change the variable you selected.
- Decide how to measure your results.

Recording Data and Summarizing the Results Your data should include charts, such as the ones you did for these experiments. They should be clearly labeled and easy to read. You may also want to include photos, graphs, or drawings of your experimental setup and results. If you have done a nonexperimental project, explain clearly what your research question was and illustrate your findings.

Related Projects Besides completing your experiments, you could prepare a model that demonstrates a point that you are interested in with regard to the chemosenses. For example, you could construct a model of the brain and illustrate the pathway of the taste and olfactory cells sending signals as they travel to certain parts of the brain. You could also try a similar dilution experiment with smell, observing the effect of varying dilutions of an odor, such as a perfume or a beverage. The effect of temperature also has an effect on smell, and you could chart people's perception of an odor that is cold, room temperature, and warm.

For More Information

Neuroscience for Kids. http://faculty.washington.edu/chudler/chsense.html (accessed March 5, 2008). Clear explanations and activities of the chemosenses.

Rouhi, Maureen I. "Unlocking the Secrets of Taste." *Chemical and Engineering News.* September 10, 2001. http://pubs.acs.org/cen/coverstory/7937/7937 taste.html (accessed March 5, 2008). Article on recently identified taste receptors and the molecules that stimulate them.

"The Vivid World of Odors." *Howard Hughes Medical Institute.* http://hhmi. org/senses/d110.html (accessed March 5, 2008). Report from the Howard Hughes Medical Institute on odor and taste receptors.

"Your Sense of Smell." *Your Gross and Cool Body.* http://yucky.discovery.com/ flash/body/pg000150.html (accessed March 5, 2008). Introductory information on smells and how the sense works.

15

Chlorophyll

Chlorophyll is the green pigment that gives leaves their color. Acting as a solar collector, chlorophyll absorbs light energy from the sun and traps it. This trapped energy is stored, then used to form sugar and oxygen out of carbon dioxide from the air and water from the soil. This extraordinary process is called photosynthesis. It is the way a plant makes its own food. But the key to this process is chlorophyll.

What's this green thing? Pierre Joseph Pelletier and Joseph Biernaime Caventou were French chemists who worked together in the early nineteenth century in a new field called pharmacology, the science of preparing medical drugs. These chemists would later discover quinine, caffeine, and other specialized plant products. In 1817, however, they isolated an important plant substance they called chlorophyll, from the Greek words meaning "green leaf." Scientists first thought that chlorophyll was distributed throughout plant cells. But in 1865 the German botanist Julius von Sachs discovered that this pigment is found within sacs called chloroplasts. Chlorophyll molecules are arranged in clusters within these chloroplasts.

One-celled plants, such as algae, contain chlorophyll. They live in water, growing near the surface and the light, or on moist surfaces. Multicelled plants—usually land plants such as mosses, ferns, and seed plants—have chlorophyll-loaded chloroplasts in their stems and leaves. These plants all need light to activate the chlorophyll. Plants such as algae require low light, and certain land plants, such as philodendron, survive well in low levels of sunlight also. Some houseplants thrive in

Chlorophyll clusters in the leaves of this healthy rhododendron plant trap solar energy. PHOTO RESEARCHERS INC.

191

An unhealthy rhododendron plant. If plants do not get enough light to activate their chlorophyll clusters, they cannot make enough food to survive. PHOTO RESEARCHERS INC.

artificial light, while other plants require high levels of sunlight.

Why leaves change color Pigments are substances that appear colored to the human eye because of the wavelengths of light they reflect. A pigment absorbs all other wavelengths of light and only reflects the wavelength that we see as a color. For example, a green pigment, like chlorophyll, absorbs all wavelengths except green. Many different pigments are present in sacs within the plant cell. There are two related chlorophyll pigments, chlorophyll A and chlorophyll B. Both appear green, with just a slight color variation from each other. Carotene, a yellowish-orange pigment, and xanthophyll, a yellow pigment, are also present in most leaves. Some plants have a red color in their petals, stems, and leaves called anthocyanin. The different pigments in a plant allow the plant to absorb different light wavelengths. Overall, the greenish chlorophyll pigment is the one that is most plentiful. It is considered a primary pigment, and the secondary pigments act as a support team to help the plant absorb more light energy.

Deciduous trees shed their leaves in the autumn. The joining place where the leaf meets the twig is called an abscission. The first step in the process that causes leaves to fall occurs when cork cells develop under the abscission. This cork layer blocks nutrients that travel to and from the leaf. Then the leaf begins to die.

Because chlorophyll breaks down faster than the other pigments, the green leaves begin their gradual color change. As the chlorophyll decomposes, the yellow and orange colors from the carotene and xanthophyll stand out. Trees with anthocyanin pigments show bright red leaves in the fall. Anthocyanin pigments need high light intensity and sugar content for their formation, so fiery red leaves usually emerge after bright autumn days. Cool nights act as a refrigerator, preserving the sugar in the leaves.

Chlorophyll and other pigments are unique in their function as food makers. Uncovering their presence in plants through experiments will help you "see" them.

WORDS TO KNOW

Abscission: Barrier of special cells created at the base of leaves in autumn.

Anthocyanin: Red pigment found in leaves, petals, stems, and other parts of a plant.

Carbohydrate: Any of several compounds composed of carbon, hydrogen, and oxygen, which are used as food for plants and animals.

Carotene: Yellowish-orange pigment present in most leaves.

Chlorophyll: A green pigment found in plants that absorbs sunlight, providing the energy used in photosynthesis.

Chloroplasts: Small structures in plant cells that contain chlorophyll and in which the process of photosynthesis takes place.

Chromatography: A method for identifying the components of a substance based on their characteristic colors.

Control experiment: A set-up that is identical to the experiment but is not affected by the variable that affects the experimental group.

Germination: First stage in development of a plant seed.

Hypothesis: An idea in the form of a statement that can be tested by observation and/or experiment.

Pharmacology: The science dealing with the properties, reactions, and therapeutic values of drugs.

Photosynthesis: Chemical process by which plants containing chlorophyll use sunlight to manufacture their own food by converting carbon dioxide and water to carbohydrates, releasing oxygen as a by-product.

Pigment: A substance that displays a color because of the wavelengths of light that it reflects.

Variable: Something that can change the results of an experiment.

Wavelength: The peak-to-peak distance between successive waves. Red has the longest wavelength of all visible light, and violet has the shortest wavelength.

Xanthophyll: Yellow pigment found in leaves.

EXPERIMENT 1

Plant Pigments: Can pigments be separated?

Purpose/Hypothesis In this experiment you will discover what pigments are present in various plants using chromatography, an identification technique based on color. You will cut up various plants and boil them in water, then add a small amount of alcohol to help release the pigments from the plants.

To begin the experiment, use what you know about chlorophyll and other pigments found in plants to make an educated guess about what colors you will find. This educated guess, or prediction, is your hypothesis. A hypothesis should explain these things:

What Are the Variables?

Variables are anything that might affect the results of an experiment. Here are the main variables in this experiment:

- the type and part of the plant being used (Example: carrot roots contain mainly carotene; carrot leaves contain mainly chlorophyll.)
- the season in which the plant was harvested (Example: if the plant was harvested in the spring, the leaves contain abundant chlorophyll; in the fall, the leaves have more carotene, xanthophyll, and anthocyanin.)
- the maturity of the specimen (Example: leaves from the heart of a celery plant are yellow from xanthophyll; as leaves mature, chlorophyll builds up.)

In other words, the variables in this experiment are everything that might affect the colors you find. If you change more than one variable, you will not be able to tell which variable had the most effect on the color.

Note: Do not use flowers, fruit, or roots for this experiment. They do not contain the pigments being studied.

How to Experiment Safely

This experiment requires the use of a stove or bunsen burner to boil the solutions. Use caution when cooking the solution and ask an adult for assistance. When handling alcohol, wear goggles and be careful not to spill it on your skin or in your eyes. Keep alcohol away from the stove or open flame.

- the topic of the experiment
- the variable you will change
- the variable you will measure
- what you expect to happen

A hypothesis should be brief, specific, and measurable. It must be something you can test through observation. Your experiment will prove or disprove whether your hypothesis is correct. Here is one possible hypothesis for this experiment: "Primary pigments, such as blue-green chlorophyll, and secondary pigments, such as yellow-orange carotene, yellow xanthophyll, and red anthocyanin, are all present in leaves."

In this case, the variable you will change is the type and part of the plant being tested, and the variable you will measure is the resulting mix of colors. A bowl filled with various food colorings will serve as a control experiment to allow you measure the effectiveness of the color separation method. If you find many different colors present in your experimental solutions, you will know your hypothesis is correct.

Level of Difficulty Moderate.

Materials Needed

- 1 cup (236 milliliters) of spinach leaves, cut up
- 1 cup (236 milliliters) of parsley leaves, cut up
- 1 cup (236 milliliters) of coleus leaves (houseplant with variegated leaves), cut up
- food coloring (red, blue, and yellow)
- filter paper (strong paper towels also will work)
- rubbing alcohol 70%
- 4 bowls
- 4 glass cups or beakers

Step 6: Four cups with pigment solutions (control, spinach, parsley, and coleus). GALE GROUP.

- cooking pot
- labels
- 4 paper clips
- measuring spoons and cups
- water
- goggles

Approximate Budget $10 for the fresh parsley, spinach, and a coleus plant.

Timetable Approximately 2 hours.

Step-by-Step Instructions

Step 7: Filter paper strip in cup, held in place with a paper clip. GALE GROUP.

1. Place one cup of water in a pot and bring it to a boil. Add 20 drops of each color of food coloring and boil for 10 minutes more. Remove the pot from stove and allow to cool. Pour the solution into a bowl and add 4 tablespoons of alcohol. Label the bowl "#1." This will be your control solution.

2. Wash the pot and add one cup of water and bring it to a boil. Add the cut-up

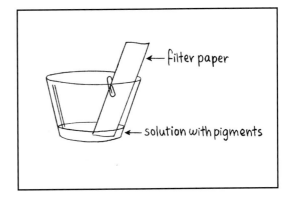

← filter paper

← solution with pigments

Troubleshooter's Guide

Here are some problems that may occur in this experiment, some possible causes, and ways to remedy the problems.

Problem: The pigment does not go up the paper.

Possible cause: The paper is wet. Make sure the paper is thoroughly dry before inserting it in the solution. Also make sure the paper is touching the solution.

Problem: The control experiment worked well, but the spinach, parsley, and coleus solutions are very light.

Possible cause: The solutions are too weak. Place more leaves into the pot and boil the solution longer. Use a low flame, and be cautious when reheating as the mixture contains alcohol.

spinach leaves. Boil for 10 minutes more. Remove the pot from stove and allow to cool. Pour the solution into another bowl and add 4 tablespoons of alcohol. Label the bowl "#2."

3. Repeat Step 2, substituting parsley for spinach. Label bowl "#3."

4. Repeat Step 2 again, substituting coleus leaves. Label bowl "#4."

5. Cut the filter paper into 1-inch-wide (2.5-centimeter) strips. These will be your chromatography papers.

6. Label the cups #1, #2, #3, and #4. Now pour 0.25 inch (0.6 centimeter) of the liquid solution from each bowl into the appropriate numbered cup.

7. Place a filter paper strip into each cup as illustrated. Use a paper clip to hold the paper to the cup. Make sure only the bottom of the filter paper touches the solution.

8. Leave the experiment undisturbed for 30 to 60 minutes. Notice how the solution creeps up the filter paper.

9. Stop the experiment when a pigment reaches the top of the filter paper. Place the pieces of paper on a clean, flat surface to dry.

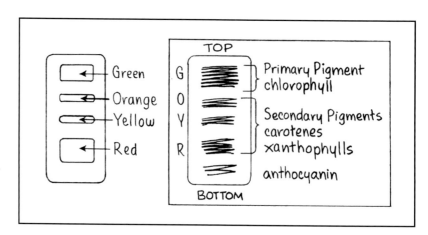

Sample diagram of chromatography paper from one of the solutions. GALE GROUP.

Summary of Results Make a diagram recording what colors appeared on your chromatography papers (see sample diagram). The pigments may fade over time, so record the results the same day.

Reflect on your original hypothesis. Were you able to detect the primary and secondary pigments present in all the leaves? Were pigments present in your control experiment? Which plant(s) contained the most secondary pigments? Which contained the most primary pigments?

EXPERIMENT 2

Response to Light: Do plants grow differently in different colors of light?

Purpose/Hypothesis In this experiment you will test the growth of plant seedlings under different colors of light. Within the cells of a plant's leaves and stems, there are various pigments that react to light to perform photosynthesis. The pigments vary in color and

What Are the Variables?

Variables are anything that might affect the results of an experiment. Here are the main variables in this experiment:

- the type of seedlings being used
- the strength of light (wattage)
- the wavelengths (colors) of light being tested
- the amount of water given to the seedlings

In other words, the variables in this experiment are everything that might affect the growth of the seedlings. If you change more than one variable, you will not be able to tell which variable most affected the seedlings' growth.

opening for light (1′ x 1′)

aluminum foil

black plastic curtain

Step 1: Set-up of boxes with aluminum foil and black plastic. GALE GROUP.

How to Experiment Safely

Incandescent light fixtures and bulbs can get hot. Do not handle or leave the lights on for more than 10 hours at a time. Never leave them on overnight. Keep them a safe distance from the cellophane filters at all times.

concentration. Each pigment absorbs all colors of light except the color of the pigment itself, which is reflected. For example, if a plant contains mostly green pigments such as chlorophyll, the plant should grow well under all colors of light except green because it reflects most of the green light without absorbing it. As a result, the plant is "starved" for light and cannot perform the photosynthesis process needed to produce food and grow.

To begin this experiment, use what you know about chlorophyll and the pigment colors found in plants to make an educated guess about how plants will grow under various colors of light. This educated guess, or prediction, is your hypothesis. A hypothesis should explain these things:

- the topic of the experiment
- the variable you will change
- the variable you will measure
- what you expect to happen

A hypothesis should be brief, specific, and measurable. It must be something you can test through observation. Your experiment will prove or disprove whether your hypothesis is correct. Here is one possible hypothesis for this experiment: "Seedlings will grow best under white light, because they can absorb more energy from the wide range of wavelengths present. They will grow worst under green light, because that is the color of the dominant pigment contained in their leaves and stems, and most of that light will be reflected instead of absorbed."

In this case, the variable you will change is the color of the light, and the variable you will measure is the amount of growth of the seedlings over a period of several weeks. If the seedlings grow best under white light and worst under green light, you will know your hypothesis is correct.

Level of Difficulty Moderate. (However, great care of the seedlings must be taken to ensure their growth.)

Materials Needed

- 4 boxes, 24 inches (60 centimeters) square in size, open on one side
- aluminum foil

- 4 light fixtures with 40-watt white incandescent bulbs, such as small desk lamps
- 4 plastic filters about 12 inches (30 centimeters) square, such as cellophane in clear, green, blue, and red
- black plastic cut from a garbage bag
- 4 shallow trays filled with potting soil
- 40 bean seeds, such as lima, kidney, or others (Use all of one type.)
- water

Note: If you are unable to get light fixtures to use, use natural sunlight and modify the setup described in the following procedure.

Approximate Budget $30–$35 for light fixtures, if necessary, and $5 for seeds and cellophane.

Timetable Approximately two months—about 20 days for the seeds to germinate, and two to three weeks before the first true leaves appear.

Step-by-Step Instructions

1. Set up four identical boxes. Line the inside of each box with aluminum foil. Cover the front opening with black plastic. Cut a hole in the top, about 10 x 10 inches, (25 x 25 centimeters), to allow light to enter.

2. Tape a different color plastic filter over the hole on each box.

3. Position a light fixture approximately 12 inches (30 centimeters) above the opening on each box and aim the light inside the box.

4. Place a tray of soil into each box and plant 10 seeds slightly below the surface of the soil. Water gently.

5. Turn the lights on for eight to 10 hours a day. Monitor the soil moisture and water gently when needed.

6. Record the seed growth in each box. Record which seedling is the tallest daily for one month after the seeds sprout or until the seedlings reaches the filter.

Step 3: Light fixture over opening of box. GALE GROUP.

Troubleshooter's Guide

Here is a problem that may arise in this experiment, a possible cause, and a way to remedy it.

Problem: The seeds did not grow.

Possible Cause: The seeds might be too old. You can try again with new seeds or accept the results if you think it was the lighting. If they died from not getting enough water, then try again.

Summary of Results Make a chart to track the growth of the seedlings. Reflect on your hypothesis. Were the seedlings more responsive to one color of light? What color stimulated growth the least? Is that color the seedlings' most dominant pigment? Summarize your results in writing.

Design Your Own Experiment

How to Select a Topic Relating to this Concept All the colors in plants and animals are due to pigments, which have many functions. Chlorophyll's function is producing energy for photosynthesis. Melanin is a skin pigment that protects people and animals from harmful solar radiation.

Check the Further Readings section and talk with your science teacher or school or community media specialist to start gathering information on questions that interest you about chlorophyll and other pigments. As you consider possible experiments, be sure to discuss them with your science teacher or another knowledgeable adult before trying them. Some pigments might be dangerous.

Steps in the Scientific Method To do an original experiment, you need to plan carefully and think things through. Otherwise, you might not be sure

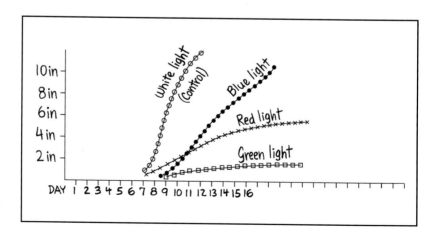

Step 6: Sample seed growth recording chart. GALE GROUP.

what questions you're answering, what you are or should be measuring, or what your findings prove or disprove.

Here are the steps in designing an experiment:

- State the purpose of—and the underlying question behind—the experiment you propose to do.
- Recognize the variables involved, and select one that will help you answer the question at hand.
- State a testable hypothesis, an educated guess about the answer to your question.
- Decide how to change the variable you selected.
- Decide how to measure your results.

When cool weather comes in autumn, chlorophyll breaks down more rapidly than carotene and xanthophyll, making leaves such as these look yellow and orange before they fall from the tree. PHOTO RESEARCHERS INC.

Recording Data and Summarizing the Results Think of how you can share your results with others. Charts, graphs, and diagrams of the progress and results of the experiments are very helpful in informing others about an experiment.

Related Projects You can create an experiment on pigments by discovering how to extract pigments from their source in nature. Or you could take an extracted pigment and find a use for it. For example, purple grape juice can be used as an acid/base indicator.

For More Information

Andrew Rader Studios. "Photosynthesis." *Rader's Biology4kids.com*. http://www. biology4kids.com/files/plants_photosynthesis.html (accessed on January 19, 2008). Provides information on plants and photosynthesis.

Halpern, Robert. *Green Planet Rescue*. New York: Franklin Watts, 1993. Discusses the importance of plants and what can be done to protect plants that face extinction.

Kalman, Bobbie. *How A Plant Grows*. New York: Crabtree Publishing, 1997. Examines the stages of a seed plant's development and includes activities on how to grow plants.

Missouri Botanical Garden. *Biology of Plants*. www.mbgnet.net/bioplants (accessed January 19, 2008). Providing information on the growth and life of plants

Budget Index

Chapter name in brackets, followed by experiment name. The numeral before the colon indicates volume; numbers after the colon indicate page number.

Level of Difficulty Index

Chapter name in brackets, followed by experiment name. The numeral before the colon indicates volume; numbers after the colon indicate page number.

EASY

Easy means that the average student should easily be able to complete the tasks outlined in the project/experiment, and that the time spent on the project is not overly restrictive.

EASY/MODERATE

Easy/Moderate means that the average student should have little trouble completing the tasks outlined in the project/experiment, and that the time spent on the project is not overly restrictive.

Experiment Central, 2nd edition

MODERATE

Moderate means that the average student should find tasks outlined in the project/experiment challenging but not difficult, and that the time spent on the project/experiment may be more extensive.

MODERATE/DIFFICULT

Moderate/Difficult means that the average student should find tasks outlined in the project/experiment challenging, and that the time spent on the project/experiment may be more extensive.

DIFFICULT

Difficult means that the average student wil probably find the tasks outlined in the project/experiment mentally and/or physically challenging, and that the time spent on the project/experiment may be more extensive.

Timetable Index

Chapter name in brackets, followed by experiment name. The numeral before the colon indicates volume; numbers after the colon indicate page number.

30 TO 45 MINUTES

3 HOURS

General Subject Index

The numeral before the colon indicates volume; numbers after the colon indicate page number. **Bold** page numbers indicate main essays. The notation (ill.) after a page number indicates a figure.

A

A groups (periodic table), *4:* 829
A layer (soil), *5:* 1066–67, 1067 (ill.)
Abscission, *1:* 192
Absolute dating, *3:* 525
Acceleration
    bottle rocket experiment, *3:* 493–501, 495 (ill.), 498 (ill.), 499 (ill.)
    build a roller coaster experiment, *5:* 934–38, 935 (ill.), 936 (ill.), 937 (ill.)
    centripetal force experiment, *3:* 501–5, 503 (ill.)
    centripetal force in, *3:* 493, 493 (ill.)
    Newtonian laws of motion on, *3:* 492, 492 (ill.)
    of planetary orbits, *3:* 579–80
Acetate, *3:* 509, 511–14, 511 (ill.), 512 (ill.), 513 (ill.)
Acetic acid, *1:* 165, *4:* 820–23, 820 (ill.), 821 (ill.), 822 (ill.)
Acetone, *3:* 511–14, 511 (ill.), 512 (ill.), 513 (ill.)
Acid/base indicators, *4:* 860
    cave formation experiment, *1:* 134, 134 (ill.)
    pH of household chemicals experiment, *4:* 861–65, 861 (ill.), 863 (ill.)
Acid rain, *1:* **1–17,** 17 (ill.)
    brine shrimp experiment, *1:* 5–8, 7 (ill.)
    damage from, *1:* 1–3, *4:* 860–61
    design an experiment for, *1:* 15–16
    formation of, *1:* 1, 164
    pH of, *1:* 1, 2 (ill.), 3 (ill.), *4:* 860–61, 861 (ill.)

    plant growth experiment, *1:* 9–12, 11 (ill.)
    structure damage experiment, *1:* 12–15, 14 (ill.), 15 (ill.), 16
Acidity
    in food preservation, *3:* 452
    in food spoilage, *3:* 478
    measurement of, *1:* 1
    neutralization of, *1:* 4
    for separation and identification, *5:* 1033, 1034 (ill.)
    of soil, *5:* 1064
    soil pH and plant growth experiment, *5:* 1074–77, 1074 (ill.), 1076 (ill.), 1079 (ill.)
    See also pH
Acids
    acid-copper reduction experiment, *4:* 813–17, 814 (ill.), 815 (ill.)
    cave formation experiment, *1:* 132–35, 134 (ill.)
    chemical properties of, *1:* 164
    chemical titration experiment, *4:* 865–68, 865 (ill.), 866 (ill.), 867 (ill.)
    copper color change experiment, *4:* 820–23, 820 (ill.), 821 (ill.), 822 (ill.)
    electricity conduction by, *2:* 334
    pH of, *4:* 859–61
    uses for, *4:* 859, 860
    See also Lemon juice; Vinegar
Acoustics, *5:* 1096
Acronyms, *4:* 700
Actions, reactions to every, *3:* 492, 494

G

H

Experiment Central, 2nd edition

N

S

W

Experiment Central, 2nd edition